MY GARDEN IN SPRING

My Garden in Spring

by
E. A. Bowles

with a New Foreword
by Brigadier Andrew Parker Bowles, o.b.e.
Preface by Charles Elliott
and Nomenclatural Update by Peter Barnes

Timber Press
Portland, Oregon

First Published in 1914 by T. C. & E. C. Jack

Reprinted in 1997 by
Timber Press, Inc.
The Haseltine Building
133 S.W. Second Avenue, Suite 450
Portland, Oregon 97204, U.S.A.

Printed in Hong Kong

Library of Congress Cataloging-in-Publication Data

Bowles, E. A. (Edward Augustus)
    My garden in spring / E. A. Bowles ; with foreword by Andrew
  Parker Bowles ; new preface by Charles Elliott ; nomenclature
  update by Peter Barnes.
        p.   cm.
    Originally published: T. C. & E. C. Jack, 1914.
    Includes index.
    ISBN 0-88192-375-3
    1. Myddelton House Garden (Enfield, London, England) 2.
  Bowles, E. A. (Edward Augustus)—Homes and haunts—England—
  London. 3. Plants, Ornamental—England—London. 4. Spring—
  England—London.
  I. Title.
  635.9'53—dc20   96-38286
                                                        CIP

CONTENTS
of the 1997 edition

FOREWORD

by Brigadier Andrew Parker Bowles, O.B.E.

MY great-great-uncle Gussie died in 1954 when I was fourteen. During those fourteen years I had spent many happy hours trailing along behind him as he bustled around his large and unique garden. If it rained we would adjourn to his home, Myddelton House, which was to me dark and exciting as he refused to have electricity and relied on oil lamps for light. There I watched him paint marvellous botanical and avian pictures. The majority of his paintings and drawings are owned by the Royal Horticultural Society (R.H.S.), but I have a collection of them which I treasure both for their expertise and the memories they hold of my beloved uncle.

Like most great gardeners E. A. Bowles was immensely generous and always urged friends and visitors to his garden to bring a large basket or box with them so that they could transport his gifts of plants back to their own gardens. When I was at boarding-school he would send me parcels of bulbs and plants and as a result, not surprisingly, I won the school gardening prize every year.

He never married and on the whole preferred the company of men to women, although the leading women gardeners of the time were his friends.

My uncle was not a man of business and like other upper-class English gardeners of that time he never had a paid occupation. He lived well off his own kitchen garden and farm and

My Garden in Spring

had a large house staff which included a butler and a cook. However his voluntary work was prodigious, both for the underprivileged of his parish and for the many botanical societies and committees he was interested in.

Besides being a gardener and artist he was also a brilliant and much-read author. This foreword is to the third printing of his famous trilogy. First editions are rare and expensive.

E. A. Bowles died on 7 May 1954, just days short of his eighty-ninth birthday. He once wrote, "May is the supreme moment of the Garden, just the climate one would expect to find in heaven." He was described as "the greatest amateur gardener of the century" and in his memory a "Bowles Corner" was created at the R.H.S. Gardens at Wisley. This corner contains most of the fifty or so plants, shrubs, and bulbs bred or discovered by E. A. Bowles or named after him.

After his death Myddelton House, its garden, and farm were transferred to London University who then sold them on to the present owners, the Lee Valley Authority, in 1968. Sadly, the garden had become overgrown and untended. In 1993 The E. A. Bowles of Myddelton House Society, a registered society, was set up and in partnership with the Lee Valley Authority are restoring the E. A. Bowles garden to its former glory. Any royalties from this book will go to The E. A. Bowles Society.

If my uncle were alive he would be amused to discover that his name is revered to this day and that his views and achievements are still widely quoted and discussed in gardening circles. But then of course he was an outstanding gardener and to me a wonderful and talented man.

PREFACE
by Charles Elliott

WHILE gardening is surely the most ephemeral of all the arts in its primary, earthbound form (even perennials die), garden writing has an amazing staying power. It is almost as if the great garden writers somehow sensed that they were bound to be defeated by frost and time, and turned naturally to words on paper for permanence. This does not explain, of course, why they were so good at it. But the fact remains that people like Gertrude Jekyll, Canon Henry Ellacombe, Reginald Farrer, and Edward Augustus Bowles—to name only a few, and all English—live on for us today less because of the actual gardens they created than because of the wonderful books they wrote about their loves and obsessions.

E. A. Bowles—familiarly known as Gus or Gussie, in spite of his somewhat austere appearance as a wealthy English gentleman gardener—is very much a case in point. His garden, at Myddelton House on the northern outskirts of London, does still survive, but what gives him a place in the dirty-fingernail pantheon is without question his books. *My Garden in Spring, My Garden in Summer*, and *My Garden in Autumn and Winter* are a trio of the most delightful and instructive volumes ever written between spells of pruning and potting.

The first, published in 1914 just as the First World War was erupting, had been suggested to Bowles by a magazine editor. The casting was excellent; Gus Bowles, then in his forties, was

My Garden in Spring

a keen and experienced gardener with time on his hands and—as it turned out—an easy, amiable, and deeply personal writing style. (His business sense was less admirable—he sold the copyright of the book outright for £80 10s., and thus made virtually nothing when it became a success both in Britain and in the United States.) To him, writing was less a bid for lasting fame than a source of pleasure closely related to gardening itself, as he implies while describing the rock garden he had prepared for his Tyrolean primulas:

> How magnificent it sounds! That is the fun of writing of one's garden: a steep bank can be a cliff, a puddle a pool, a pool a lake, bog and moraine sound as though a guide were needed to find your way across them, and yet may be covered by a sheet of the *Times*. My Dolomites lie within the compass of my outstretched arms.

The structure of *My Garden in Spring* is straightforward. Bowles simply invites the reader to join him on a garden tour. Bed by bed, section by section, pausing to comment on a rare variety or give horticultural advice, sometimes drifting off into an historical byway or an anecdote about where he found an iris or a saxifrage, he leads one with infectious enthusiasm from the rock garden to the "lunatic asylum"—the corner in which he grew such "mad plants" as a contorted hazel.

Every reader of this book will have his or her favourite bits. I treasure many, among them Bowles' three-page disquisition on the difference between daffodils and narcissus (there isn't one), and his ecstatic account of finding a prize mutation in the midst of a bed of crocuses. The latter reminds us that though he was not a professional gardener or botanist, Bowles

Preface

knew more, and wrote more learnedly, about crocuses than anyone else of his time.

Bowles was a plantsman, not a garden designer, which is probably one reason he wrote so well about plants. He cared most about making his charges comfortable. "The line of gardening I have been driven into," he writes, "is perhaps better described as collecting plants and endeavouring to keep them alive, than as gardening for beautiful effects or the production of prizewinning blossoms." The great rock-gardener Reginald Farrer, Bowles' sometime plant-collecting companion, agreed. In his preface to *My Garden in Spring*, Farrer remarks that "the essence of a real garden is the insignificance of the garden itself; the soul of the real garden lies in the perfect prosperity of the plants of which it is the home." And Bowles was in Farrer's opinion "a real gardener."

Farrer, incidentally, did Bowles few favours with his preface. Where Bowles was a man with virtually no enemies, Farrer was famously touchy, ready to pick a fight on no provocation at all. Here in the preface, sandwiched between compliments for Bowles, he inserts an attack on "the very rich" who were "out to purchase the glories of the Alps at so much a yard." Farrer had, moreover, a particular rich man in mind—one Sir Frank Crisp, a recently created baronet who had constructed an exact model of the Matterhorn out of stucco, Portland cement, and 7,000 tons of millstone grit, and adorned it with 4,000 species of rock plants and several tin chamois. This monstrosity offended Farrer, who was convinced that only he—and a few others, like Bowles, acting under his instructions—could build a rock garden properly.

My Garden in Spring

Crisp naturally reacted with some violence, and printed up a leaflet blasting not Farrer, but poor Bowles. At one point, the distinguished lady gardener Miss Ellen Willmott—previously a friend of Bowles—was spotted at the gate of the Chelsea Flower Show dispensing the leaflet from a leather bag slung round her shoulder. Farrer, never one to miss an opportunity to stir up trouble, suggested that Miss Willmott was suffering from unrequited love. "Really, you'd better marry the cankered Ellen at once and save further trouble," he wrote. Bowles, nature's bachelor, wrote calming letters in all directions. Farrer, no doubt chuckling to himself, headed off on a plant-hunting expedition to West China.

Edward Augustus Bowles survived this contretemps as he was to survive other less spectacular ones (a killing drought, black spot in the roses), and lived on at Myddelton, much loved and admired, through two world wars. It is pleasant to think that thanks to the re-publication of his books, more people will come to know him, be charmed by his approach to gardening, and learn about "my gardening basket and all its contents, almost as varied a collection as Alice's White Knight had, but certainly more useful, even the mouse-trap on too frequent occasions . . ."

MY GARDEN IN SPRING

Facsimile of the Original Edition of 1914

The Morning-room window in May.   (Frontispiece.)

My Garden in Spring

By E. A. Bowles, M.A.

London : T. C. & E. C. Jack
67 Long Acre, W.C.
And Edinburgh
1914

TO

MY FATHER

HENRY C. B. BOWLES

WHO HAS SO KINDLY AND PATIENTLY ALLOWED ME
TO EXPERIMENT WITH HIS GARDEN FOR
THE LAST TWENTY-FIVE YEARS

PREFACE

IT is a pleasure and a privilege to be asked to write about
a real garden. There are nowadays so many gardeners
that gardens are growing every year more rare. Every
one must have their "rock-work," and the very rich are
out to purchase the glories of the Alps at so much a
yard—with all the more contentment if the price be heavy,
so that their munificence may be the more admired.
Passion for display appears the ruling note in English
horticulture of every kind and in every period: we want
a show. It is now not so very long since carpet-bedding
went out of fashion with a roar of contemptuous execra-
tion; and for a short period we were all for a return to
what we spoke of as "Nature," but what was merely
wobbly anarchy reduced to a high art. But in those
days at least the rock garden was a place of plants, and
if such a thing existed in one's ground at all, it was not
a mere dog's grave to trail Nasturtiums over, but a fabric
framed because its owner really wanted to do his best for
Dianthus glacialis or *Campanula pulla.* But now the accursed
thing is once more rearing its head, and carpet-bedding is
bursting up to life again in the midst of the very rock
garden itself, of all places impermissible and improbable.
For the rich must have their money's worth in show;
culture will not give it them, nor rarity, nor interest of

My Garden in Spring

the plants themselves: better a hundred yards of Arabis than half a dozen vernal Gentians. So now their vast rock-works are arranged like the pattern of a pavement: here is a large triangle filled neatly with a thousand plants of *Alyssum saxatile*, neatly spaced like bedded Stocks, and with the ground between them as smooth and tidy as a Guardsman's head; then, fitting into this, but separated by stone or rock, more irregular great triangles of the same order—one containing a thousand Aubrietia "Lavender," and the next a thousand *Lithospermum prostratum* But nothing else; neither blending nor variety—nothing but a neat unalloyed exhibit like those on "rock-works" at the Chelsea Show. But what a display is here! You could do no better with coloured gravels. Neat, unbroken blanks of first one colour and then another, until the effect indeed is sumptuous and worthy of the taste that has combined such a garden. But "garden" why call it? There are no plants here; there is nothing but colour, laid on as callously in slabs as if from the paint-box of a child. This is a mosaic, this is a gambol in purple and gold; but it is not a rock garden, though tin chamois peer never so frequent from its cliffs upon the passer-by, bewildered with such a glare of expensive magnificence. This is, in fact, nothing but the carpet-bedding of our grandfathers, with the colour-masses laid on in pseudo-irregular blots and drifts, instead of in straight stretches; and with outlines of stone between each definite patch, instead of the stitching that divides similar colour patch from patch in the crazy quilt. Well, such artists in the grand style have their reward.

Preface

What would they say now if they were led into the garden through which we are now going to be conducted by its creator? Never before having seen a place for growing plants in, never having heard the names of Ellacombe or Wolley-Dod—or, if they have, connecting them with no vitalising work or idea—how will their noses not corrugate in scorn on merely perceiving plants—only plants, plants well grown, plants happy, plants well suited and consulted and made at home. But there are others, less rich, who will be glad of traversing such holy ground, and learning how the hills can be made to yield up their secret, and their children taught to forget the far highlands of their birth, and feel themselves contented and at home within a dozen miles of London. The essence of the real garden is the insignificance of the garden itself; the soul of the real garden lies in the perfect prosperity of the plants of which it is the home, instead of being merely, by the modern reversal of right laws, the expensive and unregarded colour-relief of its titanically-compounded cliffs of stucco and Portland cement. Come into Mr. Bowles's garden and learn what true gardening is, and what is the real beauty of plants, and what the nature of their display.

A lowly piece of ground, wandering here and there in gentle natural ravines and slopes. No vast structures, but bank added to bank as the plants require it, and nothing asked of the structure except that it be simple and harmonious, and best calculated to serve the need of the little people it is to accommodate—to accommodate, and not be shown off by. For here the plants are lords,

ix

My Garden in Spring

and the rocks take their dim place in the background as helps and comforts indeed, but by no means as the *raison d'être* and pompous origin of the whole edifice. And the result? Let the lovers of display go home abashed before a display such as not a hundred bedded-out Aubrietias can give. If it were ever to be thought for a moment that the real rock garden is a place of minute moribund plants and microscopic minutenesses, so that the only alternative lies between this and the gorgeous soullessness of the Portland cementery, let those who have held such notions only visit Mr. Bowles's garden at almost any moment of the year, and wander past great tuft after tuft of the rarest and most difficult brilliancies that have quite forgotten they are rare or difficult at all or in exile, but are here making individual masses individually beloved and tended, as full of rich colour and the blood of life as they were on the Cima Tombea or the Col de Tenda. There is no lack of show, indeed, as we wander past blazing old clump after clump of glorious Tulips that no one else can make survive two seasons, or wonder at the glowing rows of Primulas that no one else can flower, here gorgeous in their patches as on the ridge of the Frate di Breguzzo itself. Indeed, the most passionate admirer of Aubrietia will have to confess that his eye is no less completely filled here, and filled with more satisfaction and less monotony than in the most expensive show-garden, filled with plants at so much per thousand.

And what are the secrets of this display, this freshness of effect, this profound satisfaction that one takes away with one, wrapped up in sighs of envy? Far be it from

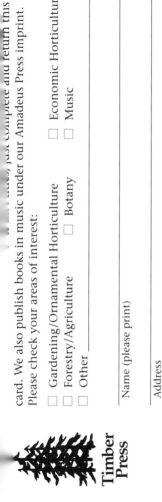

... we also offer, just complete and return this card. We also publish books in music under our Amadeus Press imprint. Please check your areas of interest:

☐ Gardening/Ornamental Horticulture ☐ Economic Horticulture
☐ Forestry/Agriculture ☐ Botany ☐ Music
☐ Other _____

Timber Press

Name (please print) _____

Address _____

City _____ State _____ Zip _____

We'd also welcome your comments on this book.

Title of book: _____

Comments: _____

_____

BUSINESS REPLY MAIL

FIRST CLASS MAIL PERMIT NO. 717 PORTLAND, OR

POSTAGE WILL BE PAID BY ADDRESSEE

TIMBER PRESS, Inc.

The Haseltine Building

133 S.W. Second Avenue, Suite 450

Portland, OR 97204-9743

Preface

me to bring a deeper blush to the cheek of Mr. Bowles
than mantles on his Primulas in May, but facts, as Sairey
has so justly said, are stubborn and not easy drove.
Therefore we must speak the plain truth : Mr. Bowles
is a real gardener, and the real gardener works with love
and knowledge and personal devotion, and not with money
and orders issued to a nurseryman.   The highest art is to
conceal art ; and accordingly the first and last essential
of the good rock garden is that it should not look like a
garden at all, but like the unharvested flower-fields of the
hills—effortless, serene, and apparently neglected.   And
to achieve this effect, as all who have tried it well know,
is the final ambition of the real gardener, and the very
last to be attained.   For nothing is harder, in any walk
of art, than to strike the perfect note of calm assurance—
which is the supreme success, and nothing short of it—
without falling into the death in life of spick and spanness
on the one hand, or the more ferocious life in death of
slovenliness and anarchy on the other.   But at first sight,
like all great works, from the Monna Lisa downwards, the
really good garden looks so simple and unaffected and
easy that those who base their admiration on a sense of
money spent and obvious artificial difficulties surmounted,
will be inclined to conclude at a glance that such a mass
of intermingled happy plants is a simple matter of luck
and neglect that any one could achieve.   And this verdict
is the crowning prize of the good gardener, more worth
than many Standard cups.   For let these complacent
people only try, that's all ; let them learn by experience
what it is to cope with things that want to be weeds, in

My Garden in Spring

such a way that they do not succeed, and yet retain their own spontaneous happiness ; then they will ere long begin to learn that right letting alone and right meddling are the beginning and the ending of good gardening, and that the simplest effects are just precisely those which defy money and ambition and effort, and everything but tireless patience, attention, and knowledge bought at first hand with pain.

Come straight from the high hills into this garden of Mr. Bowles, and it is not by any difference in the look of the ground or its plants that you will know you are not still there : here are no precious plants pining for company in a grim and tidy isolation; here are no venerable ancient persons perpetually picking weeds until all the soil between every plant is bald as a billiard ball. But here only the noxious is removed, the plants are given free scope for enjoying themselves in the company they love, and rare difficult treasures are jostled into health and happiness again by the rough-and-tumble of life as they lived it on the hills ; and the earth is clothed in a thousand new promises, each one of which may in time reveal some treasure in the way of Crocus or Pink or Pansy, until here, more than ever, does one realise the devilish damage done by weeding in the ordinary garden —where, in fact, there should be a local black-list—Cress and Groundsel, and so forth (though Mr. Bowles would even leave the Groundsel on the chance of its one day producing ray-florets or a striped leaf)—while all other offers of the gods are left to flower and show what gift indeed it was they were suggesting. There is one special

Preface

corner of Mr. Bowles's garden of which I know that he will not choose adequately to talk, but of which I, therefore, must, seeing that it has long appeared to me quite the finest piece of real gardening that I know. It is a roughly triangular piece of ground, and is filled with the Dwarf Almond, a blaze of pink and white in spring. But in spring, too, all its ground is surfaced and crammed and overflowing with rare Crocus and Primrose and Bland Anemone, and every vernal bulb that is usually looked after and cleansed and cossetted, but here left alone to make itself a wild plant and seed and establish in perfect naturalness under the eye of the gardener who knows and loves each one as a shepherd knows his lambs. So much for early spring ; and then, barrenness ? Or else digging and fussing and planting ? Not a spade touches that holy ground, any more than iron had been laid to the unharvested meadow of Hippolytus, but as the Anemones and the Crocus fade, up spring Daffodils and rare Tulips and difficult Fritillaries that are everybody else's despair and have to be treated as annuals, but here look as if they had just been poked in casually and forgotten by our late sovereign lady Queen Elizabeth, so that the whole patch, under the light trellis of the Almonds growing green, becomes anew, or continues, a dancing sea of light and colour.

And so the tale goes on, and the glories of spring give way to those of summer, till the sea turns blue with Campanulas, and the copse, for so it now has grown, is floating in blue peat-reek of *Campanula patula*, while high overhead tower the stately heads of *C. lactiflora*,

My Garden in Spring

which carry on the generosity of the world, while the great waxen snow-cup and stars of Hellebore are beginning to think of the autumn, and keep the copse in loveliness until everywhere the Winter Cyclamen light up their little lamps of incandescent carbuncle. So is the wheel of nature followed in a good garden, and loveliness brought to birth from day to day, as no money and no loveless or ignorant desire for display could ever breed it. And how different here is the apparently effortless compilation of nature's best wealth from the "display" (admirable word) of those gardens that are always yelling of the number of bedded plants they contain. There was once a man who stood upon the Mont Cenis when all the earth was indeed a burning deck of blossom, filmed into the uttermost distances with the gold and violet veils of the Pansies, and with the flanks of the great mountains snow-flaked with *Anemone alpina;* he stood with one boot on a foot-wide patch of *Gentiana verna,* and the other trampling a blossom-hidden carpet of Dryas, and he looked round with that scorn-corrugated nose of which I lately spoke, and he bitterly observed, "I don't think much of *this* for a display." Only such wealthy-minded persons, I am sure, could have such a feeling about any garden so real as this of Mr. Bowles, where nature's poor little efforts are so watched and followed, and nature's wide carpet of blue and saffron and gold and rose and violet rewoven in a tissue of loveliness, how different from the neatly-partitioned unhappiness of Alpines bought by the hundred and bedded out for show. It is from such a garden as this that one comes away both humbled and consoled

Preface

to think such things can be done, and that one has never yet succeeded in doing them oneself ; comes away also uplifted by the encouragement of the garden's wizard, as well as weighed down beneath the precious treasures he will so casually lop off and pile into your crowded basket, until at last you grow quite bashful in your efforts to avoid the crowning generosity of a Nettle with variegated foliage, or a Plantain mottled with some perennial leprosy, which may have kept this nature-worshipper kneeling in an ecstasy for a quarter of an hour upon the mountains in the teeth of a bitter snow-gale, and despite the hardly less bitter cries of his escort, not in the least enthusiastic for such things, and longing to exclaim " Excelsior ! " did not a certain lingering knowledge of Latin forbid.

REGINALD FARRER.

CONTENTS

ILLUSTRATIONS

BLACK AND WHITE PLATES

My Garden in Spring

COLOUR PLATES

MY GARDEN IN SPRING

CHAPTER I

When does Spring Commence?

IF we could take a census of opinion on the question, "When does Spring commence?" the answers would be almost as variant in character as in number.

The majority of people would most likely declare that the 21st of March was the first day of Spring, though there still exists a sentimental preference for the 14th of February, the feast of St. Valentine, while a large number of people over a certain age would insist that Spring no longer exists, and would probably endeavour to prove this assertion by lengthy reminiscences of halcyon days of yore, which provided early opportunities for picnics and thin raiment.

Who has not heard their great-aunt Georgina hold forth on the Indian muslins that in bygone Mays were all-sufficient for her comfort?

Argument with such is useless, and it is much better to pile fresh logs on the fire and shut the windows to preserve her tweed-clad frame from a chill.

"Many lands, many climates," is as true as the old saying,

1   A

My Garden in Spring

" Many men, many minds," so of necessity the answers to this question must be as varied as the aspects from which the subject is viewed, and I think some of them possess sufficient interest to warrant investigation.

First we may take the astronomical point of view, and I like the impression of powder and pigtails and snuffboxes derived from this pompously-worded quotation from an eighteenth-century writer:[1] " Spring in cosmography denotes one of the seasons of the year commencing in the northern parts of the world on the day the sun enters the first degree of Aries, about the tenth day of March, and ending when it leaves Gemini. More strictly, when the sun's meridian altitude from the zenith, being on the increase, is at a medium between the greatest and least." Which holds back Spring until the Snowdrops have departed, and the equinox gives us March, in its most violently leonine mood. To go much further back, we learn from Hesiod's *Works and Days*, which dates from an age but little later than Homer's poems, that the Greeks reckoned the commencement of Spring by the evening rising of Arcturus, sixty days after the winter solstice. Happy Greeks, with a southern sky to light the fire of scarlet Anemones on the hillsides and announce the lesser Eleusinia ! It was once my good fortune to spend early March in Athens, and enjoy the feast of the Greek Anemone (*A. hortensis,* var. *graeca*), the most glorious of all scarlet flowers. I often long to do so again, but next time I hope some epidemic may have destroyed the goats of the district, that all the buds may escape

[1] *Encyc. Brit.* 1796.

2

When does Spring Commence ?

their hungry mouths, and not only those growing among thorny plants.

Here is another view from Pliny's *Natural History*[1] as translated by Philemon Holland : " To proceed, then, the Spring openeth the sea for sailors ; in the beginning whereof the west winds mitigate the winter weather, at what time as the Sun is in the twenty-fifth degree of Aquarius, and that is the sixth day before the Ides of February."

Meteorologists give us a more exact and practical conception in dating the beginning of Spring when the average daily temperature reaches 48° F.

This of course varies with the latitude, and works out like this for Europe :

March	1.	Bordeaux, Barcelona, Marseilles, Genoa.
„	15.	Brest, Turin, Venice.
April	1.	S.W. Ireland, Land's End, Paris.
„	15.	N.W. Ireland, London, Brussels.
May	1.	Edinburgh, Moscow, N. Alps.
„	15.	N. Scotland, St. Petersburg.
June	1.	N.W. Norway.
„	15.	S. Iceland.
July 1–15.		N. Cape.

It is, however, from the gardener's point of view we must regard the question, and the wise one will follow Bacon, and be content with nothing less than *ver perpetuum* in his garden. Reference to the celebrated *Essay* shows that Bacon was satisfied with mere evergreens for the greater part of winter, and he writes : " For December

---

[1] Plin. i, ii, Cap. xlvii, C. p. 23.

3

My Garden in Spring

and January and the latter part of November, you must take such things as are green all winter ; holly, ivy, bays, Juniper, cypress trees, yew, pine-apple trees, fir trees, rosemary, lavender ; periwinkle, the white, the purple, and the blue ; germander, flags, orange leaves, lemon trees, and myrtles, if they be stoved; and sweet marjoram warm set." So that, so long as a plant bore green leaves, even though they were fully developed and no fresh growth was being produced by it, it was all he demanded to keep his perpetual Spring alive ; but in these later times, when so much more of the world has been rummaged and ransacked to provide treasures for our gardens, it must be a very poor one that, except during times of severe frost or deep snow, cannot show some plants if not actually in flower yet in active growth. Surely this starting into growth is the true Spring in plant life, whether it be an awakening due to the melting of a covering of snow as with the high alpines, or the commencement of the rains in the African veldt ; and so long as we can see some plant in the garden starting off vigorously for its annual round of existence, so long in that spot is Spring with us.

It is interesting to note how differently certain plants behave when removed from their native surroundings. Some will quickly become acclimatised, and accommodate themselves to the new conditions ; others seem to get confused, and attempt to flower at most unseemly times. This is especially noticeable with certain recently collected Alpine plants, and Soldanellas, Gentians, and certain Primulas such as *P. pedemontana, P. minima,* and *P. Auricula,* which are accustomed to form their flower buds or crowns

When does Spring Commence?

in the early autumn and then to go to rest until the Spring under a covering of snow. These evidently miss Jack Frost's annual visit to their bedsides, to tuck them up with his icy fingers, and to bid them good-night till the sunshine of next May shall pull off their snow duvets layer by layer. A November frost may close their eyes for a few days, and then a sou'wester in December with its warm rain will trick them into the belief that winter is over, and they lose their heads actually as well as figuratively, for the poor little blooms they produce all in a hurry are mere caricatures, and generally fall a prey to a roving slug.

On the other hand, I find that most species of Dianthus, Ranunculus, Anemone and Leontopodium from the same localities are never deceived into making a too early start. I think all New Zealand plants accept our seasons within a twelvemonth of their arrival, and alter their flowering time to suit them, but certain Cape and S. American plants never swerve from the traditions of their race ; thus *Oxalis lobata* from Chili, and the S. African *O. purpurata*, better known as *Bowiei*, will not learn to start into growth before autumn, although *O. vespertilionis* from Mexico, *O. brasiliensis* and *O. floribunda* from Brazil come up smilingly in early Spring. I suspect the reason is that plants which have in nature a season of rest imposed by drought or heat, of which *Amaryllis Belladonna* and certain autumn flowering Croci are good examples, have become thoroughly adapted to rushing into flower and growth with the advent of autumn rains. At the same time there is a kind of freewill, an individuality that leads plants of one genus in a similar

5

My Garden in Spring

environment to take opposite lines of action, as may be seen in two of our wild Scillas, *S. verna* and *S. autumnalis*, which are so plentiful on some of the sea cliffs but have totally different seasons of growth and flowering.

I feel I have now freed my conscience from any need to adhere to the almanac for the limitation of Spring, the plants themselves having taken a like licence, but as in the case of house-hunting with no obligation of being within reach of some special town, and the world to choose from, the difficulty of choice is enormously increased, so if we allow that any freshly-started flower brings its own Spring with it, as fire to frying-pan or Charybdis to Scylla so stands the fresh basis of choice to the old.

I have a strong conviction that the first real breath of Spring that I inhale in the garden comes from *Iris unguicularis*. I always look for, and generally find a bud or two in the last week of September, or in later seasons in mid-October, usually before *Crocus longiflorus* is fully open. The scent of those two flowers is remarkably alike. When we were children one of our favourite games was a trial of nose-power : one of us was blindfolded and the others submitted samples of leaves and flowers to be smelt and recognised. In those days we had neither this Iris nor Crocus to play with, but I feel sure the two would have proved indistinguishable. We then relied mostly on the similarity of the odours of an untimely shed cucumber, begged from the peppery but kindly old gardener, and young growths of Philadelphus crushed and matured to the acme of redolence by confinement in a

6

When does Spring Commence ?

chubby hot hand ; or a well-sucked Gooseberry skin and a spray of Shepherd's Purse or Arabis.

Many people admit that the sense of smell brings things more vividly to the memory than that of sight. I know that it is so with me, and a whiff of *Iris unguicularis* or *Crocus longiflorus*, though several other Crocuses are almost equally endowed (*C. laevigatus* and *vitellinus* among the autumnal species and *C. Imperati* in early Spring certainly are), recalls a feeling of Spring in autumn far more vividly than the sight of the flowers of a Snowdrop such as *Galanthus Olgae*, which is in bloom at the same time. We greatly want a chart of scents with descriptive names for the distinct groups, and when it comes I should like to patent the name of " Pure Spring " for the odour of these flowers. It is fuller than the scent of Primroses, with a promise of honey in it strong enough to wake any bee, yet you feel it is not such brown-heather honey as *Alyssum maritimum* and *Buddleia globosa* advertise, for there is a correcting sharpness in it, like that of lemon with the sugar of a Shrove Tuesday pancake, and such as we find in the scent of *Cytisus racemosus* and stronger still in *Narcissus Tazetta*.

Again, in the soft lilac colouring and crystalline texture and frail substance of their blooms these two Irids are markedly springlike. Except in orchids from seasonless glasshouses and *Iris Kaempferi*, summer and autumn flowers, so far as I can remember, lack the crystalline texture of Spring flowers such as Daffodils, Hyacinths, Crocuses, and all early Irises.

Begonias have it, but I do not like their fat, meaty

7

blossoms and floppy habits, and cannot be bothered with them, however much their petals may sparkle.

So as this chapter has already wandered too far, like *Campanula excisa* in the sand-moraine, I shall elect *Iris unguicularis* as the first flower of Spring, and arrange further chapters more on the flowers themselves than on the dates of their flowering.

Galanthus Imperati var. Atkinsii " Backhouse's variety."   (See p. 49.)

CHAPTER II

The Garden

BEFORE touching the flowers I must speak of the garden itself, as its conditions are answerable for many of the limitations that govern the variety and conditions of its occupants.

The garden, then, is situated in the parish of Enfield in the county of Middlesex, but so near to the Hertford-shire boundary that our postal address is Waltham Cross, Hertfordshire : and I envy but do not share the celebrated rose-growing soil of that district. By comparing a bench-mark in the wall with the Ordnance Survey maps, I learn we are 111.4 feet above the sea-level. *Helleborus niger* tells me that this is not a sufficient altitude for its comfort, and I must provide it with shade, and moisture beyond that of the atmosphere, if I wish it to " grow for me," as Irish gardeners say so pleasantly. I like the personal reciprocal touch in these words. How different a vision of mutual understanding they conjure up from that mild reproach and suggestion of wilful suicide conveyed in the other Hibernian garden phrase, " It died on me," which so neatly lays the blame on the plant.

The nearest milestone tells me it is but ten miles from London, and smutty evergreens, blackened tree trunks, and grimy fingers continually corroborate that milestone,

9

My Garden in Spring

in spite of the richness of our avian fauna and well-wooded, countrified surroundings. Fortunately, being due north of London, we do not get so many second-hand London fogs as our nearness suggests. South winds rarely follow a period of fog, nor do fogs often last for several days in London, until their own weight spreads them out as far as this place, so we do not get the genuine article so badly or so often as do Kew and Acton and other places on the south side of London.

I cannot believe there is a drier garden to be found in England. It is on the edge of that district which I think is classed with Yarmouth as having the lowest rainfall of Great Britain, and lies in a centre seldom visited by heavy thunderstorms ; the higher ground running from Enfield to Potter's Bar and Hatfield, and the Lea Valley on our other side, seem to lure away our rain-clouds. Storms often divide within sight of khaki-coloured lawns and flagging flowers to flood the railway lines at Ponder's End and Waltham, and do equally damp and doughty deeds for St. Albans, leaving us as dry as ever, an insulting sort of wind perhaps blowing down a barrowful of dead Lime leaves on to the lawn even in mid-July. This alone seems sufficient to make the garden as designed by nature fit only for xerophytic plants from desert and steppe and soilless cliff, or even the Moon itself when a collector gets as far. But the wonder is that anything else besides Opuntias, Sedums, and Houseleeks can exist through a summer, for the soil is in league with the climate. In the greater part of the garden, digging below the surface brings one face to face with gravel, splendidly healthy

The Garden

drainage to build one's house upon of course, and when it is a good red binding sample, a positive luxury for garden paths. There the advantages end, however, for although we have made plenty of paths, gravelled them unstintingly, and got out a good deal of the material from the garden itself, there still remain untold supplies below, and much of it so coarse and unprofitable that getting it out entails carting it away and finding some pond or hollow that needs filling to justify the labour. This coarse gravel discouraged all my childish schemes for digging ponds, gold mines, and that passage to the Antipodes that generally has to be tried during some flowerless month in the children's gardens. Perhaps it turned my mind off from all thoughts of engineering and drove it to the surface and the tilling thereof. As in our deepest excavations in all the upper part of the garden, we have never yet got through this vein of coarse gravel, perhaps I may be forgiven for a belief that our gravel runs right through the centre of the earth to our antipode whatever it is ; I don't know, but I hope it is New Zealand, because then perhaps the water that soaks away so quickly here may be interesting hot geysers at the other side and my nourishing manurings conveyed to the roots of antipodean Cabbage Palms and Ratas.

The greatest evil of a gravel subsoil is its unsuitability for deep roots. Trees will not enter it, but they turn their main roots out over its surface, and so go a-hunting into all the newly dug and enriched beds.

Old trees are precious possessions in gardens, and must be respected, but I do feel cross with them when I find an underground bird's nest of strong, fibrous roots

My Garden in Spring

in a vacant spot in a newly-arranged border kept empty
for a month or so for some choice plant. I have very
seldom come across a gardener who does not complain of
his soil or climate, or both, and there are but few so
happily placed that his complaints would be easily detected
as absurd and groundless, for there can always be too
much lime for some Rhododendrons or too little for an
exacting Clematis or two. Yet in grumbling at my
gardening conditions I do not feel a parallel case to the
lunatic who, in spite of believing himself in heaven, was
never happy, and told an inquirer it was because he had
a second-hand halo that did not fit and his harp was out
of tune, and I turn and rend any who base their claims
for pity and indulgence for starved plants on the possession
of a sandy soil, for well do I know the way trees make
long tap roots and find moisture deep down in most
varieties of sand, in which, besides showing an honest respect for the nutriment allotted to surface rooters, these
tap rooters anchor themselves so pleasantly and save much
labour and worry of staking. But here young Conifers
and hobbledehoy Eucalypts are sources of anxiety and
often of farewell lamentation at every equinox. So on
most days in the year I would barter my smooth, firm
paths for a good deep sand, with its storage of moisture
deep down.

Of water there seems to be plenty, for the New River runs
right through the very centre of the garden ; but though it
may carry many millions of gallons through it, clever
Sir Hugh Myddleton made its clay banks so strong that
even after 300 years they let no water soak away, and I

The Garden

smile quietly when people say, "Of course your Irises do so well all along by the river, as they get moisture from it," for I know those beds under the old Yews are about the driest in Europe. The water is there in the river bed, but as a gardener once said to me, "Yes, sir, there's plenty of water but it's very low down." I often think of his plaint when I too have been dragging it up in fat, lumpy water-cans, and wish I had standpipes and hose and sprinklers and the many luxuries of people lucky enough to have water high up, on the top of their own hill, like good old Tom Smith's ideal nursery at Newry, or in the water-tower of the neighbouring town. I must enumerate my difficulties, or my readers will not appreciate the skill and energy necessary here to grow the things they have to tear up as weeds in their own gardens, and one of my troubles is the well-known hardness of New River water. Derived mainly from chalk wells, it is so hard that one feels it would be scarcely a miracle to walk on it, and when the well nearest to us is in full work there is a distinct bluish-green colour in the river, rather attractive to look at, but as I have found by experience, rendering it an absolute poison for certain calcifuge plants. A liberal dose of New River water given in a spirit of kindness to a collection of dwarf Rhododendrons during a time of drought killed all but one in about a fortnight. The survivor is with me still, being evidently a lime lover, a hybrid of *R. hirsutum*.

With these limitations to the possibilities of watering and manuring I dread a spell of drought, and always prefer that a garden visitor coming for the first time

13

My Garden in Spring

should do so before the middle of June. A wise old farmer once said to me, in speaking of the new Parliamentary candidate, "Why, he promises 'em anything, a shower of rain every night and a shower of manure on Sundays." I have ever since felt that the fulfilment of those promises is what my garden and I need, from June to October anyway.

As gardens go, I suppose this must be called an old one, for as far as I can make out it seems to be about 400 years since a certain row of Yews were planted. They are in a crescent-shaped line, and the course of the river follows the same bend. Those who are knowledgable about the rate of growth of Yews in a hungry soil declare them to be older than the river. So it seems probable that their owner in 1609, to save his trees, insisted on this otherwise meaningless bend in the river. It was not until another century had passed that my Huguenot ancestors bought the property and settled down here, and I was always told that two quaint old Flemish figures in carved stone were in the garden when they bought it. Huguenots ought to have left a heritage of Mulberry and Catalpa. The old Mulberry tree was blown down before my day, but the remains of a Catalpa, starved and driven to a horizontal line of growth by a fine old Beech, may be of their planting, for certainly no one with a grain of gardening sense would have placed it so near even a half-grown Beech. It is so fascinating to hunt up evidence in the trees themselves of otherwise unrecorded work of one's forbears that I am sorely tempted to linger among these vegetable documents, but will try to confine

The Garden

myself to those that are necessary to explain the present condition of the ground.

The most evident signs of gardening date from the earliest years of the nineteenth century, when the place belonged to my great-grandmother, the last of the Garnaults, for on her marriage in 1799 the pleasant old French name was changed for the unromantic-sounding patronymic which I think must be the longest monosyllable in the English language, and unless carefully spelt as well as pronounced in shops and stores suffers strange vagaries in form, some of them exceedingly unpleasing to the polite eye. This Ann Garnault has left her mark on the garden by planting a deciduous Cypress (*Taxodium distichum*), which, in spite of a subsequent draining of the pond by which it was planted, has grown into a really fine tree.

In one favourable season it matured a few cones, but the catkins seldom get a fair chance of full development. They are formed in the autumn, and remain green when the foliage turns to that deep red so characteristic of this tree—the red of a fox's coat, or of Devon cattle. They remain on the tree after the falling of the leaves has covered the beds with an apparent mulch of cocoanut fibre, but severe winters bring many of them down, and even the few tassels of male catkins left generally fail to effect perfect fertilisation of the queer little solitary female blossoms for lack of dry sunny days with mild breezes in early Spring. The good example of Great-grandmother Ann has been followed by the two succeeding generations, but the younger Cypresses are of course

My Garden in Spring

far behind the big tree. After his wife's death my great-grandfather pulled down the old red-brick gabled house and built the present one of the then fashionable yellow brick brought from as far away as Suffolk, wherefore it has been my constant aim to smother it in creepers of all kinds. Some contemporary water-colours of the old house show a hearty middle-aged Larch on what was then the bowling-green, but before I can remember it had lost its formal rectangular shape and become an ordinary lawn, bounded by various paths. The Larch still stands, and is a venerable specimen, but has only been able to grow on its northern side, having always been crowded on the south by other trees. Plantations of Scots Pines shown in these drawings as saplings are now replaced by either fine old trees, or some dead and dying trunks rather puzzling to deal with, and spaces from which others have gone. For the period of active planting must have been followed by one of passive inattention, taken advantage of by certain Horse Chestnuts and Sycamores to place their greedy, grabbing offspring out in the world. How these robbers grow! They throw a light on the Psalmist's phrase of lurking in thievish corners: unobserved they get a foothold and turn their corner into a den for receiving stolen goods, and then up they go, and their betters are choked and starved by these arboreal garotters. I can scarcely believe, when looking at the garden, that I have one by one displaced such a forest of these coarse, garden un-desirables. It has been a very gradual process, spread over twenty years, for I only garden in my father's

The Garden

garden, and I hope something of filial piety, as well as the realisation of the impossibility of having one's own way under such circumstances, has led me in the path of gentle and gradual elimination of these devouring hordes, which from other views are of course trees, and therefore not to be lightly felled.

One of the last of the Horse Chestnuts dropped several stout limbs on a row of garden seats last summer, and provided a powerful argument for the removal of the trunk that shed them. So from the garden proper they have gone to the timber yard, and as firelogs serve to warm my bones instead of offending my eye. To anyone who may follow my example I offer this hint : be quite sure the wood is well dried before sawing it up for bringing into the house ; otherwise the scent of sour sap will be as offensive to the nose as the misplaced tree was to the eye. To sum up the present conditions of the garden ; climate, soil, and trees contrive to make it the driest and hungriest in Great Britain, and therefore arises the line of gardening I have been driven into. It is perhaps better described as collecting plants and endeavouring to keep them alive, than as gardening for beautiful effects or the production of prize-winning blossoms. Many find the garden too museumy to please them. I plead guilty to the charge, knowing there is more of the botanist and lover of species and natural forms and varieties in me than there is of the florist or fine cultivator. In fact I gladly give a home to the class of plant the writers in early numbers of the *Botanical Magazine* and *Botanical Register* faintly praise as being suitable for the gardens

My Garden in Spring

of the curious. It gives me more pleasure to have got together the three distinct forms—grey-leaved, golden, and major—of *Sedum spathulatum*, and to make them share a flat-topped rock with at least six other species of Sedum, than to have the same space monopolised by *Sedum pilosum*, new, rare, and lovely though it be.

Again, Euphorbias are plentiful here, but Zinnias, Clarkias, and bedding Begonias find no welcome, and Gaillardias, Cactus Dahlias, and such plants are few. After such a confession will you care to wander round my garden with me? Will you have enough patience to let me talk of the differences between the blue Wood Anemones of Norway and those of Southern Ireland or Western England and Wales? It is only fair to state that colour scheming is impossible in the circumstances, and though I have enjoyed having eight fingers and two thumbs in several iridescent pies for other folks' gardens (and some of them have proved "pretty eating," as is said in Ireland and seems to fit the metaphor), except for one effort in grouping coloured foliage with suitable flowers of which I am rather proud, most of my effects, blends, and contrasts have been the result of accident, or rather the placing and grouping of plants in surroundings I hoped would be suitable for their health rather than their appearance.

I fear I am a little impatient of the school of gardening that encourages the selection of plants merely as artistic furniture, chosen for colour only, like ribbons or embroidery silks. I feel sorry for plants that are obliged to make a struggle for life in uncongenial situa-

The Garden

tions because their owner wishes all things of those shades of pink, blue, or orange to fit in next to the grey or crimson planting, and I long to shift the unhappy *Lilium pardalinum* away from its sun-loving Alstroemeria partners and plant it across the path among the shade-loving Phloxes. The distribution of plants in this garden has been governed chiefly by a sort of extra sense that seems to be developed by many enthusiastic gardeners, a sympathetic understanding derived from a new plant's appearance only when the power is perfected ; but in others, less qualified as clairvoyants, a knowledge of its native country will often suggest its future neighbours.

One of the finest collections of trees and shrubs to be found in any private garden in England is arranged by grouping them according to their native continents or the larger countries, such as China. But that garden is so well favoured in situation and climate that almost any plant will grow in almost any part of it. Without such a strict geographical system, however, one finds that certain portions of the garden get allotted to N. American, Mediterranean, and other plants with marked preferences for sun or shade. But the sense I mean is an inexplicable knowledge and feeling, a sort of wireless message from the plant to the invisible antennae of the gardener. Such an one sits down to unpack a box of novelties and can divide them out—Trilliums to the left-hand basket for the cool border, *Viola bosniaca* to the right for the sand-moraine, with *Wahlenbergia gracilis* and *Leucocrinum montanum* for companions.

So here my sixth gardening sense, as in the last

My Garden in Spring

instance, does not shrink from associating eastern European plants with New Zealanders and Californians, and it is rather the physical geography of the borders than the native countries of their occupants that has settled the question of position.

It would be more pleasant to be able to refer to a border as China or South Africa instead of such names as position or quality of soil suggest. Here, for instance, we have the Damp Bed, but I must warn all who read that it is but a courtesy title, due to the fact that it is not quite so dry as other beds because it lies on the north side of some tall trees, and when last we turned it out during autumn manœuvres, we put a good layer of peat moss two feet underground.

CHAPTER III

Early Irises

SUPPOSE a wicked uncle who wished to check your gardening zeal left you pots of money on condition you grew only one species of plants : what would you choose ? I should settle on *Iris unguicularis*, as in summer one could get whiffs of other folks' roses and lilies and all the dull season enjoy the flowers of this beautiful Iris. It was some twenty-four years ago I first saw it in the gardens at La Mortola. Sir Thomas Hanbury parted its forelock of long leaves and displayed a mass of lilac blossoms, and then and there I vowed I must grow it, and grow it well too.

I had some difficulty in finding out where to get it, and I suppose it was not so well known then as now, as I could hear of no one among my gardening neighbours who could flower it. I was fortunate in getting hold of a good variety for my first plant, and in trying to imitate its warm home at La Mortola, I planted it against the front wall of a peach-house, where a southern exposure and warmth from the water-pipes brought it into flower within a year of planting, and set me to work to get other forms and find further suitable sites for them. So many people complain of its shyness of flowering that I feel bound to give my experiences of it rather fully, hoping to help others thereby. I soon found that the varietal forms in

My Garden in Spring

commerce had very well-marked idiosyncrasies, not only as to outward appearance but in period and freedom of flowering. The paler flowered forms are those that flower earliest and most surely in autumn. That known as *marginata* is generally the first, and the white one and the variety *lilacina* often come in a dead heat for second place. Pale colouring is correlated with early flowering, it seems, and the varietal name *lilacina* is fully justified, both it and *marginata* bearing flowers of a softer and bluer shade than any others ; *marginata* has a narrow but regular white edge to the falls, not wide or distinct enough to add to the beauty of the blossom, but sufficient to warrant the use of the name, and both forms have wider leaves than the type, and, what is better, larger flowers. I strongly advise anyone wishing for autumn and early winter flowers to plant these two forms along with the white one. Half a dozen good plants of each ought to provide buds for picking in constant succession through November, December, and in open weather in January. It is curious that the white form should flower with the pale lilac ones, as in appearance it is evidently an albino of the type, having leaves of medium width and flowers rather diminished in size, as is so often the case with an albino form.

I once heard of a larger, white form, but diligent inquiry and an ever-open eye have failed to discover it. I believe all the white flowered plants in cultivation in Britain are divisions from a single plant found about thirty-five years ago by Mr. Edwyn Arkwright when riding through the then wild scrub on the hillside near Algiers, but seedlings raised from it ought to show variation,

Early Irises

and careful selection should give us larger forms. I am watching a family of yearling babes, and hoping the leaves are increasing in width sufficiently to promise good results.

What I imagine must be the type form, because it is the commonest in cultivation, has medium-sized flowers of a distinctly warm lilac : perhaps it is not going too far to say they are flushed with rose, after the manner of the compilers of catalogues. I never expect them to flower until New Year's Day has come and gone, so in making a planting for picking purposes it will save time and trouble by keeping the early flowering sorts together, for except during spells of settled mild weather, which Heaven knows are as rare as spare moments, it is best to pick the buds a day before they open, and at that time they are not very conspicuous, as the under sides of the falls are then of a pale, dingy buff shade, slightly tinged with greyish lilac at their edges, and are very hard to distinguish from browned tips of old leaves. In consequence of this it is .often necessary, not only to examine the clumps at close quarters, but to lift the longer leaves with one's hand, and all that means stooping, and a gardener's back never requires more of that sort of physical drill than is absolutely necessary, neither is it good for his temper to hunt over clumps of late flowering forms before the reward for so doing is due.

This plan of inconspicuous colouring for unexpanded buds and closed flowers has been adopted by many winter-flowering plants. It would seem they are cryptically coloured for the purpose of avoiding observation and consequent destruction by enemies. Thus many of the

My Garden in Spring

early lilac Crocuses have the outer surface of the exterior segments coloured buff, as in *Crocus Imperati* and *C. etruscus,* or of a neutral grey shade, as in *C. Tomasinianus,* while others are striped or freckled with browns and purples in a manner that renders them very hard to see among their own leaves or grass in the case of stripes, or against bare ground on a dull day or when closed for the night if suffused externally. A spell of sunshine changes this in a few minutes, and the glowing interior of the flower shows up from afar, and is ready for fertilisation by any insect visitor which may be rendered active and hungry by the same bright spell. I have been unable to discover what are the enemies of such flowers in their own homes, but judging from the evil habits of that vulgar little pest the sparrow, one is inclined to fancy they may be birds of sorts. But for the sake of those to whose charitable sentimentality all members of the avian fauna are the " dear little birds," repaying winter doles of crumbs with spring carols, I will offer a scapegoat in the form of some beetle of the family of Cantharidae such as our British Oil Beetle, *Meloe Proscarabaeus,* to which a fresh young flower is a toothsome breakfast, for I notice that those who can overlook anything in a bird—" a dear little bird " of course, ostriches and eagles being outside their spheres of experience—are ever ready to denounce or bring about the destruction of " nasty creeping things." For myself, I am too light a sleeper to appreciate the cheeping of newly-awakened sparrows in the Wistaria round my window, and too fond of its flowers to forgive their chewing the swelling bloombuds.

Primula longiflora.   (See p 138.)

Early Irises

I think the longest word in the Greek Lexicon was invented for use in a maledictory imprecation against sparrows. One feels that to pronounce it rapidly, or to write it clearly on lintel and sidepost, ought to kill them off in flocks. Try it ; it is quite simple, only this : ὀρθροφοι τοσῦκοφαντοδικοτᾱλαίπωρος, which being translated is "early-prowling base-informing sad-litigious plaguey ways," almost as beautiful in its hyphened English as in the original Greek.

The success of *I. unguicularis* as a cut flower depends so much on careful picking, and experience has taught me how to grapple with so many sources of difficulty and injury, that details are perhaps worth recording. The first thing to note is that this Iris, after the fashion of the Crocus and Colchicum, produces no flower stem above-ground at flowering time, a long perianth tube doing duty for it until the seedpod is raised up on the true stem just before the seeds are ripe. A careful examination will show that this Iris has a short scape among the bases of the leaves, and that in healthy specimens it is about half an inch in length and bears three buds at its apex. Scape and buds are wrapped by one or two tough green spathes, and each separate bud has two more spathes of its own, of thinner texture and closely wrapped round the fragile perianth tube. The central bud of these three is always first to lengthen and flower, and generally is ready for picking before the other two show above the tough outer spathes. Therefore to avoid picking all three buds at once, and so wasting the two undeveloped ones, it is necessary to pull away the two outermost tough spathes

25

My Garden in Spring

a little, until you are sure you are holding only the two belonging to the bud ready to be gathered. Then a sharp pull will generally bring it away, leaving the other two buds to push up a week or ten days later. They sometimes do this simultaneously, and as it is not difficult to see whether the central bloom has been already gathered, one can then allow oneself the luxury of picking the whole stiff bunch of spathes and buds.

If the nights are mild it is as well to leave the buds on the plant until the perianth tube has lengthened sufficiently to stand above the surrounding spathes. But although the perianth segments when exposed just above the spathes will safely stand several degrees of frost, I find once the perianth tube is out in the world and un-protected, a few degrees of frost will render it transparent and limp, burst its cell walls in fact, and ruin that blossom's future.

So in doubtful weather I prefer to pull the buds when the coloured parts of the flower appear just above the spathes. I find it best to place them at once in water and to immerse them up to their necks. Then they lengthen rapidly, and one by one burst open and are ready to transfer to the flower vases. If placed directly after picking in water that only reaches an inch or so up their length, they are rather inclined to flag and fall over, and even to get too much exhausted of sap to open properly. Their own foliage is rather too coarse to arrange with them, so I often use the leaves of young plants of *Libertia formosa*, which are of the same shade of green but neater than the Iris leaves. They look best

Early Irises

arranged in the old-fashioned tall champagne glasses with Libertia leaves, but when they are plentiful I like to fill a bowl with some short sprigs of Cypress greenery and spear the Irises into it.

The deepest coloured variety is known as *speciosa*, and has narrow leaves and throws its blossoms up well above them, and so is much more showy in the garden than the paler forms, whose broad, arching leaves often hide the flowers a good deal. Also it seldom flowers before February, so that the blossoms can generally open and escape injury better than those of the earlier forms. Later still comes the variety now known as *angustifolia*, which has also masqueraded under the names of *Elizabethae*, *cretensis*, and latterly *agrostifolia*. This last would be a good name for it, as its leaves are very narrow and grassy, but it is possibly a result of copying *angustifolia* from some indistinct handwriting or worn-out label, as it has no authority that I know of beyond a catalogue or two and labels at shows. Anyway, this narrow-leaved form is a good thing, and when established it flowers very freely, and is a suitable subject for a warm nook in the rock garden or at the foot of a pedestal or stone in a southern exposure. I grow it in both such situations, and during March and April the clumps frequently open half a dozen or so of their showy flowers at one time. They stand up well among the leaves, and have a dainty, butterfly expression about them as the standards arch outward at a pleasant angle. They vary somewhat in the amount of white markings on the fall, but all of them have far more white than other forms of *Iris unguicularis*,

27

My Garden in Spring

some so much that the falls appear to have a white centre edged with a bluish lilac band. The texture of the flowers is rather firmer and crisper than in the larger varieties, and I find they last quite two or three days longer, either when picked or when left in the open. These endearing qualities make them well worth growing.

I grow one other form, but I do not care much for it. I got it first from Herr Sprenger of Naples as *Iris unguicularis*, var. *pontica*, and lately from Holland as *I. lazica*. It has wide leaves, which somewhat resemble those of *Iris foetidissima*, and the flowers are of a rather starry, poor form, and a washy, pinkish lilac, the falls being mottled with a yellow brown much too freely to look clean and fresh. It has some rather interesting botanical characters, such as a trigonous pedicel and markedly keeled spathe, but though I should be sorry to lose the variety I do not want any more plants of it.

The growth of the pollen tube and its passage down the style must be as remarkable and rapid in these Irises as in any known flower. If you examine the distance it has to go from the stigma down to the ovary and consider the very short duration of the blossom you will readily see what I mean. It is quite worth while dissecting a full-blown blossom and extracting the slender style from out of the perianth tube to get an idea of the delicacy and wonder of its mechanism. As great length of style is such a marked character of this Iris it is a pity that Desfontaine's name *stylosa* cannot be maintained for it, but as Poiret's *Voyage en Barbarie*, in which the first description of it occurs, was published in 1789, his name of *unguicularis*

Early Irises

must stand by the law of priority, for the other was not published until nine years later.

In most gardens the best position for planting a good row of this useful plant is along the south front of a greenhouse. It frequently happens that there is such a low space of wall quite unutilised where a narrow border can easily be made. I believe in planting them just after their flowering season, that is to say as soon as they can be procured in late April or May ; and I like to jam them up against the foot of the wall, pressing the rootstock right against it, as I believe they will flower much sooner if they cannot spread out on both sides.

I have seen good results obtained by raising their bed a few inches and placing a shallow board along the front of it to hold up the soil, and I should strongly advise this plan in moist or heavy soils. If there are hot-water pipes on the other side of the wall against which they are planted so much the better, you will be all the more sure to get flowers in the winter months. But look carefully to the guttering that almost always forms a roof over their heads in such positions, as a leak into the heart of a clump will soon destroy it. Another trouble may arise from the melting of snow on the glass of a heated house from the warmth within, and the consequent drip and formation of icicles on the young leaves. It is worth while to keep a piece of board to lay over them during such times of trouble. Once planted they need but little care. It is wise to pull away in Spring any of their leaves that have died, to let air and sunlight in to ripen the rootstock. In autumn any dead leaves that have blown

My Garden in Spring

into their hearts are best removed before they rot, and a careful search should be made from time to time for slugs and snails, which are very fond of the tender, juicy buds. By carefully bending the leaves forward from the wall and peering down among the crowns these evil gasteropods may generally be discovered ; but the caterpillars of the Yellow Underwing and Angleshades Moths are more troublesome to catch. The only successful method is to go out on a mild evening with an acetylene bicycle lamp, which will show up the marauders in their true colours.

Patience seems to be the only manure these Irises need, poor soil inducing flowering instead of production of leaf, and the older a clump grows the better it flowers, so long as it does not raise itself too much out of the ground to be able to get nourishment ; but I have some old clumps that by pressing their rhizomes against the wall have climbed up it some six or seven inches ; these aspiring individuals flower well, and I respect their ambitious habit so long as the leaves look strong and vigorous and I receive my rent in flowers.

Last winter we picked about fifty buds a week from the time the frosts had killed off the Asters and outdoor Chrysanthemums until March brought us sufficient Daffodils to keep the dinner-table supplied. As a producer of *ver perpetuum* during the dullest months of the year I feel sure no outdoor plant can beat *Iris unguicularis*.

Next in order as bringers in of Spring among the Irises come the members of that puzzling little group of

Early Irises

bulbous-rooted ones known as the *reticulata* section, from the curiously beautiful coat that covers their corms. This tunic is well worth examining with a good lens. To the naked eye it looks as if composed of parallel strands of a towlike substance, but if pulled away from the corm the strands stretch away from each other, and show lesser strands branching out from them and uniting the stronger ones, so that then it becomes a veritable network. So many local forms and varieties exist in this section that their systematic arrangement is not easy, and certain of them get chivied about as varieties of first one species, then of another, according to various authors' views, and this is the case with an old favourite of mine. I used to call it *Iris reticulata*, var. *sophenensis*, but Mr. Dykes, in his sumptuous new monograph of the genus, points out that it resembles *I. histrioides* in its manner of increase, viz. by a host of tiny cormlets surrounding the base of the parent corm, and in its stout leaves and hasty way of bursting into flower soon after the leaves and spathes have pierced through the ground, so as *I. histrioides*, var. *sophenensis*, it must now be known.

If it flowered at Midsummer we should either fail to notice it or turn up our rose and lily-surfeited noses at its humble charms, but in the darkest days of the year, in old December or young January, it is a joyous sight. Quite unintentionally it found its way into the cold frames sacred to my rarer Crocuses, and at once showed me plainly that it liked the treatment given to its neighbours, by multiplying as rapidly as the rabbits the small girl who was slow at sums envied so much.

My Garden in Spring

The small spawnlike corms are but feebly attached to the large central one, and fall off so easily that it is hard to lift the colony intact, and once off they are hard to collect, many of them being about the same size and dingy colour as the pupal cocoons of the common black ant, known as ants' eggs to bird-fanciers and gamekeepers. These soon get dispersed in the dry soil, and apparently every one grows into a fair-sized corm with babes of its own before next lifting-time. In the open border they are rather more delicate, and require a very warm, well-drained corner and frequent lifting. They are worth some trouble, for the sturdy little flowers are prettily shaded with plum-purples and deep blues, and last fresh and fair for several days, but they open so close to the ground that they are not suitable for picking, though a patch of a dozen or so is worth looking at in the rock garden at that flowerless time of year. The typical form of *I. histrioides* varies a good deal in size and in period of flowering, so that a clump of it, unless formed of off-sets from one form, will send up a flower or two at a time for some weeks. In its best forms it is very lovely, and surprisingly large and blue to be smiling at one from the surface of the cold, wet soil so early in the year.

The best form I have came from Messrs. Van Tubergen, who seem to have been fortunate in receiving this superior variety from their collector, for they allow it to appear in their list without any additional varietal name, but I have seen it labelled " var. *major*" when shown by others.

It is not only larger than the old form, but also earlier and of a better substance, and as 4s. will purchase

Early Irises

a dozen, no garden should be without a good clump of it. The variety has never increased with me as lavishly as little sophenensis does, but then I have not tried it in the cold frame which is the main source of my compound interest harvest of the ants' eggs produced by sophenensis.

I do not believe it would prove so prolific as that generous-minded midget however it were treated, for I sent a few corms of sophenensis to a friend who gardens in Cheshire, and she wrote to tell me that now after three years they have grown to the number of 168. Yet the last time I saw it shown in flower at Vincent Square its proud owner named 3s. 6d. as the price of its departure into other hands.

There are other early Irises, but they are not found here, for I have been obliged to renounce as expensive luxuries needing annual renewal such delights as *I. histrio* and *I. Vartanii.* They insist on producing long and tender leaves before they flower, and winds and frost soon take the tucker out of them, and, limp and browned, they cannot collect the necessary carbon dioxide to feed the plant, and no fat corm results for next season. Wise old *histrioides*, to be contented with those stumpy, stiff leaves until warmer days advise their lengthening ! *I. alata* ought to, and sometimes does, illuminate this dark spell, but though it lives in sunny rock-nooks here it is only after exceptionally grilling summers that it plucks up heart to flower outside. It used to do fairly well in the Crocus frame, but has been crowded out for my more beloved children.

Before the last lag-behind forms of *I. histrioides* have faded, I look to some precocious seedling forms of *I.*

My Garden in Spring

reticulata. These were surprise gifts to me from my garden, spontaneous seedlings, unbirthday presents, as the Red Queen called such pleasant windfalls. I believe their mother was the dwarf, early plum-red form known as *Krelagei*, which is a great seeder here, but, as so often happens with plants that seed freely, after producing well-filled pods it feels it has done its duty, and is content to die. Except for its precocity in flowering, and its motherliness, I do not greatly care for this variety, but as a parent I advise all to grow it until they have a generation of its babes from which to select better forms.

Experiments carried out by Mr. Dykes and others show that the purple red colouring of *Krelagei* appears in self-fertilised seedlings of the deep blue form known in gardens as the typical *reticulata.* This dark blue is furthermore the rarest colour form in its native home, and here without artificial fertilisation I have never seen it set seed. The red forms, on the contrary, bear pods in most seasons when left to natural causes for pollination. If their seeds only reproduced the squat, liver-coloured charms of their dowdy mother they would not be worth sowing. But among the gifts of the gods that appeared round my dead-and-gone *Krelagei's* label, then only its tombstone, first came a deep, indigo-blue youngster with only a slight improvement in stature, not a first-class plant, but as early as ever its mother was, then came one of the greatest surprises and joys of this garden, a posthumous son and heir to a once-cherished treasure, *I. reticulata,* var. *cyanea.* This variety *cyanea* is now nothing more than a mysterious memory. Mr. Dykes

34

Early Irises

thinks it may be identical with the form now known as *Melusine*. Both have "died on me" here, alas : but as I recall them to mind, I would gladly get *cyanea* again, but do not wish for *Melusine*. Mr. Dykes in the great monograph, says of it, " In the best examples the colour is an approach to a light Cambridge blue." If my memory is not too much affected by the weakness which makes all long-past summers warm and sunny, all childish haunts vast and magnificent, and in a fuller development turns all passably good-looking grandmothers into noted beauties of their day—my *cyanea* was fit to compare with a turquoise, and taller than all the *Melusines* I see now. Its clear blue colouring and length of perianth tube have passed into my joy of a seedling, and *so far*, it has proved of good constitution, and has steadily increased. Please note that I have said "so far," for here I must make a confession. I rather pride myself on being free from superstitions about most things, and have even lectured at local debating societies on the inconsistency of superstitious fears with a Christian belief. But I believe most people, though able to make light of certain super-stitions, and perhaps ready to walk under ladders, or dine comfortably though one of thirteen, yet cannot quite shake off some idea, probably an ingrained result of nursery teaching, that it is just as well to avoid giving and receiving scissors, or cutting one's nails on a Friday. A curious chain of experiences in the former case, and a haunting doggerel rhyme in the latter, make me weak about these. My greatest weakness of all, however, takes the form of an uncomfortable feeling, that the unseen

35

My Garden in Spring

powers lie in wait with trouble or failure for him who boasts of continued success, just as surely as the clerk of the weather does with a sudden shower, for those who venture afield without mackintosh or umbrella.

At no time am I more timid of these avenging fates than when openly rejoicing in some garden success, and more especially so in print. So often has dire calamity, sudden death, or uprooting by storm, followed the publication of a photograph and exultant note describing one of my best specimens, not only with Clematis, and Mezereon, and such "here to-day and gone to-morrow" subjects, but with many steady-going old plants, that I feel an uncanny dread creeping over me, that unless I touch wood in some way to disarm the overlooking witch and blind the Evil Eye, I had better not describe my successes. Now, as I do not wish for a blasted heath, or a landscape like that around the chemical works at Stratford, in place of my crowded old garden, and as I always use a stylograph pen made of vulcanite, and won't go back to a wooden penholder, my epistolary method of touching wood must consist of an assumed distrust in the future prosperity of my treasures, and so readers will please help me by understanding that the "so fars" and "apparently establisheds" I must sprinkle among my descriptions of flourishing colonies of healthy plants are amulets designed to protect my darlings from the maw of the mollusc and the blasting of the bacillus.

So far, then, my turquoise treasure which I call Cantab has thriven, and besides two clumps here, I have been able to send it out a little way into the world, by

Early Irises

sharing its offsets with a few friends whose openly expressed raptures have convinced me it would find a good home and loving care in their gardens.

I think it is one of the loveliest of Spring flowers, and do not believe it is only that sort of paternal pride vented in one's own seedling, that leads me to believe it is of the colour of a *Delphinium Belladonna*, and that the bee guide on the fall is just the right shade of apricot-orange to attract any flying insect and please an artistic eye with its colour contrast, producing much the same effect that you get in the deeper colouring of *Linaria alpina*.

The same crop of seedlings gave me a tall red-purple form, and yet one more that, so far as I can see, is identical with that sometimes sold as *I. reticulata major*. These two last flower in the order in which I have placed them, and are both somewhat earlier than the old garden form, which is too well known to need my praise. It is generally recommended that they should be lifted frequently, and just after the leaves have died down, to be stored in dry sand till September. But I found this plan unsatisfactory when I tried it, and prefer to replant them just as they are going out of flower. The ground is generally moist enough then to prevent their flagging, and the corms grow larger and stronger for their shift to fresh soil, and also at that time of year one can see just the sort of place and neighbours that will suit them at flowering time better than when the autumn plants are in full swing. If I have missed this golden opportunity I have sometimes lifted them in early August, but have then replanted them within

My Garden in Spring

an hour or so. They are among the plants that deteriorate rapidly when out of the ground, so when buying new ones it is as well to get them as early as possible after the bulb lists appear. Although they bloom with the Daffodils, some of the Juno Irises deserve a place among the early ones. They are queer creatures with folded leaves arranged in two ranks, bulbs that produce long storage roots from their base, which it is very difficult to avoid breaking off in planting, and yet most essential to the plant's well-being that they should remain intact, and again they have standards that refuse to stand, but either hang downwards or sprawl out horizontally. I can think of no better word to express such unstandardly conduct unless I draw upon the forceful legends on continental railway carriage windows, and anglicise them into *sporgering* and *hinauslehning*. They appear to me to prefer a stiff bit of soil to root into, but to have their bulbous body in something lighter, and unless I fuss over them they do not grow very vigorously. My favourite is the variety of *I. persica* whose right name is *stenophylla*, but which often appears as *Heldreichii*. The combination of its lavender-blue groundwork with the white and deep amethyst purple of the tips of the falls is so lovely, that I have not grudged renewing my little stock when bad seasons have brought it low. *I. Sindjarensis* is more reliable but not so lovely, but its hybrid Sind-pur Amethyst is a gem quite worth the trouble of constant lifting and rebedding in choice soil, even sand and leaf of the best the garden can produce.

The most satisfactory here, and capable of being left alone for several seasons, are the forms of *I. orchioides*

Early Irises

and the closely-allied *I. bucharica*. The old yellow form of *orchioides* is really the best, the white one having a lingering taint of the hue of jealousy too much in evidence, and the so-called *coerulea* form is a very washy affair and no bluer than a basin of starch, but I rather like *sulfurea*, its name being justified by its colouring. All are suitable for a sunny slope in the rock garden, but if you have room for only one, choose *I. bucharica*. It is a charming plant with its tier upon tier of paired, gracefully arching leaves, like some design for free-hand drawing, and its creamy-white flowers with bright yellow falls, and in my garden it is the strongest and tallest of the Junos, and I think must rank as the last of the earlies.

CHAPTER IV

Snowdrops

ONE can hardly picture an English garden without the Snowdrop. Yet not only are we forbidden by the compilers of lists of British plants to say it is indigenous to our woods, but much has been written to prove it was but little known in our gardens till well into the seventeenth century. The chief evidence for this view is found in Bacon's omission of the Snowdrop from his list of plants for the early months of the year, and Johnson's remark, when editing his edition of Gerard, published in 1633, that "some call them also Snowdrops," as though the plant as well as the name were still not well known. One great writer on such subjects, who so seldom makes a mistake that I feel almost as though I must be dreaming and ought not to believe my own eyes, has stated that Gerard omitted the Snowdrop in 1597 and Parkinson did so also in the first edition of the *Paradisus* in 1629, but it appears in both as *Leuconium bulbosum praecox minus*, and there are figures given in both books. Anyway, whatever the seventeenth century gardens contained, I should be greatly disappointed if this twentieth century one could not show me a Snowdrop at all times from late October until the advent of April brings so many other flowers that one scarcely notices their disappearance.

Primula pulverulenta, " Mrs. Berkeley."   (See p. 147.)

Snowdrops

This garden is not very well suited to Snowdrops:
they do not colonise or settle down and require no further
treatment as in cooler soils, but I take so much interest
in the various forms and seedling varieties that I have
diligently collected all I can get, and labour earnestly
to keep them here. Most of them require frequent
division and replanting, and I believe in doing this just
as they are going out of flower, and if the roots are
not broken in lifting but carefully spread out in their
new soil, they seem to gather up nourishment for the
newly-forming bulb without a check. The bulb of a
Snowdrop is well worth examining. If dug up and
well washed at flowering time, you will find it consists
of first a very thin brown skin, easily broken and rubbed
off, leaving a shining, white surface below, which is the
outside of a thick, fleshy wrapping enclosing the whole
bulb, and having a small round opening at the top, out
of which the shoot of the present year has grown. By
carefully slitting one side of this white wrapper you
can peel it off, and will see that it is about the same
thickness throughout, and has an inner membranous
lining that is only attached to it at the top and base.
What remains of the bulb appears wrapped in a second
similar fleshy covering, but by slitting and removing
this you will find that its inner surface is three times
as thick on one side of the bulb as on the other, and
the thicker side is fluted with nine or more ridges, which
remind one of those on the corrugated cardboard so
useful for packing fragile objects (and even plants for
the post when one cannot find a long and narrow box

just to fit). This second bulb scale has an inner lining similar to the first, and so has the third and innermost one, which also has one side fluted and thicker than the other, and its fluting is on the opposite side of the bulb to that of the second scale. These three scales form the whole of last season's bulb, and directly inside them you will find a long tube, thick and fleshy below and gradually becoming thinner upwards, till it emerges in the centre as the almost transparent sheathing leaf that wraps round the lower part of the two real leaves. A section of its base will show that it is of uniform thickness, and is the counterpart of the outer scale of the bulb, only a year younger, and will form the outer scale of next season's bulb. Inside this sheath come the two leaves, and if you can follow them down carefully to the point where they join on to the base of the bulb, you will notice that one grows gradually wider and thicker till it wraps right round the other, and by cutting through their thickened bases and examining them with a lens, traces of ridges may be seen, and also that one side is thicker than the other. So we learn that the bulb is formed annually of the bases of the sheathing leaf and the two true leaves, which swell out and store up all the nutriment gathered by roots and leaves during the period of growth. I do not know of any other bulb so wonderfully yet simply constructed from three pieces, and that yields up its secret so easily to the inquirer.

Another interesting characteristic of the Snowdrop that gives me annual pleasure to notice is its method of piercing through the hard ground. The two leaves are

Snowdrops

tightly bound round by the sheathing leaf, so that their tips are pressed together to form a sharp point that cleaves the ground and makes way for the fragile flower, in much the same way that you put your two hands together and hold them in front of your head when diving into the water. The point of the uprising Snowdrop is strengthened for pushing aside stones and hard substances by a thickening of the tip of each leaf into a tough white cushion, a plan also followed by the leaves of Daffodils, Hyacinths, and many other bulbous plants, but I think only in Snowdrops do these white or cream-coloured tips persist so noticeably in the full-grown leaf.

Forbes-Watson has rhapsodised very beautifully about the artistic value of these dots, but I think their mechanical service to the plant is their *raison d'être* and perhaps more admirable side.

There is much pleasure to be derived from watching the thrusting through of one's plants in the dull, wintry days. I love to see a great cracking and upheaval of the soil as forerunner to the appearance of the blunt, white nose of a really strong *Eremurus Elwesianus*, and would far rather see this vegetable mimicry of an enlarged poached egg in the border than any Venus rising from the sea. If the white, sheathing leaves appear in this knob-like form you know there is a good strong spike below, and that forking over in the autumnal cleaning up has not injured the shoot ; but if a point of green leaves first appears it is too often presage of a flowerless crown. The arch method employed by many dicotyledons is worth contrasting with the plan of spearing through adopted by most

My Garden in Spring

monocotyledons. It is marvellous what power lies in a growing shoot of a Crocus. It makes light work of a hard, well-rolled gravel path. A single Crocus leaf is a flaccid, weak instrument, but the whole series of leaves, varying from four to fifteen according to the species, when tightly bound by the tough, sheathing leaves, and the sharp and toughened points of the true leaves thus all brought together, form almost as sharp and strong a weapon as the underground shoot of one of the running bamboos. Still more wonderful are those, mostly autumnal bloomers, that flower without leaves, for in their case it is only the tips of the sheathing leaves that pierce the soil, and once through into daylight open a little way to allow the fragile flower-bud to pass upwards. But this seems to me as child's play compared with the task undertaken by the Winter Aconite, the Wood Anemones, *Bongardia Rauwolfii*, and the Epimediums, which bring their flower-buds almost to maturity below ground, and then lift them through backwards by means of an increased rate of growth in the lower portion of the floral stem and the consequent raising of the centre of the arch into which they are bent. It is the same method by which so many dicotyledons lift the cotyledons out of the seed husk, and is a case of " Don't push, just shove," as boys say, the top of the arched stem being forced straight ahead until it is not only through the surface of the ground but has gone up high enough to lift the flower-buds clear of the soil, when they will straighten up, and further growth may be uniform throughout the length of the flower-stalk.

Certain of the autumnal-flowering Snowdrops blossom

Snowdrops

before the leaves are produced, and with them, as with the naked flowering Crocuses, the sheathing leaf opens the road to the surface only, and, once there, parts to allow the blossom to emerge from its protection ; but they have not the same charm for me as those which flower with their leaves, looking rather forlorn, hanging above bare earth. Most of these come from Greece, and one, *Galanthus corcyrensis*, from Corfu, and are generally regarded as forms of the common Snowdrop *G. nivalis*.

Except in time of flowering there is not much difference between them, and they are none of them very easy to please, evidently expecting the winter to be mild and sunny and kind to their young leaves in return for their early heralding of Spring. So they are only safe in the open in specially sheltered nooks, while a cold frame makes a still happier home for them. *Galanthus Olgae* is the first to appear here, and generally does so in the latter part of October, and looks sadly out of place at that season. It has been described as a species, and retained as such by some authors, because it is said to have no green marking on the inner segments. But the original description distinctly states that when dried the inner segments appear to have no green markings, and I notice that in this form more than in any other the green fades to yellow, and sometimes disappears altogether if an elderly blossom is dried. It has been rather largely collected of late years, and can be bought much more reasonably than other autumnal Snowdrops, and is well worth a trial wherever a cosy nook can be spared to it. *G. Rachelae* is my favourite of the first comers, but alas ! it is so rare that it

45

My Garden in Spring

can only be procured by love and not for money. It was found in Greece by Professor Mahaffy on Mount Hymettus in 1884, and found a home with that kindest of good gardeners the late Mr. Burbidge, at Trinity College, Dublin. From him it found its way into a few gardens whose owners could love an autumnal Snowdrop. From Mr. Arnott's generous hand it came to me, and I am glad to say, when some years later he unfortunately lost his plants, I was able to restore him of his own. For some years it seemed to be very happy with me in the rock garden, and I was able to make two clumps of it, then the larvae of the Common Swift Moth (*Hepialus lupulinus*), one of my worst enemies, found it toothsome and hollowed out its bulbs. One clump disappeared altogether, and I am still struggling anxiously with the remnant of the other, but hoping some day to recover the lost ground, and be able to send it still further afield. When robust it sends up two or three blossoms from a strong bulb, and they are larger than those of any other early autumnal form, but for all that leafless. I have a bed I call the sand-moraine because parts of it are surfaced with granite chips, and it is provided with an underground pipe for watering, and because it must have some name, and further it is fashionable now to call any bed of carefully-mixed, gritty soil a moraine. Anyway, in a corner of this bed which is filled with yellow builders' sand mixed with a little good leaf mould, *G. Rachelae* has so far looked happy again, and has escaped gnawed vitals. I have lately been converted to this particular sand, which I believe is called yellow builders' sand by those who stock such things, meaning of course that

Snowdrops

the sand is somewhat yellow—not that the builder is a Mongolian—but it is the old friend we have bought from grocers and seed-merchants as birdcage sand, and is really a reddish-orange in colour.

Plants love it, at any rate when new, and even if it deteriorates with age I hope to find some means of doctoring it up to full fertile strength again. I should never have thought of trying Snowdrops in it but for Mr. Wilks's kindness in letting me dig up a fine specimen of *Galanthus Allenii* from his garden for me to figure ; and when I saw how clean its bulb looked, and how strong and fair were its roots in that sandy soil, I resolved it should go into this newly-made sand-moraine, and its apparent content there has caused other kinds to gather round about it. *G. octobrensis* behaved badly here, and flowered later and later each season, until it became merged with the ordinary Snowdrop. I had hoped it would have continued, and after becoming the latest of all would go on until it was a summer flowerer, and then come round to October again, but it has never done so. *G. byzantinus* is my great link between Autumn and Spring. It is interesting as being a supposed natural hybrid between *Elwesii* and *plicatus*, having the flowers of the former with their extra basal green spot, and the folded-edged leaf of the latter. I find that freshly-imported bulbs, if planted as soon as received, generally in August, will give a succession of flowers from November to February. Some of the earliest flowering forms I have removed to the rock garden, and I find, though not so early as in their first season, yet they have been in flower

My Garden in Spring

before Christmas for the last four years. So every year I like to buy a few hundred collected bulbs to make fresh colonies, and enjoy their early flowers. *G. Elwesii,* though not quite so early, yet will make a fair show in December if planted as soon as the bulbs are imported in August or September. Until I bought and planted them so early in the season I never had much success with either of these, but last season a three-year-old planting had not only increased well by offsets but seedlings appeared in most promising profusion, and especially round the *byzantinus* parents. Before the old year has gone I look for *G. cilicicus* to be showing buds at least. It is a tall, slender form of *G. nivalis,* with very glaucous leaves. Although described in catalogues as November flowering, I do not get blossoms here until late December or January, and expect it is only newly-imported bulbs that flower in November.[1] It was especially good in the winter of 1911–12, as though it appreciated the extra cooking it got that summer.

Between Christmas and the New Year I like to clean up some corners where I have clumps of a very fine form of the Neapolitan Snowdrop, *G. Imperati*. I believe it to be the one that should be called var. *Atkinsii,* after its introducer, Mr. Atkins, of Panswick in Gloucestershire, whose name lives also in the fine garden form of *Cyclamen ibericum* known as *Atkinsii*. Canon Ellacombe gave me this Snowdrop and quite half of my garden treasures besides, and it is one of the floral treats of the year to see it in January growing over a foot high under the south

---

[1] *G. cilicicus* has given me the lie, as plants love to do, by opening several flowers on the 30th November 1913 on clumps undisturbed for three years.

48

Snowdrops

wall at Bitton. As I have neither the soil, climate, nor
south wall of Bitton to give it, it is never quite so fine
here, but every season when I see it reappear I hail it as
one of the finest if not the loveliest of all Snowdrops.
The outer segments are wonderfully long and very perfect
in shape, making the flower resemble a pear-shaped pearl,
and it stands up well except, of course, during days of keen
frost. Very near to it in early flowering and stature, but
falling short in symmetry, is a form that I believe should
be known by the rather House-that-Jack-built sort of
name of *G. Imperati*, var. *Atkinsii* of Backhouse. It is a
fine thing, but very seldom produces a perfectly symmetrical flower, for either one of the inner segments is as
long as the outer ones, or there are four outer segments,
or yet again a petaloid bract may appear just below the
ovary but not quite so purely white as the flower proper,
and all these vagaries give a clump rather an untidy
appearance when looked at closely. I find it hard to say
which I consider the most beautiful Snowdrop, and
should pick out four as candidates for the prize, but I have
never ranged them all four together for comparison, so
when I look at any one of them I wonder whether the
others can possibly be more beautiful. I think if only I
could grow it here as I once received it for figuring straight
from its home in Ireland, the Straffan Snowdrop would
win the golden apple. It is a Crimean form, and like its
relations bears two flowers from each strong bulb, one
rather earlier and taller than the other. It is a fine large
form, but so beautifully proportioned that it is not a bit
coarse or clumsy, as I think some of the very globose

forms of *G. Elwesii* are. It is known botanically as *G. caucasicus grandis*, and is a late flowering form of the Caucasian form of *nivalis*. It was brought to Straffan by Lord Clarina on his return from the Crimean War together with bulbs of *G. plicatus*, which was the Snowdrop that spoke so sweetly of home to our soldiers when the Spring melted the snow and the trenches were covered with white blossoms instead. Lovely *grandis* has never been really comfortable here, and I fear is decreasing in numbers, though its few flowers were very lovely last March.

As this beauty returns my affection and care so coldly I turn to a more generous-natured form which the late Mr. Neill Fraser sent me without a name, so shortly before his death that my letter of thanks and inquiries was too late to bring an answer. The bulb he gave me has grown so well that I am now re-minded of his pleasant friendship from several corners of the garden, but the original clump is the best placed. It is at the foot of a large bush of *Erica scoparia*, a heath seldom seen in English gardens, as it has little to recommend it save a very graceful habit and good ever-green colour, the flowers being very inconspicuous, small, and of a brownish green, but an interesting plant, as it is one of the species of heath which produce burrs or knots on the roots, and though the best are those from *E. arborea*, in the Landes district (where *E. scoparia* is very plentiful) its root-burrs are collected and exported for making the pipes known here as briar-root pipes, a corruption of the French name Bruyere. I grubbed up my plant in the woods round Arcachon, and though I

Snowdrops

tried many that looked like removable seedlings, it was some time before I hit upon one that had not a root fit for a pipe-factory with many large knobs already formed, and even if such as these were likely to live I jibbed at the postage I should have to pay. Now, twenty years after, it is a fine bush five feet in height, and at its feet and under its spread my souvenir of Patrick Neill Fraser attracts everyone in February more than any other Snowdrop clump in the garden. I take it to be a hybrid, and the parents probably *nivalis* and some form of *caucasicus*. It is rounder in flower than the Straffan one, but has much the same graceful outline on a slightly smaller scale, but has not inherited the Crimean character of bearing a second flower from each pair of leaves. It is at its best as the Bitton *Imperati* is going over, and while the Straffan princess is still a sleeping beauty, so these three can reign as queen each for her season.

The fourth claimant may not appeal to everyone, for it is somewhat of a freak, the best-known of the so-called white Snowdrops, which means the flowers have little or no green marking on them. It is known as *G. nivalis poculiformis*, and appears now and then among the typical common Snowdrops. It originated at Dunrobin among seedlings raised by Mr. Melville, who kindly sent me plants of it. It is inclined to revert to the normal form, but when a flower is as it should be, it makes up for a few lopsided ones. The inner segments should be long and pure white just like the outer ones, and in this condition it is very graceful when half expanded, as without the usual stiff green-

My Garden in Spring

spotted petticoat to hide the golden anthers they show
out more, and set off the purity of the six equal segments. It is a lowly gem, but it is worth bending
one's back and knees to enjoy it from its own level,
rather than playing King Cophetua. In fact, no Snowdrop looks so well plucked as growing, unless one cuts
it off at ground level, so preserving it between its twin
leaves and bound by the sheathing leaf, and Heaven
forbid I should so treat and sacrifice *poculiformis*. Mr.
Allen raised an interesting seedling from it, which he
called Virgin. The inner segments are about two-thirds
the length of the outer, and curiously shaped, their
sides being rolled and forming two semi-cylindrical tubes
with the tips bent inwards, and the usual green horseshoe mark is reduced to two round green specks ; it is
curious and interesting, but not so beautiful as its mother.
One Snowdrop time, when Mr. Farrer was here, he
astounded me by scorning the charms of *poculiformis*,
even of a perfectly-formed blossom, because he said
he possessed a much larger, taller, and finer form,
also earlier in flowering, and therefore over for that
season, so I bottled up my curiosity for eleven months
until, in the following year, he bade me make pil-
grimage to Ingleborough and see the marvel. It was
a long, cold journey, and how I hated it ! but at last,
on my knees before the object, I felt well rewarded,
for it was a fine form of *G. Elwesii* that had poculiformed
itself with great success. Moreover, it had increased to
an extent that permitted of division, and my kind host
and I dug it up, replanting the bulbs with great care,

52

Snowdrops

with the exception of one fine specimen, with which he sent me home rejoicing. Both our gardens have benefited (so far, of course) by this replanting. He tells me his have been much finer ever since, and mine was replanted and spread out a little this February. It has a solid, waxy white flower of great beauty, not so dainty as the *nivalis* form, and of rather a colder or greener white, but is a noble and early white Snowdrop.

Yellow Snowdrops sound abominable, and look somewhat sickly when the blossoms are young, for the green of the ovary and inner segments is replaced by a rather straw-coloured yellow; but on a sunny day a well-expanded bloom, showing the yellow glow that the markings lend to the inside of the flower, is not to be despised, and makes an interesting change from the green and white garb of the rest of the family. The best known is *lutescens*, a form of *nivalis*, but a larger and more robust form is called *flavescens*. Both were found in gardens in Northumberland, the first by Mr. Sanders and the other by Mr. W. B. Boyd, who has a better collection of Snowdrops and knows more about them than anyone else. To his generosity I am indebted for roots of the lovely double-yellow one which was found in a garden near Crewe, a loosely-formed, graceful double, with the usual markings of the inner segments of a good bright yellow, and a very charming thing when looked full in the face.

It seems to revert occasionally to its ancestral green markings, and I was rather dismayed to see so much green where I looked for yellow this season, but Mr.

My Garden in Spring

Boyd tells me it behaves similarly with him after removal, but after a season or two repays patience with pure gold.

Green Snowdrops suggest the dyed atrocities seen in continental flower-markets, and even our own streets at times, whose unopened buds have been placed in ink instead of water, and so forced to drink up the dye and fill their vessels with gaudy hues foreign to their nature. But several Snowdrops have chosen to add to their greenness by natural means. One of these is a charming little plant. It appeared in the Vienna Botanical Garden, and from thence travelled into Max Leichtlin's garden at Baden Baden, that wonderful centre of distribution for rare plants which, alas! is now a thing of the past. It is said that he sent two bulbs to England, one to Mr. Harpur-Crewe, the other to Mr. Allen, and I believe all that exist over here now are descendants of that brace of bulbs. It is known as *virescens*, and thought to be a variety of *G. caucasicus*, though except that it flowers very late in the season it has no character that I can recognise as connecting it with that tall Russian. It is a very dwarf form, with glaucous leaves and stem, and the outer segments of the flower are striped from their junction with the ovary for two-thirds of their length with a delicate duck's-egg green, and the inner segments are wholly green, except for a narrow white margin that gives a delightful finish and charm to a very lovely flower. Better known is a very curious freak form of *G. nivalis*, which was found in a wood in Western Prussia and named *G. Scharlokii* by Prof. Caspary of Königsberg after its discoverer. Its claim to greenness rests in a patch of short green strips on the tips of the outer seg-

Snowdrops

ments, but its chief peculiarity is the very curious pair of leafy spathes that replace the narrow green keels with their membranous connective that are common to all other Snowdrops. In *G. Scharlokii*, these queer little leaves stand up and spread out over the flower with an expression like that of hares' ears. In some seasons a number of the flowers may have the leafy spathes partially united, even for about half their length, and then after a year or two all may be divided to the base again. Mr. Allen raised some seedlings that showed a slight inheritance of these characters, but they are not improvements : one of them is a double flowered form, and I think quite the ugliest Snowdrop I possess, only having enough suggestion of green on the outer segments to make it look dingy.

I have also a form known as *Warei* which has the green-tipped segments without the leafy spathes, and is rather pretty. The greenest of all I have saved to the last, a double green Snowdrop that doesn't hang its head, which sounds what children call " perfectly hijjous," but I assure you it has a quiet beauty and charm of its own. One might not wish for a bouquet of it, or to decorate a dinner-table with nothing else, but when Mr. Boyd kindly sent it to me I greatly enjoyed examining and painting it, and am very proud of possessing so great a rarity. It was found at Ashiesteel near Melrose, in a garden where no Snowdrops but the common *G. nivalis* are grown, so its peculiarities must be entirely its own invention, a parallel case to that of the small girl charged with biting, scratching, and spitting at her dear kind nurse, who in answer to Mother's explanation that such behaviour was very bad as being put into her head by the

55

My Garden in Spring

Devil, replied, " Perhaps the biting and scratching were, but I assure you the spitting was entirely my own invention." But it is a very curious case of a sudden mutation, for every one of the segments have become long and narrow and heavily striped with green as bright as that of the leaves. The outer segments are slightly longer than the inner, which still retain the emarginate apex, to drift into botanical terms, but in more ordinary English, the little snick round which the green horseshoe mark is generally found. The whorls of these segments occur fairly regularly and alternately till a tassel-like flower is formed, but instead of hanging as tassels, and good little Snowdrops should, it holds its head up with a " bragian boldness " unsurpassed even by Bailey Junior.

I have a pretty form of *G. plicatus* with green markings on the outer segments, and have had, and heard of, similar vagaries in forms of *Elwesii*, and Mr. Allen had some very well-spotted forms of *Fosteri*, so green spots evidently run in the family, and encourage the idea that perhaps a cross between a Snowdrop and the Spring Snowflake might be possible.

Many of the species hybridise freely, and some beautiful seedlings were raised by the late Mr. Allen of Shepton Mallett. Unfortunately many of these have quite died out, and are only known from the mention of their names in his paper on Snowdrops in the *R. H. S. Journal* of August 1891, in many cases, alas! without any description. These seedlings were never distributed by the nurserymen, and so are only to be found in a few gardens of the personal friends of Mr. Allen, and as I began collecting this family too late to get in touch with him I am indebted to the kindness of his friends for most of my varieties. I think

56

Magnolia stellata in the Rock Garden. (See p. 170.)

Snowdrops

Robin Hood is one of the best of his hybrids; it is *Elwesii* × *plicatus*, and a fine bold flower with a great deal of deep green on the inner segments. Galatea is a very well-formed, glistening white seedling, apparently *nivalis* × *plicatus*. A distinct one is Magnet, in which the pedicel is very long and slender, and the large nivalis-formed flowers hang and sway in the breeze in a way that reminds one of a Dierama. He also raised a double form with the same peculiarity of a long foot-stalk that I like very much, because, like another of his doubles called Charmer, there are no more than three outer segments, the doubling consisting entirely of a neat rosette of inner segments, instead of the mixed muddle of inner and outer segments found in the ordinary double form of *G. nivalis*. The beautiful *G. Allenii* named after him is a wild species, and very remarkable for its immense leaves, which at maturity measure about a foot in length and an inch and a half in width. When the flower is at its best they are much shorter, however, but even when first they unfold they look more like the leaves of some Tulip than of any Snowdrop. The flower is very round in form and of a good size, though not in proportion to the promise of the leaves—for then it would have to be as large as a good-sized Daffodil.

There is more than one form of this species, and I have some that it is hard to decide whether they should be placed as varieties of *Allenii* or of the much smaller but similarly-shaped *G. latifolius*, a dull little thing that might be attractive if it could be induced to flower more freely. The leaves have a very cheery appearance, being very bright green and beautifully polished, but here the flowers are always few, and too insignificant for the foliage. There

57

is another broad-leaved Snowdrop, *G. Ikariae* from the Island of Nikara, which is a much better thing, and valuable as being one of the latest to flower. Its broad, glossy leaves look as though they belong to some species of Scilla, but are charming in the way they curve outwards and set off the large flowers, which are of a very pure white, and have a particularly effective, large green spot on the inner segments. In one part of the garden it is sowing itself freely, and I hope for great things from these babes in years to come. I think it likes a warmer situation than most other Snowdrops, except perhaps *G. Imperati*, for both of these do best under a south wall or in a very sunny spot.

I have never seen more than one variety of it, that is an early flowering seedling with deeper coloured leaves that appeared under the celebrated south wall at Bitton. A bulb, kindly given to me by Canon Ellacombe, has retained its character here, and is always over before the true *Ikariae* is out. By the side of this in the rock garden I grow another beautiful seedling given me by Mr. Elwes, who found it among a group of *G. Elwesii* at Colesborne. I call it Colesborne Seedling, and believe it must be a hybrid between *Elwesii* and *caucasicus*, as it has the inner segments marked with the second green spot of the former but has the leaves of the latter. The flowers are very large and of a fine globose form, but it has too short a stem to lift them up sufficiently, otherwise I should rank it among the most beautiful of all. I suppose I must not linger much longer over my beloved Snowdrops, nor mention all the forms I grow, but must say a word in praise of a few more. One of these is *G. nivalis*

58

Snowdrops

Melvillei, another Dunrobin Snowdrop, and named after its raiser. It is a very well-shaped, round flower, but still quite of the *nivalis* type, and very slightly marked with green ; in fact in one form I have, sent to me by Mr. Melville, the horseshoe has disappeared, leaving in its place only the heads of two of its nails, little round green dots on each side of the nick. It is a dwarf form, but so sturdy that it lasts a very long time in flower. Dwarfer still is a curious seedling of *Elwesii* that my own garden gave me. When first it begins to flower the immense globular flowers are borne on such short stems that when the buds hang free from the goldbeater-skin covering of the spathe, their tips rest on the ground, but later the stems lengthen and lift them. Mr. Farrer suggested the name of " Fat Boy " for it, when he first saw its solid obesity, and it now behaves as strangely in his rock garden in Yorkshire as it does here. The most curious thing about it is that it produces three and sometimes four flowers from between each pair of leaves, and these follow each other, and each succeeding one is lifted on a taller stem above the swelling ovary of the last and now fading flower. So that it begins as a dwarf early form and ends as a tall and late one. Among some imported bulbs of *Elwesii* I picked out a very late flowering one ; I see by the figure I made of it that it was on the 6th of March 1906. It was also very large, and had the second green spot converted into a band across the centre of the inner segment. This one bulb has flowered every year until this, but has made no increase, and in some seasons the flower has lasted quite fresh into April, being the latest of all my Snowdrops. This year

59

My Garden in Spring

I noticed it had failed to open its flower-bud, so I dug it up to see what was wrong, and found some evil underground grub (the Swift Moth, probably) had tunnelled right through it. I much doubt whether it can possibly recover after such an injury, and I shall have to rely upon one of Mr. Allen's *plicatus* seedlings called Belated to keep up my Snowdrop supply from October to April by filling up the last fortnight after *G. Ikariae* has turned its attention to seedpods.

The Spring Snowflake is so nearly a Snowdrop and flowers with the later ones that I shall praise it here. My favourite form is that known to science as *Leucoium vernum*, var. *Vagneri*, but which lies hidden in catalogues and nurseries as *carpathicum*. Both are larger, more robust forms than ordinary *vernum*, and strong bulbs give two flowers on each stem, but whereas *carpathicum* has yellow spots on the tips of the segments, *Vagneri* has inherited the family emeralds. It is an earlier flowering form than *vernum*, and a delightful plant to grow in bold clumps on the middle slopes of the flatter portions of the rock garden. Plant it deeply and leave it alone, and learn to recognise the shining narrow leaves of its babes, and to respect them until your colony is too large for your own pleasure, and you can give it away to please others.

L. Hernandezii, also known as *L. pulchellum*, has won a place in my affections by its useful preference for wet feet. Like the larger and finer, but later *L. aestivum*, it thrives well on the very edge of water, and looks so much better there than anywhere else, that I advise such a planting. *Hernandezii* flowers over a long period, throwing up a succession of flower-stems, and it comes in Daffodil days, at a time

Snowdrops

when other white water-side flowers are asleep. A clump of it that has been slightly overrun by our beautiful evergreen Sedge, *Cladium mariscus*, makes a pretty picture every Spring, growing an extra few inches under shelter of the Cladium. How seldom one sees this grand plant in a garden, and I think no nurseryman stocks it. Yet there are acres of it in the Norfolk Broads, and half of Wicken Fen is full of it—too full for my taste, for it is only fed upon by one of the rare insects of the district, and crowds out reed and other suitable food plants, and seems to be increasing rather fast in the fen. My plants I hauled up and lugged home from Norfolk—not a very easy job, as I was entomologising at the time, and a pocket-knife and my own fingers were my only digging weapons, whilst its root system is a wide-spreading mass of the toughest fibres, interlaced with those of every imaginable sedge and rush and weed. Once home it made up for all pains of transit, and its great arching leaves are a rich green throughout the year, unlike those of any other water-side plant, resembling some extra fine Pampas-Grass. With the exception of the New Zealand *Arundo conspicua*, which alas ! is none too hardy here in wet places, nor too vigorous in dry ones, Cladium the Fen Sedge is, so far as I know, the only truly evergreen plant of similar bold grassy habit, fit for the water-side. The effect of its deep green among the tawny browns of reeds and bulrushes in autumn and winter is very fine. Nurserymen take note, also take a holiday in the Broads, take a spade and a sack, and make a fortune out of three-and-sixpenny snippets in thumb-pots of *Cladium mariscus.*

CHAPTER V

Spring Crocuses

FOR me, starting this chapter, there are great searchings of heart, compared with which those of the divisions of Reuben were as nothing. If but one of them possessed a flat object with diverse and recognisable sides to it they might toss up and decide whether to go and help smash up Sisera or stay and listen to the music of their baa-lambs, and they seem to have decided pretty unanimously for the ovine concert. But for me, the very inmost cockle of whose heart glows more for a Crocus than for the most expensive Orchid, every cockle in me (though I haven't a notion what portion of my internal anatomy is meant by that borrowed appellation of marine molluscs) is full of searchings and divisions how to do justice to my first garden love and avoid wearying and driving away readers to whom my raptures may appear the vapourings of a love-sick monomaniac.

We treat Crocuses *au grand sérieux* in this garden, giving over two double-light frames to their service in the very sunniest part of the kitchen garden, and we always have two sets of pots sunk in ashes containing the seeds or seedlings of two past seasons, finding that method the best way to prevent the worm who will turn from waltzing the seeds of one variety into the middle of a patch of another,

Spring Crocuses

as invariably happens when they are sown in parallel lines in open ground. Also Crocus seedlings have a habit of descending about an inch each season, and not always perpendicularly. Their method of obtaining what Maud's young man desired in his delirium is curious and worth noting.

They bury themselves deeper by forming a peculiar outgrowth called a starch root, which is a semi-transparent, fleshy affair, something like the storage root of an Alstroemeria, and at first serves the same purpose of containing a store of nutriment, but there the similarity ends, for Alstroemerias retain these storage roots throughout their resting period, whereas a Crocus at the ripening-off season loses its starch root, its store of starch being absorbed into the newly-formed corm. The starch root withers and contracts in a series of corrugations after the manner of closing of a concertina, and as its long lower end is firmly fixed in the soil the corm is pulled down lower into the space formerly occupied by the once plump starch root, which has now grown as lean as the soup-hating Augustus of the Struwwelpeter. It frequently happens that one of these roots grows out from one side of the corm, and will then cause an oblique descent, and in two seasons carry a corm more than an inch out of the line in which it was planted.

So that what with worms and starch roots it is necessary either to leave a wide space between each row of seedlings or to place buried slates between them to prevent the different stocks becoming hopelessly mixed. Slates are costly and space is precious, for I hate a vacuum

My Garden in Spring

in a bed of good soil as much as Nature does universally. So we sow each variety of seed in a separate pot, and sink the pots, and their gradually narrowing sides not only prevent the wandering of the babes but force them to draw nearer, and after two years in pots, if all is well with them, it should be possible to turn them out in August and find a layer of corms, each about the size of a pea, a tender young green pea of the first picking, and all at the bottom of the pot. Raising Crocus seedlings has proved such a source of interest and pleasure to me, and such a means of enrichment to my collection, that I wish I could persuade more garden lovers to carry it on. It has certainly the great disadvantage of a wait of at least three years for the first flowering, but years pass only too swiftly in a garden, and once that period is over every succeeding season brings fresh babes to flowering strength, and I know no garden joy equal to a visit on a sunny morning to the Crocus beds when seedlings are in full flowering. To see a dozen, a score, or better still a century, of some old favourite reproduced in a new generation is good, but still better is the thrill of spotting a pure white bloom in a row of orthodox lilac ones. Forms with larger flowers, deeper or lighter colour, or extra markings as compared with the normal type, fill the heart with joy and pride when found in one's own seed-beds, and it is a happy being who carefully lifts them out from among the common herd with the only instrument really suited to the purpose, a cook's fork. Poor mere man that I was, I stumbled along for years in unenlightened masculine ignorance, using a mason's trowel, old dinner-

Spring Crocuses

knives, and such bungling, root-cutting tools for the fine work of seedling selecting, until a practical cousin of the fairer sex caught me using one of the best silver forks that I had taken out in a bowl of breakfast scraps, the daily portion of my gulls, and she said, " What you want is a cook's fork, and I will send you one." How was I to know cooks had forks designed by Heaven for the use of gardeners ? But when it came I wanted others, and as I often leave them stuck about in jungles of the rock garden I am a frequent customer at the ironmongery counter of the Army and Navy Stores, where cook's forks are obtainable. Go thou and buy two, one of the largest size for general use and one a size smaller for weeding out grass, *Poa annua* especially, among delicate bulbous things, and you will bless me every time you use them, or ought to do if your heart is not of stone. The Crocus treasure-troves go from the seed-beds into the Crocus frame, and generally suffer no check from their removal, but ripen up a good bulb for next August's lifting. I wish I could breathe some germs of the Crocus Seedling Fever into the words I write and set all who read aflame to embark on such interesting work. Do start this very spring. When you see your Crocuses wide open in flower sally forth with a stick of sealing-wax or the amber mouthpiece of an old pipe in your hand, not as a charm, talisman, phylactery, or whatever you call that sort of thing, but for practical use. Rub whichever of the two unusual accompaniments of a garden stroll you have chosen, on your coat-sleeve if it be woollen, and hold the rubbed portion as soon as possible after ceasing rubbing near the anthers of an open

65   E

My Garden in Spring

Crocus, and you will find the electricity thereby generated will cause the pollen grains to fly up on to the electrified object, and, what is more, to stick there, but so lightly that directly they are rubbed against the stigma of another Crocus they will leave the amber and be left where you, and Nature before you, intended them to be. For fertilising flowers with small pollen grains you will find this plan much more satisfactory than the use of a camel's-hair brush. The sealing-wax can be wiped clean very easily between each crossing, but pollen grains work in between the hairs of a brush, and are not easily induced to leave it and adhere to a stigma, so that it is hard to be sure you have not left some to work out afterwards and muddle up your crosses. It is best to label the bulb with the name of the pollen parent, and either to remove other flowers from it or fertilise them with similar pollen as they appear. The ovary of a Crocus flower is below ground, of course, at flowering time, and does not appear in the upper world until the seeds are nearly ripe. From early May onwards and throughout June the ripening capsules may be looked for, and it is best to pick them before they split and scatter their contents. A gentle pinch will soon tell you whether the seeds inside are hard enough for gathering. I find the nested willow-chip boxes used so much by entomologists very useful for keeping the seed in : the capsules ripen well in such dry quarters, and the names of the sorts can be written in pencil on the lid. Next best and less bulky are those strange wee packets sold for about nothing three farthings the hundred as pence envelopes. I have often wondered who uses them for their original purpose, buying

Spring Crocuses

them by the hundred for it, but cannot imagine a grade of society so refined as to clothe their pennies in these paper jackets.

For seed collecting they are A1 though, and I generally wear half a dozen in the ticket pocket of my coats, even my Sunday best, and have often acquired a new plant by having one at hand when a pod or two of poor little orphan seeds were crying out for adoption. Next time I go to the A. and N. Stores for some cook's forks and pence envelopes shall I find a queue at either counter ? The seeds are best sown as the year's harvest is gathered in, but they will be none the worse (unless lost or devoured of mice) for being kept unsown until the middle of September. Then you will remember the pots are plunged out in the open in a bed of ashes for two years, until the cormlets are gathered together as peas in a pod at the bottom of the pots.

Then they get turned out in August, cleaned a little of worn-out coats, and are pricked out in rows in a specially prepared bed of rather gritty soil in an open, sunny place, and are left there to flower. Here we always have two seasons' pots sunk in the ashes, and three seed-beds, each with one year's seedlings in it, so that in their third year the seedlings go out into a bed and should begin flowering, but it is in their fourth year that the main crop of flowers should appear, and in the fifth the lag-behinds should show if they are good for anything. After that we turn that bed out, sort out what is left, and prepare it for another batch of two-year-olds.

Yes, we treat Crocuses seriously here, even alluding to them sometimes as Croci, but I could never bring myself to

67

My Garden in Spring

use the correct Greek pronunciation and call the first syllable Crock. I should like to do so if I could remember, and thought anyone would know what I was talking about, for I like to be consistent, and one always uses the short *o* for Crocodile, and it would be pleasant to try to believe in the derivation of κροκο-δειλος (Crocus-fearer) given by some of the ancients.

It is not very likely that the huge reptile of the Nile, than which, according to Pliny, " there is not another creature againe in the world, that of a smaller beginning groweth to a bigger quantity," ever came in contact with the Crocus, or would take the slightest notice of it if he did, unless he turned up his nose at it, as his movable upper jaw would permit. But one must remember that the word Crocodeilos was also used for smaller Saurians, even for his poor relations the lizards, and on the authority of Stephanus we learn that Saffron mixed with honey was good to anoint beehives and scare off the land Crocodiles.

It is interesting, too, to note that the Latin name Crocus has entirely supplanted the English one of Saffron in popular use for the plant, providing a handy argument against the inventing of lengthy and often confusing new English names for plants, such as Cape Fuchsias for Correa and Cape Cowslip for Lachenalia.

Saffron is now used almost entirely for the drug, and Meadow-saffron as a name for the Colchicum is not commonly used for the garden forms, and I hope never will be, for the Crocus and Colchicum are too frequently confused as it is. "What is the Crocus found in the meadows in the Alps, or Germany, in the autumn?" is a

Spring Crocuses

question I am asked so frequently I have sometimes thought of having a short reply form printed to hand or post to the inquirers. It should state that a Colchicum belongs to the Lily family, and shows it by having six stamens, while Crocus, as an Irid, has only three.

This very elementary fragment of botanical lore once stood me in good stead. Very many years ago, more than I care to count up exactly, when I was a fledgeling gardener and beginning to learn and collect plants, I was taken to Coombe-Fishacre, a veritable Golconda of floral treasures, and Mr. Archer Hinde, their kind custodian, was, I knew, a great authority on plants. Imagine, then, my nervousness when on going out to the garden I was asked the name of a group of rosy-lilac flowers. " A Colchicum," I cautiously replied, " but I am not sure which," and then came the reassuring remark, " Oh, that will do. It's *speciosum*, and I knew, but I always ask people, and if they call it a Crocus I won't give them a thing."

I still grow and value many of the plants I carried away with me that afternoon, and bless my luck in having known just enough to avoid calling a Colchicum a Crocus.

I feel Meadow-saffron to be almost as bad a misnomer, for Saffron is only the Arabic Zahferan, and in but slightly altered forms the word is found in both Oriental and European languages to denote *Crocus sativus* itself or the drug procured from it.

Crocus must be one of the oldest names given to a flower and still in common use. If there is an older I cannot recall it. It is the Latin form, from the Greek, of a very ancient word-root which appears in Sanskrit as

My Garden in Spring

Kunkuma, in Indian languages as Kurkum, and in Hebrew as Karkom. In these Eastern languages the consonants are more important than the vowels, and are written first, the vowels being mere dots and dashes placed above or below the line. So K.R.K.M. would represent this word, the name of the drug so highly prized in the ancient world as a sweet scent, a golden dye, and a medicine. It is easy to imagine how merchants would carry it about the world for sale, and how nations speaking different languages would alter the name a little ; Crocum is a form found in the writings of some Romans, and doubtless the result of their not quite catching the pronunciation of the name by which the Phoenician merchants called the precious drug. We have plentiful instances in our own land of the way a vowel gets tranferred from before to after an *r* as one tracks the word northward.

I shall not speak here of autumnal Crocuses, though I know it is not quite consistent with my plan and the way I treated *Iris unguicularis* and the Snowdrops, but I like a change, and hope you do. The Spring and Autumn bloomers are not varieties of the same species, unless *graveolens* be, as botanists declare, a form of *vitellinus.* Nor, except in the case of three widely differing species, do any flower continuously from Autumn to Spring. Of these last, two (*C. caspius* and *laevigatus*) flower mainly in the autumn, with just a few poor remnants of flowers for the New Year, so are best classed as autumnal. The third species, *C. Cambessedesii,* is the only one with sufficient originality of mind to baffle all attempts at classification by time of flowering.

Spring Crocuses

It is a lovely but tiny species, endemic to the Balearic Isles, and was quite lost to cultivation until a few years ago, when a cousin of mine, who lives in Spain, kindly managed to get some collected for me ; but not before every species of Merendera, Romulea, and Colchicum found on Majorca and Minorca had arrived here, triumphantly announced as the precious Crocus. This is ever the case when the amateur collects some wild Crocus for me, and in many places Sternbergias are also to be met with, and come along regardless of their weight for postage ; and then, when all these members of other genera are exhausted, if my friends' patience holds out there will arrive a specimen of the real thing, with the query, " Can this common weed be the one you want ? It is so common here, we thought it cannot be any good." So *C. Cambessedesii* came at last. It is one of the smallest of all, and looks as though it might have been the fairies' first model when they were designing *C. Imperati*, being very much like it, only so much smaller, and only just washed with colour. Its segments are about half an inch long, palest lilac within, and the three outer ones are pale straw colour externally, and beautifully marked with purple featherings. The flowers appear at intervals from October till March, among leaves almost as slender as a hair. I always like to pay a visit to the Crocus frames, on my way back from church on New Year's Day, to see what promise of Spring they have as a present for me. For many years I have been greeted by newly-arrived blooms of the typical brilliant yellow form of *C. chrysanthus*, and in most seasons it will have appeared, in the open border

My Garden in Spring

too; and as among the autumn Crocuses only the first, *C. Scharojanii*, and the last, *C. vitellinus*, are yellow, and both of these are very rare, the golden buds of *C. chrysanthus* are a veritable foretaste of Spring. It is quite otherwise with Spring-flowering Croci, a large proportion of which have either yellow flowers or at least the three outer segments of some shade of buff or straw colour on the outside. Of those now in cultivation, for the one truly autumnal yellow, *Scharojanii*, we have eleven Spring ones, with flowers entirely yellow on the inner surface, four that have yellow forms as well as white or lilac ones, and several with buff outer segments, at any rate in some of their forms. They may be divided as follows:

Normally yellow:

Aureus, susianus, stellaris, ancyrensis, gargaricus, Korolkowii, Olivieri, Suterianus, graveolens, Balansae, chrysanthus.

With yellow forms:

Candidus, reticulatus, biflorus, aërius.

With buff exterior:

Imperati, suaveolens, dalmaticus, etruscus, versicolor, and vernus.

The two last are seldom seen with any yellow about them, but I have some *versicolor* collected near Mentone that in some forms have straw-coloured outer segments, and a seedling I got here from *vernus* Mme. Mina has quite a Nankeen tint outside when in bud. I have never seen a yellow Crocus growing wild, and without close acquaintance with them in their homes it is impossible to say what causes this preponderance of yellow in vernal species.

72

Some of the lunatics. (See p. 178.)

Spring Crocuses

It may be more conspicuous to insect visitors among withered grass and stones or bare earth, while the lilac and white of autumnal species form a greater contrast with the browns and tawny reds of fallen or dead leaves.

I have before alluded to the way external stripes, after the manner of those of the zebra and tiger, render the buds and closed flowers inconspicuous, and it is worth noting that these stripes are particularly well developed on Spring Crocuses, and in the yellow species; in fact only three, *gargaricus*, *Olivieri*, and *Suterianus*, have so far never been found with stripes or feathered markings, for *ancyrensis*, which has been described as never varying in this way, has of late years given me seedlings with featherings and suffusions of dark brown. The most extreme of all in this respect is *C. Balansae*, one form of which has the three outer segments externally of a deep mahogany colour, and in bud looks nearly black and is very hard to see, but the moment these deep-coloured segments part, the rich orange of the inner segments makes a most conspicuous and beautiful object of the flower. A half-expanded one forms as striking a colour-contrast as any flower I can think of. Every one who sees it for the first time is astonished at its beauty, and can hardly believe it is real, like the little girl at the Zoo, who after gazing at the Anteaters said, " But there aren't really such animals as those, are there, Nurse ? " Other forms of *C. Balansae* are pretty, especially those well feathered with bronze on the orange ground, but they are quite credibly tame and dull after the mahogany one. It has never borne a varietal name, so it is not possible to buy

73

it for certain from any nursery I know of, and it does not come quite true from seed.

Of yellow Crocuses the best known is the old Dutch form of *aureus*, too well known to need description, but it deserves mention as it is a very curious plant, for though its anthers are larger than those of any other Crocus it has a deformed, atrophied stigma, and is quite sterile, never producing seeds, and has been like that for a very long time, and so must have been propagated solely by offsets, by vegetative instead of sexual reproduction, and yet it shows no sign of deterioration, and is, I should say, one of the most widely cultivated of all plants that cannot be raised from seeds, for there can be but few gardens that do not contain a few hundreds of the common yellow Crocus. The Saffron Crocus (*C. sativus*) is another similar case. It has been cultivated for centuries for the sake of its stigmata, which being dried become the Saffron of commerce, from Kashmir to the Bay of Biscay, and was at one time largely grown in England at Saffron Walden. But it has never produced seeds in the memory of man or since he has written about it. I have a curious, dull-coloured, and smaller flowered form of *aureus* that in other respects is much like the Dutch Crocus, but does produce a few seeds in favourable seasons. I cannot trace its origin, but have heard rumours of a stock of yellow Crocus that exists in Holland and is of an inferior quality, and I suspect it is my fertile but dingy old friend. The wild type of *C. aureus* is a very free seeder, and varies a good deal in its seedlings. The best forms of it are of an intense glowing orange: one I get from Mr. Smith's

Spring Crocuses

wonderful nursery at Newry under the name of *moesiacus* (which is rightly but a synonym of *aureus*) is larger and deeper in colour than any other orange-coloured Crocus that can be grown outside. I think these deep orange *aureus* forms grow best in slight shade such as is given by some small light bush, and when they are allowed to seed about and colonise are simply glorious in the rock garden.

Sometimes I get a seedling which is the form Dean Herbert named *lutescens* and figured in the *Botanical Magazine*, a beautiful flower of several shades, as though cream were mixed with apricots, and there was more cream than apricot at the edges of the segments. This season I have a white seedling which is of course the old named form, v. *lacteus*, but I hope from this year's behaviour it will prove an earlier flowerer like the type, a few flowers of which generally flare up before the paler Dutch appears, whereas the old *lacteus* is the latest of all the forms of *aureus* to pierce through, and often manages to keep back a flower or two to be company for *vernus* var. *obesus* and compete for the honour of being the last Crocus of that Spring. *Lacteus* is an ivory white in colour, distinct from any other, and you can see it is a yellow turned white, reminding one of that beautiful softened shade of white that in old age replaces red hair of the shade euphemistically called auburn, but colloquially carrots or ginger.

No present-day seedlings of the orange wild *aureus* are anything like the old Dutch variety, whose origin is lost in mystery, as also is that of another section of this

My Garden in Spring

species, which is most likely of garden origin. It is of slender build and pale colouring, and is known as *sulphureus*, and there are three varieties of it : a self-coloured one known as *sulphureus concolor*, almost as pale as butter ; a rather faded-looking one, shading nearly to white at the tips of the segments, which is *sulphureus pallidus ;* and the other, *sulphureus striatus*, is slightly larger and deeper in colour than *concolor*, and striped outside with reddish brown. All of them are pretty and interesting, especially in the rock garden, and they have always been perfectly sterile, and the anthers are reduced to mere rudiments. It is curious that *C. aureus* should have been so sportive long ago and produced such widely different breaks and then ceased to give more, and the sterility of the new forms is so contrary to general experience with a sportive form, which nearly always, if the flowers are not double, shows greater fertility. Every garden ought to have large clumps of the old yellow Crocus to brighten up the bare soil in February, and I find a good place for such is towards the back of borders, round the feet of deciduous shrubs or permanently planted herbaceous plants that cover a large space when in full leaf. They have a fine effect in such places, especially if planted in a thick central mass and with outlying smaller groups as if naturally spreading from the main clump, and to my mind look better than when in bands or small clumps in the front of a border, and they are quite capable of taking care of themselves in the middle distance, whereas the edge is so valuable for more delicate plants. Wherever they can be planted in grass that can be left unmown till their leaves ripen they

Spring Crocuses

show to the very best advantage, and the yellow Crocus is best planted alone, unless some early flowering white *vernus* form be mixed with it, each in fairly large clumps, and a few outliers of both kinds hobnobbing occasionally.

I meant to treat of the yellow Crocuses first, but find it a bore to be too systematic, and I want to go on talking of bold plantings in big borders and grass. The fat, prosperous, gone into trade and done well with it, garden forms of *Crocus vernus* are best used for colour masses. The individual blooms strike me as coarse after the refined true species. But used as I like the Dutch Yellow, they look well. Margot, a soft lavender one, is best of all, and looks more like some species—a giant *Tomasinianus,* perhaps—than a florist's *vernus,* and I should like to have it in thousands, and generally plant a new patch of about a hundred each season. *Purpureus grandiflorus* is a fine effective thing, especially if near a clump, and the scouts of either army intermingling, of some lilac or striped variety such as Mme. Mina or Sir Walter Scott. I do not care so much for large clumps of any white form. At the back of the borders they look too cold, and suggest unmelted snowpats. One of the lawns here is divided from meadow land by a light iron fence, and as usually happens the mowing machine spares a strip a few inches in width of the grass at the foot of the fence on the lawn side. I noticed in a Norfolk garden a charming effect, where such a sanctuary was peopled with a long line of Harebells and Lady's Bed-straw, and the following autumn we turned back our turf at the foot of the fence and planted Crocuses as thickly as we could set them, and replaced the turf

My Garden in Spring

counterpane, tucking them snugly in bed. In the first stretch I planted we mixed up three forms, *purpureus grandiflorus*, Mme. Mina, and Mont-blanc, stirring them well together, but in a later planting we did a stretch with one colour, and then began mixing in another form, about one of the new to four of the old, and gradually increased the percentage of the new until we had used up our stock of the old, and the line became all of one sort again. This has a very good effect, and if colours that blend prettily are chosen is the better plan to follow.

Now back to the Yellows. Among them are some very dainty gems, suitable for the rock garden. *C. ancyrensis* has several good points; it is inexpensive, early, seeds freely, and sows itself, and it has such a rough netted jacket that it is avoided by mice (has been so far, I must write, or perhaps to-morrow I shall find holes, empty corm tunics and room for repentance). That does seem to be a fact, though: they will dig out certain species with soft jackets, especially *Salzmannii* and *Tournefortei*, and finish off a whole clump if not trapped first, but they leave *Sieberi, susianus*, and such reticulated armoured kinds alone. I suppose it would be rather like having the tennis-net entangled in our front teeth to chew such tunics. *C. Korolkowii*, especially Van Tubergen's large forms from Bokhara, are good for a warm nook, and often commence flowering in the old year. They are mostly of a glistening clear yellow, like that of a Lesser Celandine, and have deep bronze and purple frecklings on the outside. They make the largest corms of any Crocus I know, and when first sent from Bokhara were planted for a Gladiolus species. The older form of *Korolkowii* from

Spring Crocuses

further East is a washy little imitation of these better forms, greenish on the back, rather the colour you sometimes find on the outside of the yolk of a hard-boiled egg, and suggestive of dirty metal—German silver, or Britannia metal, "which goes green and smells nasty," as Mrs. Brown knew by experience. *C. Olivieri* is for all intents and purposes an orange-coloured *Balansae* without external markings but *gargaricus* has character of its own, its first flowers coming without leaves, and they are of a soft warm orange, like the reflected depth in the heart of a Van Zion Double Daffodil. It has an original sort of corm too, very small and round, and it splits up in some seasons into a multitude of little yellow pills, very hard to collect out of the soil at lifting time, and you know will require two seasons to grow to flowering size again. But a patch in flower on the rock garden makes up for it all. One little yellow Crocus has an obnoxious trait in its character, and is a little stinking beast, as Dr. Johnson defined the stoat. It is well named *graveolens*, and its heavy scent is generally the first intimation I get of its having opened its flowers. Sometimes I get a whiff of it even before I reach the Crocus frame—an abominable mixture of the odour of blackbeetles and imitation sable or skunk, or one of those awful furs with which people in the next pew or in front of you at a matinée poison you. A dried specimen of this Crocus retains its scent for years, and so does the blotting paper it has been pressed in. I think it emanates from the pollen grains, and I suppose it must be of some use to it in its native country—perhaps attractive to some insect of perverted olfactory tastes. It is a vegetable

79

equivalent of the egg of the Fulmar Petrel, which retains much the same awful scent for years after it has been blown.

Though I began with a reference to it I have saved my account of *Crocus chrysanthus* for the last of the Yellows because it is my favourite, and also it varies into so many other colours it will lead us away from the livery of jealousy. In most of its forms it is one of the smaller-flowered species, but it produces buds so lavishly that a few corms give a solid colour-effect when in full bloom, though of course this means they should be placed at the edge of the border among choice and neat plants, or in the rock garden. One race of *chrysanthus*, of which more must be said later, shows promise of great increase in size, and there may be a great future for my favourite if size can be added to its other charms of varied colouring and beauty of shape. It is what the older Crocus-lovers called gourd-shaped, and would have borne the latinised equivalent *laganae-florus*, better than the form of *aureus* to which it was once applied. I greatly admire a gourd-shaped Crocus ; it means that the throat is wide and full, and the segments ample and rounded, at least at their bases, so that an unopened blossom has a distinct waist about two-thirds of the way down, and below that there is a second swelling oval formed by the throat ; when fully expanded the segments bend outwards from above this waist, forming a round rather than starry flower, as the segments in well-developed gourd-mimics overlap well. In bud, then, we have the outline of a Pilgrim's-bottle Gourd, standing on its head but not flattened

Spring Crocuses

enough to stand the other way as a real one should, and in an open flower we get a solid effect that would charm the eye of such a florist as the great Glenny.

I wish I could show you the Crocus frame and the seed-beds on a sunny morning in early February, that you might see these gems in the flesh instead of through this printed page. Let us be childish enough to "make believe" we are doing it. I will take my garden basket and all its contents, almost as varied a collection as Alice's White Knight had, but certainly more useful, even the mouse-trap on too frequent occasions, while the cook's forks to extract new treasures, and painted wooden labels to mark them withal, are indispensable. It is noon, for I have waited for you, my visitors, and your train was late, delayed by a fog in town which here was only a rime frost and white mist that the sun has conquered, and the lawns are only dewy now in the shadows, so we can take the short cut over them, passing the Snowdrop clumps and Aconite carpets and hurrying on to make the most of the sunshine, over the New River by the bridge guarded by the weird lead ostriches, which are six feet high and give some visitors a turn when they first see them. Into the kitchen garden, and don't look at the peach-house Crocus clumps yet, but hurry along past the vineries round by the stove and then—are they open? Yes, even in the seed-beds in the open air bees are busy on the lines of colour. There are several lines of uniform lilac—without a break of a pure white or deep purple original-minded babe ; the labels at their heads tell us they are *Sieberi* or *Tomasinianus,* while solid yellow families are proclaimed

My Garden in Spring

as *ancyrensis, Korolkowii,* or *aureus,* but the variegated lines
are our objects of veneration, where white, cream, sulphur-
yellow, and lilac look as if all the seeds of the season had
been mixed. The label on one such will perhaps say
chrysanthus good white, another *c. pallidus,* or even striped
seedling, but except those labelled *c. superbus* there is no uni-
formity, thank Heaven. You must not mind if I suddenly
yell with joy, for perhaps yesterday was an R.H.S. day, and
I was in Vincent Square from early till late, and Monday
was wet and no Crocuses open, and Sunday had so many
services and Sunday-school classes, I have not seen my
seedlings since Saturday. So, if there is an extra fine
white flower with orange throat, a deeper blue self than
ever before, or some specially peacocky chameleon with an
inventive genius for external markings, I shall shout and
flop on my knees regardless of mud and my best knickers
donned for the visitors, and the cook's fork will tenderly
extract the prize, and you can admire it without going on
the knee, while I am writing a label for it, and before it
goes into a place of honour in the frame. It is not every
day, though, that my variety-spotting eye lights thus
easily on a tip-topper, and even now we must look carefully along the flowering rows for promising breaks,
bending some flowers to one side if fully open to see
what external markings they carry. Some will be replicas
of good forms selected in former years, but very seldom
sufficiently exact a copy to be mixed with that stock, so
they, and some that are obviously from the same studio
but by a prentice hand, can be cook's-forked out for you
to carry away if you are bitten with Crocomania. Now

Spring Crocuses

move on to the frames. They have four divisions, but two only are ablaze, for the other twain are devoted to autumnal varieties, and now contain leaves only, save for a few rare and tender bulbous plants that share their home, Romuleas that came masquerading as Croci, and such people. In the upper part of the frames are squares of twenty-five to fifty of some Crocus that has increased well, but nearer the front we get almost as many labels as plants, for here are the seedlings selected during the last few seasons, and the miffy, peevish, no-pleasing-'em kinds that simply won't increase ; but among them are some of the loveliest, and you will see at a glance that there is a very large preponderance of varieties labelled as *chrysanthus* seedlings, and yet no two are quite alike. When I see them here I long to be transported by magic carpet to the Bithynian Olympus, where *C. chrysanthus* is found in its most variable mood. George Maw records in his magnificent monograph of the genus that it was from thence he brought the white form he named *albidus*, the white with blue external markings which is his variety *coerulescens*, and best of all the sulphur form now known as variety *pallidus*, which has proved the best seed parent of all, and given us the race of Anakim of this species which I have mentioned.

They originated at Haarlem in that centre of creation of new plant forms, the Zwanenburg Nursery, where Mr. Van Tubergen and his two nephews, Mr. John and Mr. Thomas Hoog, always have some fresh revelation of beauty awaiting the visitor, and frequently delight me by most kindly posting me some new development among Crocuses.

83

My Garden in Spring

One season they sent a large white form with cream-coloured outer segments richly suffused with crimson purple, asking what I thought had produced this sudden break among seedlings of *chrysanthus pallidus*. Three years previously I flowered a batch of seedling *chrysanthus* here, among which were forms almost identical with the Haarlem wonder, but raised from forms of variety *coerulescens*, so I was able to reply that I believed them to be pure *chrysanthus* in descent, and this has been proved by the seeds of this blue and white form, which is now distributed and known as "Warley Variety," giving a percentage of typical *pallidus* forms at Haarlem.

These blue and whites are lovely forms and very strong growers, and I recommend a free use of Warley Variety for the rock garden and also as a seed parent. For the best form of my kindred race I have an even greater affection, perhaps as my own raising to begin with, but it is a rounder flower with more cream colour in the outer segments, and the crimson markings are divided into more distinct featherings. I call it Bowles' Bullfinch, having adopted the plan of calling the best of my *chrysanthus* seedlings after birds' names. Yellow Hammer, a light yellow striped with deep brown, Siskin with bright yellow exterior to the outer segments but the inner pure white, a very effective little chap, and Snow Bunting, white with grey lines on cream-coloured outer segments, have gone forth into the world, and I wish them to bear the genitival form of my patronymic before their avian pet name, so as to distinguish seedlings raised here from others that I know are coming along in friends' and neighbours' seed-beds. The 22nd of February

Spring Crocuses

1905, stands out as an event in the Crocus world for me, for a little packet post-marked Haarlem lay on my breakfast table, and had brought me five blooms from Mr. Hoog of *C. chrysanthus pallidus* seedlings which for size and delicious creamy moonlight yellows surpassed anything I had dreamt of. One had a band of deep purple on the outer segment, another greenish-blue feathering, and the largest of all was as soft a yellow as the pat of butter in front of me, and with a feathering patch of warm brown-madder at the base of each segment that set off the yellow in much the same manner as the apical patch of brownish black does on the forewing of the lovely Pale Clouded Yellow Butterfly. My admiration of this new race went to Holland by return of post, and had a pleasant sequel in a generous gift of corms of these varieties and the naming of the butter-coloured giant after me. I wish I possessed a tenth of the vigour and good temper of my namesake! " So far " he has increased well and smiled back at me in the weak wintry sun, in Crocus frame, rock garden, or ordinary border, and every one singles it out at a glance as the best of all the Yellows. Except in the typical, early-flowering yellow form, the stigmata of these *chrysanthus* forms I have described are bright scarlet, and give a brightness and finish to the open blossoms, but there is another race of *chrysanthus* with gourd-shaped throats but then a falling off, for the segments are rather pointed and make too starry an open flower. This race is invariably freckled or feathered externally with brown of various shades, and they were called by Maw vars. *fusco-tinctus* or *fusco-lineatus* according to the patterns of their freckles. They all have plain yellow

85

stigmata, and a curious line of their own in anthers, the ground colour instead of yellow being smoky-grey or greenish-black, which, of course, is most conspicuous in a newly-opened one, before the anther valves have rolled back and the pollen broken loose. These dusky anthers seem to be correlated with starry flowers rather than the brown markings, and are puzzling to account for without getting inside a bee and seeing with its compound eyes and thinking with its decentralised ganglionic brains. In the other *chrysanthus* forms, with very rare exceptions the little barbs at the base of the arrow-shaped anthers are tipped with black. There again, what can that be for ? Why should *chrysanthus* alone of yellow Croci benefit by these minute spots ? One has to look rather closely to see them at all even in an expanded flower, and they cannot be visible to a bee until it has settled on it, and I cannot think they are put there to help good patient botanists to recognise this otherwise variable species, or they would surely be on the *fuscotinctus* forms too. At the same time they do often help to point out a *chrysanthus* without reference to the corm tunic, but I have known them absent in some pure yellow and *pallidus* forms.

One of the smallest of Crocuses, known as *C. biflorus Pestalozzae*, but deserving specific rank I believe, and which I hope some day to reinstate in that proud position, always has minute black spots just where the filament joins on to the perianth, making the flower look as though some grains of soil had dropped into it. Again, *C. Crewei* and a very strange rare little blue one thought to be a form of *C. tauri* and called v. *melanthorus*, have

Spring Crocuses

the anthers jet black, and so has a winter flowering one from Palestine, *C. hyemalis*, var. *Foxii*.

Without the means for private interviews with the bees of their native land these questions must remain unanswered, and for the present be placed with those things "no fellah can understand."

Another of these insoluble riddles is why Miller in the great Dictionary originated the name *biflorus* for his species No. 4. It is quite the ordinary rule for Spring Crocuses to produce at least two flowers from each set of leaves wrapped round by a spathe or sheath as Miller puts it. *C. gargaricus* is the only one I can recall that is usually one-flowered, but Miller knew others bore two, and described his No. 3 as so doing. Dean Herbert goes further, and in his diagnosis states "scapo (vidi ipse) interdum furcato bifloro," so reading a deeper meaning into Miller's simple words. Like the Snark :

> " He summed it so well that it came to far more
> Than the witnesses ever had said."

But expositors of Browning and commentators on the deep sayings of other poets as well as Herbert are equally Snarkish in their powers of summing.

C. biflorus in some forms is hard to distinguish from *chrysanthus*. There is a sheet of specimens in Maw's herbarium in the British Museum, collected above Scutari, and labelled *C. biflorus nubigenus*, but most of them have the tell-tale black barbs, and I find living plants of them that I have here give me regular *chrysanthus* seedlings.

87

My Garden in Spring

I have lately raised and received from others forms intermediate between the two species, of the build of *biflorus* v. *Weldenii,* the Dalmatian form of this widely-spread species *biflorus,* but instead of a white ground-colouring they are of exquisite shades of pale sulphur, and variously freckled or feathered externally, like some *Weldenii* forms, with soft lilac, and are very lovely things apart from their interesting intermediate relationship. Their mixed blood is further shown by a tendency to grey on the anther, either as spots on the barbs or on the whole length. This Dalmatian form *Weldenii* is represented further east in Servia and Bulgaria by a large form known as *biflorus* v. *Alexandri* with yet more intense external markings, and when these form a broad band of amethyst purple, leaving only a narrow margin of white, it is one of the most lovely of Spring Crocuses ; the contrast of the pure white inner surface and the rich purple outer segments is a thing to sit down and look at. I have now seedlings that have the ground colour of various shades of lilac and the outer markings as in *Alexandri.* The first one appeared without warning in the rock garden, evidently self sown, and another unbirthday present from the garden, a little thing of its own compose, as the parish clerk called his doggerel version of the Psalm of the hopping hills, for it appeared a year before I had obtained the wild lilac-grounded *biflorus* var. *Adami*—a pretty form from the Caucasus but not over-robust in the open ground.

C. *biflorus* is best known in its old garden form of the Scotch Crocus, large flowered and white, beautifully striped outside with deep purple, and like other old garden favour-

Double-flowered Anemone appennina. (See p. 208.)

Spring Crocuses

ites quite sterile. Many smaller wild forms come from Italy, especially from round Florence, where they have a pale lilac ground-colouring, and vary into the pretty form *estriatus*, which has no stripes on the external buff of the outer segments. This, as a hardy, dainty, and early flowering form, should be in every rock garden and sunny border where tiny bulbous things have a chance. "Crocuses everywhere" is my motto here, and the lower shelving slopes of the rock garden make splendid homes for the rarer gems, but even there they must fit in with herbaceous plants such as *Œnothera speciosa*, *Veronica filifolia*, &c., which cover the ground after the Crocuses have finished with it. And here you will find the forms of *aërius*, which one would say was a blue counterpart of *chrysanthus* from its round shape and narrow leaves, but below ground it has a thin jacket instead of the hard, shell-like covering of *chrysanthus*. Some of its forms have rich outer markings as nearly crimson as one can hope for in a Crocus, and its variety, major, is one of the finest of all lilac Crocuses, almost deserving to be called blue. There is no real blue one so far as I know, the nearest approach to it being a quaint, rather ill-tempered midget Messrs. Barr imported as *C. tauri*, but not a bit like the great tall thing Maw figured under the name and pronounced to be more robust than any Eastern form of *biflorus*. The autumnal *C. speciosus* is in some forms nearly blue, but in many forms of *biflorus* there is a spot or line or two of real Prussian blue at the base of the inner segments, and if only it could be persuaded to spread over the segments we might have a turquoise-blue Crocus. How dread-

My Garden in Spring

fully its colour would fight with the present mauves and lilacs of its family !

I must not prattle of the multitude of Crocus forms for which I have labels. They all possess distinctions and differences for me, but in many cases are better seen than read about, and even I am beginning to be alarmed when I see the rows of labels sticking up in the frames and seed-beds in August just after replanting. " Looks rather like a cemetery, doesn't it ? " friends mockingly ask. " I don't mind," say I, " so long as it has an annual resurrection." I may be forgiven, however, for discoursing of what should be everybody's Crocuses, such as *Imperati* for the first. There are two distinct races going about under the name. One is the wild plant from the country round Naples, the other I have never yet traced to its native home, and rather suspect it is of garden origin. Herbariums appear to have only the Neapolitan fellow. The two are very distinct ; the unmistakable point of difference is in the spathe valves, those wonderful wrappings of living tissue-paper that enclose every Crocus bud in its youth. There are either two or only a single one, and as a rule the number of these floral spathes is a good specific feature, and a whole species has either a monophyllous or diphyllous spathe, but in *Imperati* all the wild Neapolitan ones, so far as I can find out, have diphyllous spathes, and every author who describes the wild plant mentions the two spathes but makes no mention of a form with a monophyllous spathe. Both have the same colour-scheme, warm rosy lilac within, and the outside of the three outer segments striped or feathered

Spring Crocuses

with purple on a buff ground, but from a garden point of view the diphyllous form is in most respects the better plant, having larger flowers and varying endlessly in the degree, or even absence, of the outside purple featherings, and even varying in this respect from season to season, I am sorry to say, for I have sometimes selected especially fine seedlings for their richness, or absence, of feathering, but after a season or two they have reversed their scheme of decoration.   Except a few forms of *C. versicolor* I have never known another species of Crocus vary as to the markings of the offsets.   The diphyllous form flowers over a long period, and that means that one seldom gets a mass out at one time on a clump.

On the contrary, the monophyllous form scarcely varies at all in feathering, and is most punctual in blossoming in the early part of January, and almost every plant in a clump will be flowering at the same time.   It stands up higher among its upright leaves than the diphyllous one among its longer recumbent foliage.   I used to know which of the two forms the different nurserymen stocked, but both forms have done well here, and it is years since I bought any, and so have lost touch with their sources.   The diphyllous form has sometimes been listed as *C. Imperati longiflorus*, or *purpureus*, and such a name would, I expect, still bring you that form, but there was never any distinguishing name to the monophyllous race. There are some good white forms of the diphyllous—one pure white except for a cream-coloured exterior to the outer segments, which is the var. *albiflos* of Herbert. Another has the rich purple featherings of the type on the white ground, and is a fine variety. Both forms are delightful in the rock garden or in any sunny corner, and the diphyllous race are great seeders, and soon colonise in a kind home where hoes harrow not too harshly.

C. Sieberi is another indispensable—one of the earliest to appear, generally showing up about Twelfth Night. It is chubby in shape and a cool, bluish-lilac in colour, with a very rich yellow throat ; it is a good increaser both from seed and offsets, and though it comes from sunny Greece is very hardy, and the blossoms stand snow and frost better than many others. Max Leichtlin sent out a good deep-coloured form of it as *C. atticus*, but it is certainly no more than a good variety of *Sieberi*. The Cretan form is one of the most glorious of all known Crocuses, for the ground is white, the throat a very rich orange colour, and the outer segments are marked externally with bands or streaks of a curious shade of purplish-crimson unlike that in any other Crocus. Unfortunately it is very rare in gardens, and has not been collected for a great many years, as it is said Cretan brigands will murder even good little plant-collectors—honest root-gatherers as Parkinson would call them—for the value of their skins, and *C. Sieberi versicolor* grows up among their mountain strongholds. Although it has as large and conspicuous scarlet stigmata as any Crocus it produces but little pollen, and flowers later than other forms of *Sieberi*, so I, and a neighbour who has caught Crocus fever from me, have hard work to get any seeds from this variety, and think ourselves lucky if we can sow half a dozen each season. Some of the results have been very encouraging, and we have got a few with the red markings on a pale lavender ground colour.

Spring Crocuses

C. Tomasinianus is the Crocus for spreading by seed into natural drifts, or filling a border or slope of rock garden. It replaces *vernus* in Eastern Europe, and it is not easy to find any definite botanical character to distinguish it from that variable species. Here it certainly hybridises with some forms of *vernus*. Maw states that its glabrous throat distinguishes it from *vernus*, but I have never yet seen a flower of it that lacks a plentiful supply of white hairs in the throat, and can only imagine he had some peculiar form of it. On the other hand, I have a beardless form of *vernus*. *Tom*, as I feel inclined to call it for short and knowing him so well, is a variable plant; some races have nearly white outsides and in bud look dull, but half-opened and showing the lavender interior are very pretty. I prefer the deeper-coloured ones though, and have selected some warm, rosy-purple forms, and have got still deeper-coloured seedlings from them. I have also a pure white that is good for contrast, but not an improvement in a species whose chief charm lies in its peculiarly amethystine shade of lilac. One day I went into the garden to try and forget a raging toothache, and nearly succeeded, for a lovely *Tom* seedling caught my eye, a rosy-hued one with the addition of nearly white tips to each segment, and under each white mark a spot of violet-purple, after the style of the form of *vernus* called *leucorhynchus*. The treasure was removed to the frame and has increased to hundreds, and has gone into many other gardens, but if you want to know the end of the tooth you must ask my dentist ; it passed from my keeping to his. I want to get *Tom* freely grouped in the grass, but it does not increase much there : in a sunny border it conquers new territory

93

My Garden in Spring

at a surprising rate, being a great seeder, and also splitting into many small offsets from the larger corms. It is appearing in tufts all along the path edges of the rock garden, the result of seeds getting swept in among the edging stones.

C. versicolor is the last I shall insist upon your regarding as a garden necessity, and if you cannot get hold of the wild form from the Alpes Maritimes or the Riviera, variable, delicately coloured, and feathered beauties of endless kaleidoscopic possibilities, you should grow a garden form known as var. *picturatus*, with white ground-colour and crimson-purple featherings. *Versicolor* is the one Crocus in which the inner segments are as a rule striped or feathered on the inner surface. A few garden forms of *vernus* and the wild one *siculus* are slightly so, but *versicolor* seems to take a pride in internal decoration beyond all others.

I cannot pass to another chapter without mentioning *C. Fleischeri*, a starry little creature, but one that wears a scarlet feather in the centre, the finely-divided stigmata of course. They are so brightly coloured that they glow through the white segments of the closed bud much as the yolk of a woodpecker's egg does through the shell, giving it a pink glow that, alas! disappears as soon as it is blown. Then too there is *C. carpetanus*, which is peculiar in two respects; it has a pale lilac stigma, but not so handsome or bright as that of the autumnal *byzantinus*, and it also has a leaf that in section is semi-cylindrical, with raised ribs on the under side, and no lateral blades as in other Crocuses. It has a very pretty soft lilac flower, but is not a robust grower. Underground even it is peculiar, and wears a covering of fibres more like tow than the coat of a respectable Crocus.

94

CHAPTER VI

Numerous Early Comers

FOLLOWING close on the heels of the Crocuses come *Scilla bifolia* and *Chionodoxa sardensis* racing *Anemone blanda* for the honour of forming the first blue carpeting of the year, for not one of these is much use as dots or stiff little rings in front of a large label, and all are quite unsuitable for the modern millionaire's made-by-contract, opulent style of gardening—a thing I hate rather than envy, so don't make mental remarks about the proverbial acidity of the immature fruit of the vine. The filling of so many square yards of prepared soil with so many thousands of expensive bulbs, to yield a certain shade of colour for a fortnight and then to be pulled up to make place for another massing, gives me a sort of gardening bilious attack, and a feeling of pity for the plants and contempt for the gardening skill that relies upon Bank of England notes for manure. But I love a large colony of some good plant that you can see has spread naturally in a congenial home, aided by the loving care of an observant owner. It has the same charm of refinement and antiquity that one gets from an old house where the Chippendale chairs and cabinets have stood on the same polished boards and time-toned carpets ever since they were new. It is a case of good taste and knowledge from the first, and watchful care and apprecia-

95

My Garden in Spring

tion and absence of the weathercock giddiness that is influenced by gusty Fashion with a large F if you please. Buy as many *Scilla bifolia* as you can afford, then, but choose them a permanent home. Among the roots of a wildish group of briar roses is a good situation, or even among dwarf heaths, so long as they are not the red *carnea* —the flowering periods of these two coinciding and proving somewhat too competitive to please me ; but almost anywhere will do among permanently planted larger plants that can stand a spring carpet of blue at their feet. Then leave them alone to seed and multiply and replenish the earth.

There is a great charm about the red, polished noses they thrust through so early, and which, on a sunny day, suddenly split asunder and reveal the neatly-packed flower-buds, looking like a blue ear of wheat. This is only promise, and the reward comes when the two leaves lie close to the ground, and the blue spikes are feathery sprays. It sometimes happens that the collected bulbs have a few Chionodoxas mixed among them, but there is no harm in this, as the colours do not fight at all, and the Chionodoxas carry on the flowering for a week or two. I have purposely mixed them in a large bed of briar roses that I am allowing to carpet itself with them. The Scilla comes first, then *C. sardensis*, followed by the interesting bi-generic hybrid forms known as Chionoscillas, which are sure to appear wherever the two genera are grown together. I believe *C. Luciliae* enters into most of these rather than *sardensis*, but the early flowering of Scilla is almost always inherited, and the hybrids flower before *Luciliae* is fully open. The most easily noticed distinction between Scilla and Chionodoxa is the difference

Numerous Early Comers

of the filaments of their stamens ; in Scilla they are filiform, that is slender and threadlike, but in Chionodoxa they are flattened out, wide at the base, and tapering upwards, so that they lie close to one another, forming a cone in the mouth of the flower, and are conspicuously white. In the hybrids they are of every intermediate width, and readily catch the eye even if they are the only mark that shows the mixed parentage. *C. gigantea* can be used to follow *Luciliae,* but its colouring is rather too pink a blue to carry on the same effect, and the form sold as *Luciliae* Boissier is a better colour, being very nearly *Luciliae* only flowering later and having more white in the eye, and leading on to *C. Tmoli* (wrongly spelt Tmolusii sometimes, as if named after a man instead of the mountain), but which I, and also the Dutch growers, find has a habit of dying after seeding, otherwise it would be a pleasant wind-up to the Chionodoxa season. Some of the Chionoscillas are worth looking after, and several have been named. Mr. Allen took an interest in them, and selected several good ones. His variety, Volunteer, is one of the best of a good *sardensis* blue and very free, and his Queen, a charming soft pink, is one of my most precious gems, but alas! a great rarity. Now and then, a large or extra bright one has appeared here, and tempted me to burrow to the bowels of the earth for its bulb, so as to remove it to a safe corner of the rock garden. This burrowing is difficult when one has to go some eight or more inches among the plants, and I use another special tool of my own compose for it. An ordinary "lady's fork" of four tines furnishes the raw material for my inventive genius to work upon, a coarse file my coadjutor : mind and muscle and metal

My Garden in Spring

then get to work, and off come the two outer tines, and I have a lovely giant's toothpick that almost always accompanies me when in the garden. Hark to a list of its virtuous uses. It goes to the root of the evil in cases of Dandelions and Docks unlike any other weapon : a plunge, a twist, and the tap-rooted fiend lies vanquished at my feet. More gently and lovingly inserted, it fetches up a choice bulb, a rogue among the Tulips, or a new seedling of great price and depth. Again, when the gardening visitor comes with a basket and wants a bit of something good, nothing removes a side crown so neatly, without disturbing the main plant, or so unerringly extracts the very piece your critical eye selects as best spared, and your affection for your guest settles the extent of, as this two-pronged walking-stick. It nearly got patented and put on the market by an enterprising firm who read Mr. Donald McDonald's praises of it after a visit here, and I gave measurements and inspected models, but the Bowles Fork has not appeared, and being so easily made from the four-tined variety is perhaps not yet needed.

I have a very superior form of *Scilla bifolia* here, that we call var. *taurica*. It was given me many years ago by Dr. Lowe of Wimbledon, one of the many mementoes I possess of his kindness and generosity, and a very pleasant friendship that has left many marks of betterment on me and my garden.

Although it is many years since the Scilla came to me, I have but one small clump, for it never bears seed, and increase by offsets is rather slow, as friends admire it so, and I have such a foolishly soft heart that will persuade me I can spare just one more bulb. Its great beauty lies in the crimson anthers of a freshly-opened flower, and a neatness of habit, stiff, sturdy stalks, and close-set spikes of larger flowers, and a softer tone of blue than in the type. Those I have bought at various times bearing the same name have been nothing but strong bulbs of ordinary *bifolia*. It is hard to get hold of the forms of *bifolia*, for few lists include any but *alba* and *carnea*. The former is a lovely little thing, most suitable for the rock garden, and *carnea* is very much like it but only *carnea* by courtesy, for, unless within a few hours of its opening, it will have faded to an ivory white. The rare old var. *rubra* is a lovely thing, rosy-salmon in colour, and so big and strong-looking you would expect it to ramp and fill the garden, whereas in reality it seldom makes an offset, and has never set seed here. Mr. Allen's seedling raised from it and called Pink Beauty is rather earlier and a fainter, more rosy pink, and rather better at increasing. Another of his raising, var. *purpurea*, has deep-red stamens and a purplish tone of blue, and is distinct but rather heavy in colour, and not so pleasing as the type unless looked at closely. There is a little colony of these forms in the rock garden, in a flat bed that is overrun later in the year by *Convolvulus tenuissimus* (the plant generally wrongly labelled as *C. althaeoides*, which has a much larger and paler flower with purple eye, and is more tender, living but refusing to flower here), which throws a veil of silver leaves and bright, rose-coloured flowers over the summer sleep of the Scillas.

In the same bed I have the form I like best of *Scilla sibirica*, known as var. *multiflora*. It won my affection by its habit of blossoming three weeks earlier than the type, and I prefer its lighter, less aggressively Prussian blue colouring

My Garden in Spring

for associating with other Scillas. It seeds freely, and its children inherit the parental colouring and early rising habit. The white *S. sibirica* grows near, and is also lavish in seminal increase, and a few early-flowering whites have appeared that I am watching anxiously, and hoping they have inherited the best traditions of both families.

Hyacinthus azureus is one of the most exquisite of the small and earlies, but like eating soup with a fork, one never gets enough of it. It is cheap enough, only three shillings a hundred, yet I never saw a garden that could show so many. I vow that next planting season I will let six sixpences go bang and try to grow a century of spikes of its pure turquoise bells. It is very lovely grown beside *Crocus aureus;* their colours are not too violent in contrast, as at their early appearance there is plenty of brown earth for background. Two quaint, squat little Ornithogalums flower in the very beginning of the year, opening a flower at a time during any intervals of decent weather ; one is *O. Haussknectii,* which I advise the inventors of English names to call the Horse's Necktie Bird's-milk, and the other *O. libanoticum,* and Pompey and Cæsar are very much alike, especially Pompey. I won't say they are strikingly beautiful, but in January one is pleased to see their greyish-white, green-streaked flowers flattened down among their rosettes of leaves. One dreadful winter I was obliged to spend in London helping to nurse my brother through typhoid fever and all its complications, and on a dreary December day kind Dr. Lowe came to inquire, and brought with him from his garden of treasures a bulb or two of a charming little Muscari in full bloom. He told me he went round his garden to see what he could bring to cheer me, and this bright little Grape Hyacinth suggested itself. It lived in my window in that London square until I could bring it and my Convalescent home, so for association's sake alone I should treasure it, but I also rejoice in its wee blue flowers, which never fail to appear in a succession from December to March.

I never had a name for it, but have called it Dr. Lowe's ; it is probably a form of *M. botryoides,* and I have forgotten, if he ever told me, where he got it from. He was one of a delightful old school of amateur gardeners, a friend of Miss Hope, Harpur-Crewe, Miss Marianne North, Isaac Henry, and many others, only venerated names to me, but many of their treasures have passed into my hands through Dr. Lowe's kindness to me when a struggling beginner. *Puschkinia scilloides,* the Striped Squill, I owe to him, a pretty little grey thing like the ghost of a Scilla come back to earth ; and if you buy what is offered as *P. libanotica* you will get *scilloides,* for they are but one and the same, though often listed as distinct, and sometimes you are invited to pay more for one than for the other, so always buy the cheaper.

Cyclamen Coum and *C. ibericum* and their garden-raised hybrid offspring *Atkinsii* should have been showing crimson or white buds lying on the earth since mid-December, and be raising them up and turning back their petals before the days grow perceptibly longer. The two first are constantly confused with each other, but are easy to distinguish, as *Coum* has plain green leaves, while those of *ibericum* have more or less of handsome, grey spotting or zonal bands, and it is altogether the larger and handsomer plant. I won't say that puzzling hybrid intermediates besides Atkinsii do not exist, for I believe there are several in Bitton Garden, where the two species have grown side by side for nearly a century, that are distinctly intermediate, but not large and handsome enough to rank for garden purposes as *C. Atkinsii*, which is a bolder plant with larger flowers than those of either parent. *C. Coum album* is a difficult plant to obtain. Many lists contain the name, but the plants that arrive bearing it are either *C. ibericum*, as rosy as red tape, or *C. cilicicum*, an autumn-flowering member of the family with conspicuously mottled leaves. One or two such names seem to exist in catalogues simply to provide aliases for plants. It is rather amusing to gamble with some and see what you will get for them. *Crocus lactiflorus* I especially recommend ; it is a bran-pie, lucky dip, and surprise packet all in one ; you never know whether an order for half a dozen will produce an autumnal or vernal species, and many of my rarities came to me so named. *Lathyrus magellanicus* is another, *Anacyclus formosus* a third. I imagine no plant is grown by the author of the list under these names, and so the packer turns round three times and catches what he can. I am not sure that I am not getting rather extravagant over Cyclamen. I love them so that I order a few hundreds each season, and sow seeds as well, but I never yet saw a garden containing too many of them, and it will be a long day before this one provides enough to please me. With one species and another they are in flower very nearly all the year round. *Coum* and *ibericum* begin with the year, and before they are over *C. repandum* has opened out its ivy-shaped leaves, pushing them along underground until they come up far away from the centre of the corm, making you think they must

Numerous Early Comers

belong to seedlings. They appear above-ground folded in two like a butterfly with closed wings, and soon after them come the buds. I was greatly pleased with a form I got from Holland in the autumn. It is called var. *roseum*, and is a pretty pale pink and marvellously floriferous. I used to have a fine plant of a pure white form, but it died and I cannot get another as good, all I have bought lately for white being nothing but a faded or overworn pink as the sixteenth century gardeners call it. The bright, rosy type form is very good, and carries on the season until *C. europaeum*, the sweetly-scented gem from Italian woods and Tyrolean hillsides, begins to flower. It does so about the end of May here, and goes on until September is middle-aged and the truly autumnal forms are in full swing. The largest flowerer of the hardy forms is *C. libanoticum*, unfortunately rare, rather expensive, and none too easy to grow. The happiest I possess are on a burnt-up dry slope of rock garden overhung by an old thorn ; the soil is dry as dust all the summer, and I suppose the slopes of Lebanon are not very different at that season, and so it feels at home where nothing else but a few Sempervivums exist for long together.

I am very fond of the Spring-flowering Colchicums, but unfortunately slugs are also, and those greedy gasteropods and I have a race for who can see the flower-buds first. If I win I go out after dark with an acetylene lamp and a hatpin and spear the little army of slugs making for the tea-party at the sign of the Colchicum. *C. hydrophilum* and *libanoticum* are two closely-related eastern species ; the former from the Taurus has the more richly-coloured flowers, and the Lebanon one the larger and better shaped.

My Garden in Spring

Both are attractive so early in the year, but the two I like best are *C. luteum*, the only yellow one of the family, and *C. crociflorum*, a charming, little white flower with purple lines running up the back of each segment, a very good imitation of a small Crocus. They have existed for some years in the rock garden in ordinary soil, but I believe the sand moraine with underground waterpipe would suit them best. It certainly agrees with their wilful cousin *Bulbocodium vernum*, a plant I could never induce to settle down and be cosy until I indulged myself in the luxury of what, for want of a better name, I call a sand moraine.

As I suppose it is inevitable that I write of my moraines, we might as well discuss the subject here. No one would read a gardening book nowadays that did not deal with this latest fashion in gardening. The name and popularity and prattle of the thing are new, but many good cultivators had their porous, gritty, raised or sunk beds for alpines, whatever they called them, long ago. Mr. Wolley-Dod laughingly called his narrow raised mounds "potato-ridges." But they proved the ideal home for many difficult plants that would not exist domiciled otherwise on the cold, sticky clay at Edge Hall. The ridges were, as I remember them, about twenty yards long, and mainly composed of grit and leaf soil, and ever full of rare and healthy plants. The ridge system was the important factor of success at Edge, but in the hungry, arid, gravel soil at Cambridge, Mr. Lynch found a sunk bed of gritty soil made a happy home for Saxifrages that repined and went into a decline under other treatment. Then arose the prophet. The abundant rainfall of Ingleborough and the local limestone (three or four lumps of which make any sort of rock gardening a thing

Anemone nemorosa purpurea. (See p. 213.)

of beauty if only one side of the block be bedded up with earth), aided and abetted by river silt from the lake's mouth and chips of all sizes from the mountain side, were only waiting for Mr. Farrer's master mind to plan their combination and lo! a new era dawned. The most discontented of his alpine treasures flourished, the great news went forth to the world, a series of books in slate-coloured covers became the foundation of conversation, even at dinner, to the great annoyance of those who wait and therefore should expect all things to come to them. This is a fact: a head gardener, in speaking of the extraordinary wave of the fashion of gardening, told me that the men in the house complained bitterly that, whereas once upon a time they picked up innumerable sporting tips and had much interesting gossip to listen to, nowadays the talk at dinner was all Latin names and about soils and gardening books. Now the moraine holds the field. I wonder will the name live unrivalled until these words are published, or will someone invent a terse term for the bed with underground pipes that promises to replace the plain granite chip arrangement? I hope it won't be called the glacier; it is bad enough to misname as moraine a square yard or two of a hole in the ground filled up with road-mending material and bristling with labels, but underground-water-bed savours of chronic invalids and hospitals, and is also cumbrous. Melting-snow sounds Japanesque and is what one is trying to imitate, but as I did not invent the system I do not feel bound to name it, and I hope it will be in common use and have gained a familiar name before this is read. Mr. Grove has perfected the idea in his marvellous garden near Henley, and I have seen hosts of plants

My Garden in Spring

that I believed were impossible, in health and vigour and jostling each other in his piped beds, and we must look to him for light and guidance. Mr. Malby has experimented on a smaller scale with beds with impervious floors and an inlet above and outlet below, and has found them very successful.

Of course I was an early victim of the moraine measles after my first visit to Ingleborough, and when next the Moraine Magician came to see me, he helped in planning my first attempt at a granite chip one. My previous experiments had not been over successful; a range of the rock garden had been built with the débris of broken Welsh slate, the result of the re-roofing of my brother's house, but I and the plants find it rather uninteresting—too dry and lean, like a diet of cracknel biscuits or pulled bread. Another mound composed of old ceilings, brick rubble, cinders, and gravel exactly suits my outdoor Cactuses and other succulents, of which more anon. A sloping pocket of the slate-roof range was cleared out and filled to the depth of two and a half feet with granite chips, smaller in gauge than Mr. Farrer usually advises to meet any arid climate half-way, and mixed with leaf soil it has suited some plants admirably, but contrary to all my hopes needs watering morning and evening in dry weather, and so is not much better in labour saving than any ordinary bank of the rock garden. In it *Androsace hedraeantha* is happy and seeds about; *Cerastium alpinum*, var. *lanatum*, which refused to live with me before, now wishes to fill this bed. Edraianthus species have ceased to be an anxiety, and give me pleasure and flowers. *Saponaria lutea* is as happy as the proverbial

Numerous Early Comers

king, though no more yellow than the paper of the typical bun-bag, and were it not a rarity and collected by myself in happy hunting-grounds I should not greatly care if it miffed itself away as under former treatment. But some of them do not like overhead watering in hot weather, so I tried experiments in a corner of this bed to see whether I could keep it from burning up so quickly by mixing sand, my favourite birdcage variety, with the chips and leaf soil. Plants loved it and grew wondrously, but wore it out rather quickly, and still it needed watering oftener than I liked. The next new bed was made on the opposite side of the path, and planned to hold a rather richer compost of leaf soil, peat and sand, with occasional surfacings, admixtures, or even unadulterated patches of granite chips : but the most important innovation was a leaden pipe with a funnel-shaped mouth at one end to receive water, and two rows of holes bored on the under surface at intervals of 3 inches. This is buried in the bed at a depth of 6 to 8 inches according to the slope of the bed, and the funnel comes to the surface and is covered with a flat stone, that can be easily lifted off when it is wished to pour a can or two of water in. We arranged the fall of the pipe so that the water ran out fairly evenly from all the holes, and found it needed to be very slightly lower at the end farthest from the mouth. This bed is now nearly two years old, and has been great fun. In the richer peaty end *Primula pedemontana* and *P. Bowlesii*, the latter a hybrid from *P. pedemontana* and *P. viscosa*, have recovered their strength after the shock of being collected when in full flower, and flowered well this Spring. *Astrantia minor*, said to be impossible in England, has done well and given me a fine crop of seed. *Gentiana verna,* collected forms from Mt. Cenis, mostly of the *angulosa* type, and *G. brachyphylla* have spread into good tufts. *Campanula cenisia* is a good test plant, and has settled down in the chippy patch, while *Papaver rhoeticum* looks as happy as it did in its Tyrolean shale beds.

Then in the following Spring the rock garden was enlarged, a new wing thrown out, and there was a chance for a fresh venture in underground watering. A steep bank was divided into large pockets, and some slabs of old slate from a demolished water-tank were used to pave the bottom of the pockets, following the line of the slope. Partition walls of brick and cement below ground and stone above were arranged so that water, poured down a portion of drainpipe at the top of the hill, would fill each pocket up to a certain height and then flow through to the next. It took some time to construct and harden, and so was empty for a week or two, and I was chaffed by all my garden visitors on my fish hatchery or filter beds, and many pleasantries arose from my adopting Mr. Malby's ingenious plan of inserting half a hock bottle at advantageous corners, so that in winter the corks might be removed and the beds drained. But once filled up with various cunning mixtures of sand and leaf in some parts, and old mortar rubble, or even our local gravel screened and stirred up with something a little more feeding in others, it looked like any ordinary new rock garden bed, and many things have astounded me by the way they have approved of it and spread or seeded. *Viola bosniaca* never liked me and my ways before, and I was quite as much ashamed of myself as any really keen

Numerous Early Comers

gardener need be, for so constantly begging bits of it from more successful growers. Now I weed it up as well as supplying all who come. *Douglasia Vitaliana* never lived here long enough to make it worth while looking up its synonyms, so as to make up my mind whether to call it Aretia, Androsace, Gregoria, Primula, Macrotybus or *Vitaliana primuloides*, for it has received a new name almost as often as it has died under my tender care. After a year in the fish hatchery it has spread into a grey mat and flowered this Spring almost as solidly as it does on Mont Cenis, and I have turned its history up in Pax and Knuth's Primulaceae volume of *Das Pflanzenreich*, and hope it will live here as long as it shall remain a Douglasia, for surely no one will dare alter the genera as settled by that redoubtable pair during my time. Of course one must always discount such successes by realising that many plants will flourish in newly-disturbed soil for a season or two and then either render it unsuitable for them or they themselves grow sick of it. *Linaria alpina* is an instance of this ; even in the Alps it is only on landslides or new earthworks that one finds it in profusion. I have even seen it on a heap of grit that had been left by the roadside after a part of it had been used for mixing cement for a new house. Here it will always thrive in a newly-constructed bit of rock garden, and after a year or two refuse to grow even if carefully sown. But to see Soldanellas, *Primula frondosa*, and the alpine form of *Parnassia palustris*, growing in apparently dry sand, and a little way below *Lewisia Howellii's* salmon and orange-coloured flowers contrasting deliciously with that exquisite gem of Campanulas called *C. caespitosa*

My Garden in Spring

Miranda by Mr. Farrer (but with a big query at present, and which I owe to his generosity, for it goeth not forth for pelf at present), the rounded bells of which are a pearly grey of indescribable delicacy—to see all these so contiguous and so happy makes my visitors wonder and fills me with pride in my fish hatchery. The New River is so close to the top of it that it is an easy job to pour a can or two of its contents into the mouths of my two drainpipes, and this done once a day even in the hot dry time of the last summer proved sufficient to keep the lower soil moist.

That, then, is the history of my moraines. I call the first granite chip one the "Farrer" moraine, the second the "sand" moraine, and the "lead pipe bed" and "fish hatchery" will refer to the others.

Now to go back to the *Bulbocodium*, which flourishes in the lead pipe bed, but do not imagine, in spite of this lengthy digression, that the moraines were made on purpose to accommodate it. I put it in there because I was so pleased to see the way it grew among the Gentians in certain gullies by the Mt. Cenis lake, and then found my little purple friend liked it. I am hoping it will also agree with the Spring-flowering *Merendera caucasica* and *sobolifera*, for although the autumnal *M. Bulbocodium* is fairly happy here the other two require frequent renewal, and I am so fond of their quaint wee flowers, so much like a Colchicum when first open but so ragged and untidy when the segments part company after a day or two of prim neatness. The mark of this genus is the lack of a perianth tube: the segments are connivent at first opening, that is, they hang together at the throat, but when they rise a little out of the leaves each segment

starts away from its neighbour, and you see that they are
divided right down instead of joining to form a tube as in
Crocus and Colchicum. *Bulbocodium vernum* behaves in
the same way, but the segments of the perianth are
furnished at the base with spurlike outgrowths which
make them arrow-shaped, and keep them together longer
and more perfectly than in Merendera. I like to grow
these plants and to admire the transition they show from
free perianth segments to the long, perfectly-formed tube
as found in Colchicum.

Tucked away in a sunny corner among Sempervivums lives another of my minute favourites. I have
often been accused of growing and loving too many
microscopic plants, and perhaps *Allium Chamaemoly* is
alone sufficient evidence to convict me. For some years
I was surprised to find seedpods and yet to have
missed its flowers, then a sharp look-out showed me
that they appeared much earlier than I expected, and
were very much smaller than I had hoped. A careful
search in late December and throughout January generally
reveals a flower or two. They are certainly very small,
about the size of a bee's knee their detractors might
say, but they are dainty little green and white stars,
and in January it is very pleasant to find anything
that is a flower.

Another first comer of the year, but different in
every way from *Chamaemoly*, except that you do not see
it in many gardens, is the Toothwort of the Pyrenees,
Lathraea clandèstina. It ought to be in every garden,
for it is very beautiful when in full flower, looking like
a colony of some very dwarf purple Crocus, but when

My Garden in Spring

you look closer you see the flowers are of an unfamiliar shape, more like those of some large Sage or Dead Nettle, but not a labiate ; indeed, it is a plant hard to place, for its relations, the Orobanches, are not as a rule well known to gardeners. The fact that it is a parasite makes it difficult to establish. First, one must find a suitable host in a suitable place, and with roots in a condition to be pounced on by the Lathraea. Poplar and Willow are the most likely trees to prove hospitable to it, but it is a queer, cranky sort of plant, and you cannot reckon on what it will do. After careful planting it may apparently die away, and then after two or more years some January day may reveal its white scales— leaves it has none—breaking through the ground perhaps a yard away from the place you planted it in; a few years later still, when seeds have had time to form and fly and grow, it may appear, healthy and vigorous, far from the range of the roots of the tree. I know of an instance where it chose to board itself out on a Gunnera, and in Cambridge Botanic Gardens it thrives as well across the streamlet in the grass as on the other side among the willows. Here I chose a Weeping Willow for its foster mother, thereby paying off a small grudge I owed it. I made a luxurious bed of good soil at its feet some years ago for Japanese Irises, but the Willow said, " First come, first served," and ate up the fatness and starved out the *I. Kaempferi*, filling the bed with its fibrous roots. Among these I planted a sod or two of Lathraea, some of them kind gifts from Mr. Lynch, others sent by my Spanish cousins, and later on some seeds also from Cambridge. I cannot

Numerous Early Comers

say which attached themselves, but I know I was planning a fresh attack, both on the Willow and Mr. Lynch's generosity, as after three years of waiting I saw nothing of the Toothwort, and then it appeared in several places, and since then has spread rapidly. First it pushes the scale-clad stem out of the ground, a strange-looking creamy-white mass, of seaweedy or coral-like appearance—or is my memory playing me tricks? Yes, I think it is, and you had better not believe me, good reader, for now it dawns upon me that I really mean neither a seaweed nor a coral, but two products of the Mollusca that one finds washed up at high tide level. The first is *Flustra foliacea*, sometimes called Scented Seaweed, but really the dry house of a dead colony of one of those strange compound molluscan animals called the Polyzoa, and the other is the empty egg mass of the whelk, both when dry being of the same creamy white as the Lathraea's scales. Yes, these are what I am reminded of by the rosette of scales.

It is a foolish plant to appear so early, for although the white scales seem to be unhurt by severe frosts, the purple buds which emerge from between them are ruined by a very few degrees, and look brown and sick after a cold night. In mild spells of weather I have enjoyed the soft lilac mass of colour in late January and February, but it is not until the Crocuses are over, that is to say early April, that one gets the full effect from it. It pushes up fresh flowers out of the rosettes for some weeks longer, and as the grass grows and shelters them the later flowers are larger and more attractive than the earlier ones.

My Garden in Spring

They are followed by fleshy capsules of a dull purple, not beautiful, but of great and exciting interest, for when the seeds are ripe enough to go out into the world the walls of these capsules become tensely turgid and the two valves press inward on each other very powerfully, so that a slight shock or touch at the summit causes them to split, and each valve to curl inwards with such force that the two enclosed seeds are shot out to a considerable distance. I greatly enjoyed taking some examples of ripe capsules up to one of the meetings of the Scientific Committee of the R.H.S., and as they were new to the members present, aided by my position as acting chairman at the head of the long table, while I was describing the mechanism I gave them a pinch, and startled the members at the other end of the table by the sudden impact of several Lathraea seeds. At the right season I can always get some amusement by inducing a visitor to press a bunch of ripe capsules and noting how high he jumps when the seeds fly into his face, and after this initiation we aim over the pond with other capsules to see what distance we can shoot the seeds into the tell-tale water. This season a self-sown plant has appeared in the grassy bank of the pond, perhaps the result of one of these contests.

I have sown our native *Lathraea Squamaria* on Hazel roots several times, but have not yet seen it above-ground. Experience with its more showy relation preaches hope and patience, so I still look for its appearance, but shall continue to sow seeds or plant clumps whenever I can get them.

The list of earliest arrivals cannot be closed without

Numerous Early Comers

mention of Winter Aconites. The common one, *Eranthis hiemalis*, like Chionodoxa, is one of the test plants of the established maturity of gardens: your parvenu, architect-planned, and colour-schemed affair can seldom include such a fine drift of its cheery yellow faces in their green Toby frills as one may see in the garden of many a parsonage or quiet old grange. It is difficult to establish a new colony of it unless one can rob an old one, for it is one of those plants which suffer terribly from being kept out of the ground any length of time, and here I find the best time to transplant it is during its period of flowering. Roots bought in autumn are generally sick unto death.

This season the extraordinary mildness of early December brought it into flower quite a week before Christmas, and the blooms were small, dingy, of thin texture, with no staying power in them, and they came out a few at a time and so made no display, being one of the few flowers that are better for a severe winter if it comes before their flowering time. Gerard knew this, and writes: "The colder the weather is, and the deeper that the snow is, the fairer and larger is the floure, and the warmer that the weather is, the lesser is the floure, and worse coloured." This I have noticed, and take to mean that the flowers are better for being kept back until they are thoroughly matured as under a covering of snow, and then burst out with the thaw in full strength and numbers.

The behaviour of seedlings is worth noting: they content themselves for their first season with no leaves other than the pair of cotyledons, but find them all-sufficient to gather enough carbon dioxide from the air to add to their root-collected store of nutriment to form a neat little tuber before the summer heat dries them up. *E. cilicica* is worth having too, as it comes after the older species has gone out of flower, and its red stems and more finely divided frills are attractive. It is beginning to colonise here by self-sown seedlings, but I fear will never rival the friend of one's childhood, which is in more than one sense first in the field.

Are you nervous of scorpions? If so plant a wide ring of Winter Aconite, and during its growing season at any rate you can feel safe in the centre of this magic circle, for Gerard tells us quite gravely it "is of such force, that if the scorpion passe by where it groweth and touche the same, presently he becometh dull, heavy, and senseless, and if the same scorpion by chance touch the white Hellebor he is presently delivered from his drowsinesse." What fertile imaginations those old gentlemen had!

CHAPTER VII

Daffodils

THE people who talk about flowers may be roughly divided into two classes, those who ask and those who are expected to answer the question, " What is the difference between a Narcissus and a Daffodil ? "

I appear to belong to the latter division, and answer, " None whatever, one being the Latin and the other the English name for the same plant " ; but the other class are never satisfied therewith, for they want a difference, and like a certain fretful baby we have all seen pictures of—won't be happy till they get it. So I take down Parkinson's *Paradisus* and, having impressed them with the antiquity and authority of that great man, read them his words of wisdom, for he writes : " Many idle and ignorant Gardeners . . . doe call some of these Daffodils Narcisses, when, as all that know any Latine, that Narcissus is the Latine name and Daffodill the English of one and the same thing ; and therefore alone, without any other Epithite cannot properly distinguish severall things." If that does not subdue their inquisitive spirit Gerard may be called as second witness to testify that "Generally all the kindes are comprehended under the name Narcissus, in English Daffodilly, Daffodowndilly, and Primerose Peereless."

Clearly these two great fathers of English gardening

saw no difference except of language between a Narcissus and a Daffodil. All the same it would be useful to have a name for those Narcissi that we somehow feel ought not to be called Daffodils, even though we may not be able to find one better than the word Daffodil with some "other Epithite." In spite of Gerard and Parkinson we shall be in good company in feeling thus, for Turner in *The Names of Herbes* writes: "This that we take for Daffodil is a kind of Narcissus." So in 1548 it was felt that though all Daffodils were Narcissi yet some Narcissus might not be a Daffodil: but where they gave Parkinson a chance of calling them hard names, was in the way they used the Latin name of the whole genus for certain members of it, instead of choosing some distinguishing English word for that particular group. In much the same way now people use the generic term Viola as though it belonged only to the particular race of perennial garden-raised Violas that have been well named Tufted Pansies. It would be equally wise to start calling the Irish Single Tea roses, Rosas, or those hairy oubits of dogs, the now fashionable Pekinese, Canis.

It is unfortunate that our modern idea of a true Daffodil is not that of Parkinson's day. Hear him on the subject. "Now to cause you to understand the difference between a true Daffodil and a false, is this: It consists ónly in the flower, and chiefly in the middle cup or chalice; for that we do in a manner only account those to bee Pseudonarcissos, bastard Daffodils, whose middle cup is altogether as long and sometimes a little longer than the outer leaves that doe encompasse it, so that it seemeth rather like a trunke or long nose than a cup

Daffodils

or chalice, such as almost all the Narcissi or true Daffodils have." In fact all those long-nosed ones which we like to call true Daffodils he calls bastard, which is not a pleasant "Epithite" to give to an honest flower.

Still we need not let Parkinson's views weigh too heavily on our conscience, for does he not include as Narcissi, Sternbergia, Pancratium, and Zephyranthes, this last as he says "not finding where better to shroud it"? A still more glorious dispensation may be found in Sprekelia's appearance as the Indian Daffodil with a red flower! Narcissus Jacobæus!! The vaunted pink daffodils, this year's most sensational exhibits, cannot vie with this crimson glory. Their stripes or flushed yellow perianths remind one of a hen's egg that was left too long under the maternal breast to be appetising when boiled, or "lightly poach" we will hope, for as Mrs. Green knew, "A poach hegg you sees naked before you, an' if it ain't what it should be, back it can go without no committin' of yourself in the way of a broken shell."

Furthermore the word Daffodil is such a thoroughly home-made English corruption of Asphodel that it was probably made for our one unquestionably wild species, *N. Pseudo-narcissus*, the Lent-lily, which is certainly the swallows' precursor of Shakespeare, and the Daffodil of Herrick and the poets generally.

The initial D has never been satisfactorily accounted for, according to the New Oxford Dictionary, and one must bow down before its pontifical authority, even though one misses certain traditional derivatives that lack documentary support, omitted by its strict plan of relying only on historical evidence. I am sadly disappointed if an

My Garden in Spring

English history omits the tale of Alfred the Great's failure as a cook, and would like to believe many fanciful derivations of words to be true. It is a tempting text for a philological sermon that D, but I must not give you unto fifthly and lastly, so condense it into the half sheet of notes which, if cunningly concealed in a book, gives a preacher or lecturer a reputation for extempore fluency. (1) The D may be due to playful distortion, as in Ted from Edward ; (2) part of the definite article ; (3) the final *d* of *and*, or the Flemish article *de*. I hope it is the playful friendliness of No. 1.

Anyway in English use it was at first confined to the Asphodel, then confused with the Narcissus, some think through both plants once bearing the fanciful name *Laus tibi*, but I would rather try to believe it was from a desire to find some wild English equivalent for the Asphodel,[1] and what would give us as flowery a mead as the wild Lent-lily ? Both Turner and Lyte testify to this confusion. Turner speaks of " Asphodillus . . . in English whyte affodil or duche daffodil." Lyte writes of his third kind of Asphodel " in English also Affodyl and Daffodyl." Botanists, after unsuccessfully resisting this mis-application, compromised the matter by retaining *affodil* for the Asphodel, and accepting the more popular *daffodil* for the Narcissus, which has lived on as a familiar word, while the other has been rectified to a form nearer its classic original. That Daffodil is Affo dyle, " that which cometh early " has been confidently asserted by some (see Sowerby's *English Botany*

---

[1] Turner, *Herbal*, I. b. iii. 6, supports this : " I could never se thys herb (asphodelos—ryght affodil) in England but ones, for the herbe that the people calleth here affodil (or daffodill) is a kind of narcissus."

Anemone sylvestris grandiflora.   (See p. 218.)

Daffodils

for an instance), but is ignored by the Oxford Dictionary, and as I have found no evidence for it beyond bare assertions, this time I thankfully avail myself of the authority of the great work. Again, that Saffron-lily has given us Daffadowndilly, and thence Daffodil, is argued by Dr. Prior, but he confesses the explanation is merely conjectural, and wants the test of historical evidence. It is a modern idea, though, that a Daffodil must be yellow, for both Parkinson and Gerard speak freely of white Daffodils, in describing *N. poeticus*, both double and single, and also for polyanthus varieties, so there is no reason why we should not talk of Poet's Daffodils instead of using the Latin name Narcissus for that group—or we might revive Gerard's name Narcisse for them, and Parkinson's name Peerless Daffodil seems to me a charming one for the Incomparabilis section, better than the contemporary ones " nonpareille," " nonesuch," and " incomparable," and the hideous modern nickname of " incomps " one often hears from the lips of Daffodil growers. Then the scientific name Narcissus might be reserved for botanical purposes, when the species or their wild hybrids and varieties are referred to.

Do not expect me to write of the Daffodils of this garden as an expert. I sit among the great of the Daffodil world, and see their latest productions, but the garden knows them not. Birds must be of a feather to flock together, and Croesus and White Emperor consort not with paupers. So I have no list of latest novelties to make your mouths water, only some few that, though neither new nor worth double figures in pounds, yet are beautiful enough to be worthy of a sentence or two. Many are mementoes of kind friends and their richly-stored gardens.

My Garden in Spring

I shall begin with my greatest favourite, Dawn, a very appropriate name for a first comer. I need hardly describe so well-known and much-shown a flower, but must rejoice in some of its good points. It has a butterfly expression in the reflexed white perianth and the graceful way the segments stand out at rather variant angles, especially where the twin flowers of each stem touch each other, and push the segments forward, and cause their tips to bend over. The slender stem and pendant twin flowers make it charming as a cut flower, and the flat, yellow cup is of such a pure colour that it sets off the white perianth to perfection. I have hitherto grown it in the peach-house border, a warm and sheltered home reserved for new and precious plants until they increase enough to send out their offspring to test their powers of endurance in less secure quarters. It is a long, narrow bed facing due south, backed by the peach-house and its low wall, with water-pipes, heated in Spring, just behind it. It has been a successful nursery for many a good thing, when not only protection from chills, but also constant watching is advisable. I believe many a treasure has done better here, because the border is so narrow, and the delicate things are so easily got at to be fingered, or have their surrounding soil pressed down or scratched up, or some other slight attentions paid to them, which sometimes make all the difference to a plant while still half-hearted about living and growing, much as those of a watchful and tactful nurse can help an invalid to recovery. Next Spring I hope to see Dawn out of this nursery, or nursing home, and waving its butterflies in the rock garden. I have not outgrown my admiration of Weardale Perfection. There

122

Daffodils

may be more beautiful bicolors for millionaires, but they have not come my way yet. Lord Muncaster was taking a proud place in lists quite lately at six guineas each, and I felt much inclined to sell all mine but one, and lay out the result in Weardales, but I have never yet sold a plant, and I hope I am too old to begin. So his lordship is still here.

I will try to tell you what charms I find in Weardale. It is quite large enough for me. I do not want to sit under a trumpet during a shower. Beyond a certain point, size nearly always means coarseness, and I greatly dislike the huge race of trumpet Daffodils so much to the fore in some Dutch gardens. A small man might almost feel nervous of looking down some of their trumpets, for fear of falling in and getting drowned in the honey, and a life-belt or two should be hung among the beds. As we have not yet come to viewing our gardens from aeroplanes, we can do without *Rafflesia Arnoldii* in the rock garden, and the Waterbutt Trumpet Daffodil for mixed borders. Even the loveliest of fair damsels, magnified to the size of two and a half elephants, would be an appalling object to the stock-sized suitor, and until I have to take to much stronger spectacles, Weardale is large enough for me.

I like its proportions: the trumpet has not ceased to be a trumpet and become instead a gramophone's mouthpiece, but the wide, overlapping perianth segments make the balance more perfect than would be the case were the segments of a narrower type such as in the variety Duke of Bedford. But I lay most stress on the colouring, and the soft blending of its two main shades that is so delightful to look at or imitate in paint. The base of the trumpet pales a little at its base, and also picks up

My Garden in Spring

some reflected light from the perianth, so that its high lights are almost of the same tone as the main ground-colour of the segments, and the soft lemon-yellow of the trumpet runs out a little at the base of each segment, preventing any sudden break of colour, and I always marvel at the amount of pearly grey in its shadows, especially in the channelling at the sides of the broad central beam of each segment. This beam when present in a Daffodil adds greatly to my delight. It strengthens the lines of the drawing so well, and generally proclaims a firm substance and good lasting quality in the flower. I do not despise Duke of Bedford. It is a fine flower both in the border and cut, but for lingering over, painting, or dining in front of, I prefer the softer blending of lemon and cream of Weardale to the amber and milk of his grace, but both are lovely flowers, and fortunately they may be bought for shillings.

For a self-yellow trumpet, if there really is such a thing, or near enough to be called one if there is not, Hamlet has proved sturdy and generous with its soft, canary-coloured blossoms, and is one of the earlier flowerers ; as a late one I can recommend The Doctor, a tall, clear yellow Æsculapius with a hearty, breezy look that must mean a cheery bedside manner. All of which good qualities, save the colour, are typical of the popular physician for whom, as Americans say, it was named, and who I believe is now growing Daffodils as well as he does Sweet Peas. This flower, The Doctor, is very welcome in the garden, in sickness or health, as he comes when other big trumpets have given us up (this season he was at his best about the 20th of April), and there is a charm about the long, narrow

Daffodils

perianth segments and the fascinating backward curve they take when fully blown, which added to the King Alfred type of colouring urges one to send for this Doctor. Monarch I like and I give him a little square kingdom of border. Golden Bell is very effective for an irregular planting; my best group is among some species of Rosa, but I think its wide-mouthed bell too heavy for cutting. On the other hand, I can never quite forgive the long-nosed, drainpipe effect of Mme. Plemp's trumpet, and even Dorothy Kingsmill's lovely colouring is marred by the narrow mouth, and I feel as if the glove-stretchers should be applied gently at an early stage. On the other hand, in the Pyrenean wildling *N. muticus* the use of Nature's scissors has balanced the flower, and I like the stiff, straight trumpet. One of my greatest treasures (I feel tempted to write "so far" as a recurring decimal to guard it from ill for aeons) is the white *muticus*. It has been found more than once in Pyrenean pastures, but so far as I know the only stock in cultivation came from a single bulb found by Mr. Charles Digby, the Rector of Warham. It increased slowly with him, but his generous spirit led him to give away a bulb or two when offsets appeared, but nowhere have they proved very vigorous, and many have died out. A promising youngster came to me from Warham, and a happy inspiration caused me to plant it on a northern slope of the rock garden. The cool conditions and good drainage have suited it *so far;* and I had seven of its lovely white blossoms this Spring, and learning of its total disappearance at Warham had the great pleasure of returning three bulbs to its kind discoverer. White Minor is another of the very elect of the earth : it was found in an old Irish garden, and has not gone

My Garden in Spring

far afield yet, but arrived here last autumn, a token of the kindly heart and good memory of Mr. Bennett Poë, who recalled my raptures over its refined beauty when I saw a bunch of it in his drawing-room at one of those delightful gatherings for a cup of tea after a long R.H.S. day, alas! too seldom possible for me, who throughout the Spring have ever a train to catch to be in my place at a night school that has grown to be part of my existence. Even among the choicest orchids and rare exotics from his collection of rare and lovely plants that always fill his vases, and make one feel the R.H.S. Hall ought to have a subterranean passage ending in a door into that room, to let Fellows see what cut flowers for decoration of a room should be like— even in such company, White Minor held its own as a gem. I was a prisoner in a sick-room when it flowered this year, but it came to my bedside and filled me with pride and gratitude and hope for next season. It is just the plant for a choice corner of the rock garden, a fitting companion for *N. triandrus, cyclamineus, minimus,* and their hybrid off-spring *minicycla,* an early flowering, long-lasting darling, with the charm of both parents. *Minimus* is not so pro-lific here as I wish: it once seeded along a path edge, and I hoped would go on doing so, but no further strays have appeared. *N. juncifolius* is rather a late flowerer, but very charming even though the rock garden is by then full of flower, and all the Hoop Petticoats in the world may come to me if they like and I will try to find room for them. I once collected bulbs of *citrinus* near Biarritz, and by getting my feet wet in their boggy home caught a bad cold, but learnt a valuable lesson as to the right position for this thirsty soul. This year I flowered and have seeded the

Daffodils

true *N. dubius,* kindly sent me from its wild home by M.
Denis of Iris fame. It is *very* small, but such a perfectly
formed little flower, and so white that one longs to give a
doll's dinner-party to decorate the table with it. It loves heat
and drought, so I am hoping it will thrive here, and some
bulbs I keep in the Crocus frame have been lifted and replanted, and I found they had increased in size. I like any
wild Narcissus in the rock garden, and some of the distinct
hybrids, such as Dawn, Moonbeam, and other *triandrus*
crosses, but the beds and shrubberies are the homes for
most Daffodils. I have tried to group some of the cool-
coloured ones in the centre of the piece of ground I have
alluded to as my sole bit of colour scheming. This grouping
contains Poets such as Rhymester, Almira, Cassandra and
Lovelace, a few *Leedsii* varieties, White Lady and Ariadne
among them, and nothing more yellow than Argent, Albatross, and Seagull, and coming between a mass of grey-leaved
things and golden-leaved forms, with silver variegations
among the daffodils, and the whole backed by purple foliage,
the early Spring effect is delightfully clear and cool. White
Lady is fine for this use, being far enough in the middle of
the bed for the cup to pass unnoticed. I quarrel with her
name on account of that cup, for no lady would go out with
so clean and fresh a white skirt over such a bedraggled
petticoat—worse than bedraggled, it is a lace-edged one, but
with the lace frayed and torn and wanting mending. The
distant effect may be a white lady, but close at hand the
rags spell white slut. Argent I could never over-praise
either for the border or as a cut flower, whatever rich and
rare adjectives I might bestow upon it: the mingling of its
silver and gold is charming. I have thoroughly enjoyed

My Garden in Spring

trying to paint it, and though failing to express the brilliancy of the reflected gold of the scattered sections of its cup on the glistening silvery perianth, yet my dull daub brings back some reminiscence of the real thing. I think it the very best of all double Daffodils, as it has gained in contrasting light and shade by its repeated sections of cups, and is not a bit heavy, owing to the length and scattered position of the perianth segments.

Plenipo I like, but not nearly so much, as the perianth is of too deep a yellow to make the contrast so pleasing.

I could fill many pages with prattle of my newer, choicer treasures, the ordinary garden furnishing of other folks' beds most probably, so I will only say that they live in what we call the Pergola garden, where some paved paths divide it into rectangular beds, and one of our later additions, the New Wall, cuts off the east wind, so that there is found a sheltered home for good little daffs, and one can get at them easily to admire their beauty or fuss over their needs. Lemon Queen, White Queen, Solfatare, Lord Kitchener, Great Warley, Outpost, Incognita, and May Moon are some of this pampered company, and the end of one bed is filled with a double row of a fine giant *Leedsii* of Dutch origin, named H. C. Bowles after my father. At first we thought it rather shy flowering, and I was a little disappointed at its likeness to an enlarged White Queen, only with a less symmetrical base to the cup. But it has certainly improved since it became a British subject, and has shown a remarkable vigour of growth and freedom of flowering, and has a great deal of substance in it, so that as a cut bloom it lasts a long time, and the pale sulphur of its cup gradually tones down with age to a most delicate ivory white. White

128

Daffodils

Queen is not to be despised, but she must play second fiddle when this anglicised Dutchman tunes up and plays his best.

Another naturalised Mynheer is Whitewell. I have always admired it since the day I first saw it among its sisters and its cousins and its aunts, more numerous than those of that First Lord who could be reckoned by dozens, Whitewell's went into hundreds, and yet among them all this fine cream and soft buff-orange thing kept on catching my eye. I was in Holland, and for the first time in my life in that part of the country which is the real Holland for a flower-lover. I had the good fortune to be there with Mr. Joseph Jacob, and therefore under his wing, and for his sake found a kindly welcome in many a quiet, out-of-the-world nook where the making of new garden plants was going on. Pleasant as are my memories of those sunny or showery April days, none please me more than the mornings in Mr. Polman Moy's holy of holies, where the pick of his last season or two's seedlings are gathered together under mystic numbers. Mr. Jacob was choosing some of these to go to England to keep up the reputation of Whitewell Rectory for the good things that are always to be seen in Spring in the long, straight beds of his garden.

He was good enough to pretend he valued my advice in this selection, and extol as he might the charms of others, I always declared I preferred this X over a thing like a fish's tail, No. 1234, and so many notches, or whatever other hieroglyphics then guarded the identity of the future Whitewell. I loved the set of its perianth, three ears forward and three back. Not show form, perhaps, but so good to look at, and the forwards casting such delicious shadows on the backwards in the sunlight.

My Garden in Spring

My constancy and a close comparison with other attractive stocks gradually eliminated its rivals, and one morning when we met at breakfast I heard the news that an early visit to the bulb garden had ended in the arrangement that the stock of my favourite was to go to the Rectory in Wales. I am glad to say Whitewell made a successful début on the show stand and was eagerly sought after, and its purchaser often tells me he is glad he was overruled by the fascination the flower had for me. My plants of it were a gift from him, and every Spring they recall pleasant memories of my first visit to Haarlem and its bulb gardens. Hall Caine I first saw during that same visit, and was much struck by its beauty. A large, loosely-built, sulphur-tinted Peerless (I mean to live up to my views and use this name), it seemed just the thing for cutting as well as for a good effect in a broad planting. The veteran grower who was showing us his stocks declared it to be "just incomparabilis," and quoted what we thought a ridiculously low figure for it, and we made vows to invest largely in this "just incomparabilis," but alas! at the office we learnt it was an unnamed seedling, and thought too much of to be acquired as easily as we were expecting. Now it has a name, and though it is a very charming thing its price is not prohibitive. It is soft and uncommon in colour, and with a fine tall stem and graceful poise, and is none too well known.

The celebrated white trumpet Peter Barr is among my choice and petted forms in the bed under the new wall. I wish he were a trifle taller in the stem and knew how to make more of his beauty. He came to me by means of exchange. I did not give fifty guineas for him—fifty shillings would be more than I should dream of giving for any one

Daffodils

bulb—and I often wish Mr. Pope had never set the big price ball a-rolling by paying down £100 for those three bulbs of Will Scarlett.

I was one day asked what I thought the most beautiful novelty of the Daffodil shows of the year, and with happy unconsciousness replied without hesitation, "Lavender, which I saw at Birmingham." "How nice of you," came the reply; "it is one of my raising, and as you like it you shall have a bulb," and in his characteristically generous way my host led me to a newly-planted line and extracted the treasure just beginning to root, and each succeeding Spring I have revelled in the delicate colouring of that cup. The poor dear's perianth is not a thing to boast of, buckling and curling unless treated in some cunning way unknown to a simple soul who, like me, is not up to the tricks of the showing profession, but the cup would save it even if the perianth were made of spiders' legs. It is more like some enamelled jewel than a flower. The central hollow is of a soft emerald green of solid opaque enamel, then the flattish cup glistens all over and shows radiating lines of brightness and has an almost indescribable touch of pink in it. (In painting it I found a wash of Rose madder needful but difficult to subdue.) I think it suggests a transparent white enamel laid over engraved copper, or gold heavily alloyed with copper. Then the rim of the cup is stained with soft orange, of almost a salmon shade, and exquisite in combination with the green of the eye. This lovely beauty must never be stared at by the sun, but should be gathered directly the bud bursts and brought into the house to open, and I am rather glad to feel that some flowers are best gathered, and enjoy a vase of Lavender

My Garden in Spring

all the more for the knowledge that out-of-doors it would not look so happy.

Writing of gathering leads me to the final aspect of Daffodil-growing that I must dwell upon. I grudge picking blossoms so much from even well–flowered groups, that we have planted some lines of useful cutting varieties in the spaces between the currant and gooseberry bushes, not needing that space for the crop nurses told us in our early days emanated from that special bit of ground. The daffodils get a bit of protection there and grow stiff and tall, and are out of the way before fruit-picking begins. What have we put there? Let me see now—Sir Watkin of course, a fine healthy lot of bulbs of giant proportions from a certain Dutch field of many acres I once crossed with Sir Watkin up to my knees. I never saw such a sight, and vowed I must test their vigour here. In this their first year they have surprised all who had not seen them at Noordwyk; and now comes the question, Will they be able to do so again? Queen Bess is another indispensable as she is so early. Hall Caine, whose praises I have already sung Mrs. Camm, as she is one of the most useful, a delightful size for old and tall champagne glasses, delicate in colour and lasting well. Mr. Camm is there, too, but not so much approved of. Seagull, Albatross, several Poets, and a long line of mixed Dutch seedlings are those that come to my mind as most successful. Some beds of Tea Roses are planted pretty thickly with *Barrii conspicuus*, the Camms, and Golden Mary, and provide many a good bunch, while I hope and believe the Daffodil leaves protect the Rose shoots. It is good to see that *Barrii conspicuus* is still in favour even with experts, for in the voting list returns as

Daffodils

shown in the R.H.S. Daffodil Year Book, it heads the list of cut flowers from the open, those suitable for planting in grass, and also of the yellow-perianthed *Barrii*, and is well up in lists for other purposes. William Backhouse must have been a happy and proud man when he first saw it in his seed-bed. I have a great affection for its white peri-anthed sport Branston, and am amused rather than annoyed when some of the flowers come half and half, and look like cream poured on custard.

CHAPTER VIII

Primulas

I USED to think this garden was unsuitable for Primulas other than the commonest forms of Primroses, but patience and a certain amount of manoeuvring have somewhat increased the possibilities, though still an extra hot and dry year like 1911 frizzles up the double garden varieties and parches *P. rosea* beyond recovery. The earliest to flower is *P. megasiaefolia*, or perhaps I should say to try to flower, for from December onward this foolishly precocious plant gets a flower-bud irretrievably damaged about once a fortnight, and seldom succeeds in opening one. *P. cashmireana* often shoots up a mushroom-shaped mass of buds in January only to be blackened and end in decay, but *P. marginata* manages better and, by keeping close under its leaves at first, opens the earliest of its flowers with the Hepaticas. It is such a good-tempered and lovely thing, both in flower and leaf, I wonder one does not see it oftener. In a real Primrose-beloved garden it should be possible to have edgings of it, and how lovely they would be. Here I have to find a cool corner with stones to keep its roots moist to make it happy, and some clumps in the rock garden reward my care with a fine show of flowers : one is a particularly blue form, and having deeply-toothed leaves is good to look at all its days—

Primulas

pays rent all the year in fact. I have a rather interesting set of named forms with widely-differing shapes of leaves and the much-praised garden form Mrs. Hall Walker, whose flowers I have not seen yet, but have great hopes of them next season founded upon the present fatness of the central crown. I spent a very happy day up in the Cottian Alps this last June collecting some lovely forms, and hope to make a good planting as soon as I can get them out of the sand frame where they are making their new roots after being pulled to bits.

I once thought I did not greatly care for Alpine Primulas, they seemed to me so much given to thin magenta colouring, but a few weeks among them in Tyrol, with Mr. Farrer as interpreter of their charms, converted me, and he likes to remind me of my declaration that I should not collect more than two or three of each and the contradictory reality of the full tins I carried on my poor old back down those mountain sides. A few of the purple, almost blue, bells of *P. glutinosa* on the Venna Thal enlightened me, and a mountain side rosy-purple for a mile or more with *P. spectabilis* in full bloom, as a Scotch hillside might be with heather, finished the work. But then both in their native hills are revelations of what Primulas can be. Picking out the largest white-eyed forms of *spectabilis* and selecting the most rosy and least aniline I found as fascinating as any bit of collecting I had ever done. Just picture to yourself a turfy mountain side, worn by weather and sheep, or goats, into countless horizontal miniature terraces such as one often finds in a steep bit of the South Downs, and under the brow of each terrace fancy clumps of a dozen to twenty rosettes of a green-

My Garden in Spring

leaved garden Auricula whose large heads of flowers are of every shade of rose and crimson, so that looking up the hill you get the full stare of their friendly eyes and every one you look at seems to possess some varietal charm of its own—a clearer white eye, a warmer rose tint, or fuller and rounder flower. Can you wonder that I was on my knees every other minute plunging my trowel into the tufts to extract half a dozen of the rosettes? Just two or three of the best indeed! that tin was a heavy load to carry down, and there was much work sorting and packing my chosen few. Just the same when I found myself face to face with it in another district, and where, meeting with *P. minima*, there were interesting hybrids, exciting to look for and so entrancingly beautiful when found that I discovered I could not bear to live without *P. Facchinii* and *P. Dumoulinii*. *P. oenensis* had to follow, and *longiflora* with its charming, mealy stem filled my gardening soul with greed and every spare corner of my tin with its neat rosettes, and eventually the boot-bag I carry in a pocket in case of overcrowding had to come out and hang round my neck to hold that mealy-leaved golden glory *P. Auricula Bauhinii*.

A few days later Mr. Farrer took me to another ridge just to look at other interesting Primulas, but I think he had long ceased to believe in my intention of just gazing and then picking out a trinity of mementoes of the vision, so he was not surprised that, when I had at last got over staring at the unbelievable, fantastic beauty of the great Dolomite peak that hung over our heads, I fell to eagerly on the crevices which harboured *P. tyrolensis* and hunted the open turf for its very local *minima*-bred hybrid *P. Juri-*

Primulas

bella, and at last owned myself vanquished by the beauty of Alpine Primulas at home, when I saw the peaty hillside blue with *P. glutinosa,* there as common as Cowslips in a home meadow, instead of dotted singly as on the Brenner. Home they went in the largest tins I could cajole out of reluctant head waiters, and how will they behave here is now the burning question. On arrival they were all pulled asunder, and as separate rosettes planted in lines in a frame in almost pure sand and leaf soil. By the autumn they looked fat and leafy above, and by experimental liftings were proved to have made long, white roots and to be ready to go out. An overgrown portion of the rock garden, hitherto sacred to Geranium species, was torn down and rebuilt to imitate the Tyrolean homes from which I had exiled my Primulas. I had to leave out the Cimon della Parla and the Drei Zinnen, but hope the carefully-mixed soils I have given them will make them so happy that they will not look up and miss such trifles.

Peat in small quantities, leaf mould used generously, a stiffening of the soufflé resulting from these two by a liberal dose of the old soil, and the main geological formation of this miniature range was ready for adaptation to the special wants of its flora. Feeling too poor to invest in granite chips or even birdcage sand, I commandeered a load of our native red gravel, well screened, from the estate mason's storehouse and worked it into my too sticky compost in varying quantities. The lower slopes, reserved for *P. minima, longiflora,* and *glutinosa,* had only enough to make the soil feel sharp and gritty, but vertical crevices prepared for *Auricula* and *tyrolensis* had the upper two or three inches well reddened with the gravel. The hybrids had a middle

My Garden in Spring

position of intermediate grittiness and *spectabilis* has gone to the upper slopes. How magnificent it sounds! That is the fun of writing of one's garden : a steep bank can be a cliff, a puddle a pool, a pool a lake, bog and moraine sound as though a guide were needed to find your way across them, and yet may be covered by a sheet of *The Times*. My Dolomites lie within the compass of my outstretched arms, and there is not much wasted space now the Primulas are settled in. So far they have thriven amazingly, and this Spring, when the curtain rang up, the *Auricula* forms first took the stage. The *Bauhinii* troupe were quite as fine with their large Daffodil-yellow, white-eyed flowers on stout stems as on their own hillside. The *ciliata* lot with their deep green mealless leaves gave blossoms as nearly orange as when found wild. *Oenensis* took the next turn, and pleased me more here than when at home : the flowers looked less aniline in colour and had such pleasant white eyes, but perhaps I had picked out the best forms only. *Longiflora's* was the star performance, however. Before going to rest for the winter they formed fat crowns like small cabbages, and this May each rosette sent up two stems, and the main one bore twenty or more blossoms, instead of the half dozen or so I had found them contented with at home. I had never seen this species alive before I went to its home to meet it, as it is apparently seldom grown in gardens, and in spite of all this appearance of vigour I cannot help feeling there must be something wrong about its constitution to have prevented its sharing cottage-garden edgings with Thrift and Daisies.

So I have saved some seeds to prepare for squalls, and

Primulas

I noticed that where the rosettes have waxed so strong they insist on sending up ridiculous, dwarfed, flower-crowded stems at intervals all the summer through, and doing nothing towards a fat cabbage for next winter's sleep. Several have gone off yellow, as its near relative *farinosa* so often does after a good orgy of flowering, and I rather expect it will be best to starve *longiflora* into less ambitious displays or, if it comes easily from seed, treat it as a biennial. If it can be so grown it will be well worth the trouble: the mealy calyx and reddish-purple flowers—"reether redder than I could wish" as Bailey Junior said of his imaginary beard—were wonderfully good to see when at their best. *P. glutinosa* lives and grows, but, as I believe to be only too usual in English gardens, has offered no trace of a flower. No more has *tyrolensis*, but has made such deep green rosettes and wide leaves that they must surely mean a promise of good things later on. *Minima* and the hybrids looked so chubby and cheery on their return to greenness I expected great things of them, but never a bud appeared until I had given up looking for them, and at the end of June I was astonished by a goodly sprinkling of rosy-purple and a few pure white blooms, all as large and well-coloured as when I selected them. But the stupid things were so pleased at pleasing me they have tried to go on with it, and through the Dog Days have kept on sending up mean, flabby, starry caricatures of their former successes. *P. spectabilis* opened a very few eyes, but has been so busy working up a stock of large green leaves that it had no time for such frivolities as flowers this season.

P. pedemontana behaved in the same way its first season

My Garden in Spring

in the pipe-bed, and made up for it by a charming display this May. Its ugly duckling hybrid child *P. Bowlesii* shot up its taller scape too. It is ungrateful of me to speak slightingly of this plant after its dedication to me, but in case you are thinking of rushing off to Mt. Cenis to hunt for it I had better be honest and say it is very scarce : a whole morning of careful search this June rewarded Mr. Farrer and me with three plants of it, and between us we do not miss much when we hunt for a thing systematically. Also it is fair to say that in spite of its lovely parents, rosy *pedemontana* and the true *viscosa* of imperial purple, it is a mawkish magenta in all the specimens we have found save one, which was a cheery crimson-purple, and so good that at first sight I thought it too good to be true Bowlesii.   I wonder how this name will be pronounced should it be tried by Poles and Russians, Germans, Turks or Prooshians, or an I-talian.   I rather fear it will become Bovvleaysiee.   Anyway I was glad to be the first to flower my Primrose, and to be able to send a scape and leaves to the British Museum, though it was not in time to appear at the Primula Conference.   It has made the most curious long and narrow leaves this summer, and at present looks totally unlike either parent.

P. frondosa is a good plant for the sand and water-pipe moraine even in fullest sun, and never looked so well here with other treatment.   Whether it be the true *frondosa* of Janka or no, has been much debated, and at present it is comforting to know that the latest authorities pronounce it genuine, as the type specimen is suspected of having lost its mealiness through maturity, and therefore Pax and Knuth's upsetting decree that it must be without meal

Primulas

need not be regarded.[1]   Where *farinosa* refuses to settle and
be comfortable *frondosa* makes a fine substitute, though it
lacks in my eyes the grace of our native plant, and is
rather too leafy and clumsy in build.   The new Chinese
P. Knuthiana is a still larger form of the same type of
Primrose, but after flowering appears to make rosettes
without sufficient roots, and so is liable to turn flabby and
then yellow in hot weather, and seems hard to restore to
health.   Old plants look very queer here now, in the pipe-
bed, but what appear to be self-sown seedlings are racing
along to fill up their places.

P. *Juliae*, the new comer from Trans-Caucasia, has
behaved here as a real lady, just as the bearer of such a
name should.   Two tuffets came from Herr Sündermann
early in the year, their canary-coloured labels the showiest
part of them.   Cossetted for a little in a frame and then
put out in cool, leafy soil they flowered brilliantly in late
April.   The astonishing crimson-purple of their flowers is
in such sharp contrast with the brilliant yellow eye that every
one exclaims "Oh!" "Marvellous!!" "My stars!!!"
"Crikey!!!!" or something else according to the richness
of their vocabulary, when they first see it.   Not only have
they developed their characteristic runners with new crowns
at their ends, but when I parted the leaves to enjoy a sight
of these promises for next year I found they were indulging
in a little quiet practice for next Spring's flowering, and had
several half-sized blossoms hidden away below, but as
brilliant in colouring as ever.   Of the two I possess, the
plant in fat soil in a half-shaded border has done better

---

[1] Since writing this I have seen a plant straight from its native Balkans which
is as mealy as any miller.

than the other in the poorer soil of an old portion of the
rock garden, and it looks as though the right treatment
for it is the same that one would give to the choicer
double Primroses.

They, poor dears, are not very happy here, except in
wet seasons, and a Spring visit to Ireland always fills me
with envy, and longings for a climate that can produce
such double whites, French greys, and lilacs, and also
clumps of Polyanthus of such size, and flowers of such
texture and colouring. Short of digging a ditch for them
I fear I must not expect to see them thrive here.

In this neighbourhood Cowslips are wild in some of
the meadows, but Primroses are very scarce, only occurring along a ditch or two, and possibly not truly wild
there. Among the wild Cowslips in one of our meadows
there occurs an interesting form in which the orange
spots, so characteristic of the plant, are wanting. I have
brought it into the garden, and it remains perfectly true,
and is seeding about freely, and I hope to soon observe
how large a percentage will resemble the parents. I
always look at Cowslips in other places to see if they too
show this variation, but have never seen it elsewhere.
Knuth in his *Handbook of Flower Pollination* mentions
that "Flowers devoid of this (orange-red) patch have
been observed by Kirchner in Wurtemberg and Appel
(as he tells me in a letter) at Würzburg." I have a
great affection for Cowslips, and so grow all the forms
I can get now, and long for the curious green and
double ones figured in the old herbals. A beautiful orange-
coloured form was given to me by Mrs. Robb, who told me
she remembered it from her early childhood, but had

Primulas

lost sight of it for many years, till, staying at her old home Great Tew, one of the children came to say goodnight and carried a bunch of Cowslips, among them the orange one. "Don't take that dear child to bed, Nurse, until she has found the plant she picked these from, and put in a stick beside it," said this imperious old lady, and as she was generally obeyed the Cowslip found its way to her charming garden at Goldenfield and thence to me. "Pick out the best you can see," she bade me ; "they won't all come true, but you might as well start with the best form," and I greatly treasure this memento of her generosity and happy days at Goldenfield. A silver Cowslip of palest yellow Canon Ellacombe gave me, and other interesting forms are due to my always collecting a plant or two from every alpine district in which I meet with it. Most of them are the form known as Columnae, with cordate leaves on long petioles and flowers approaching *P. elatior*. On Mt. Cenis one finds every sort of intermediate, and a botanist might spend years there cataloguing their variations. *Elatior* itself has overrun a portion of the rock garden, but is so charming it may keep on running as long as *Charlie's Aunt.*

There have been bold men who declared true *elatior* never hybridised, but Mr. Wolley-Dod gave me some living proofs that such statements were inaccurate, for these plants have *elatior* form but the colouring of various red and pink Primroses, and I myself have found several seedlings with flowers bearing traces of Primrose characters. Pax and Knuth give no less than two pages to the various hybrid forms due to its liaisons with *P. acaulis* and *P. officinalis.* One of them, *P. anisiaca,* has been praised for its floriferous character by Mr. Farrer, and he kindly gave

My Garden in Spring

me part of each of his forms of it, but here it suffers so from thirst in summer that it does not flower through the whole Winter and Spring as with him, but is a dwarf and Interesting form.

I am very fond of the various purple or lilac forms of Primrose that come from Turkey and the Near East. The good old plant, sold so unblushingly as *P. amoena*—the true plant belonging to that name not being in cultivation at present—should be known as *P. acaulis*, var. *rubra*, say Pax and Knuth, but Dr. MacWatt has raked up the name of *Sibthorpei* Pax for it, in spite of the great man and his coadjutor having placed it as a synonym in their monograph. It is the single form of the old double lilac, and in its best forms of that same charming cool colour. I have also a deeper form, almost a purple—another of Mrs. Robb's good things. She saw it on Mount Olympus, and much to the annoyance of her magnificent dragoman, who was dressed in a uniform richer in gold lace than that of the most distinguished general, she insisted on his dismounting from his horse and digging up some roots with a broken potsherd, the only weapon that offered itself. She told me its purple glory always reminded her of the rueful face of that glittering dragoman.

These forms require, at any rate here, frequent division and replanting in soil freshened by leaf mould and cow manure. They dwindle if left alone for more than two years, but if well looked after are very charming in good broad plantings. *P. cortusoides* and its garden descendants, who have not descended but have very much gone up in the world as to size, appearance, and general affluence, need more leaf mould and choicer, cool corners than the

Primulas

garden can commonly afford, so they are not broadly planted, and only to be found in a few nooks of the rock garden, where the white and lavender forms of *Sieboldii* are very welcome to spread if they will do it on their own responsibility.

P. Veitchii I have tried to like, and failed to do more than tolerate. A white form I could love, but the type is so defiantly aniline in its choice of red that I should neither cry nor purchase a successor should it die of my cold neglect. On the contrary the smaller-flowered, equally aniline, *Cortusa Matthioli* has a firm hold on my affections, perhaps grounded in the memories of pleasant mornings in the cool gully, where among fallen boulders and a dwarf forest of *Alnus viridis* I first saw its downy leaves and crimson buds planted by Nature's own hand. It is a strange place, that gully, part of the only woodland for miles around, on the shady side of the Mt. Cenis lake. You must mount up to the col and cross into France and begin to descend before you find another thicket of the Alder, but there you will find no Cortusa, for on the Cenis it is wholly confined to this gully. There it is very abundant under the straggling stems of the Alder, growing in rich leaf soil, or tufts of moss, or apparently nothing but rock and atmosphere, but always, always in shade. Snow lies late in this hollow, and must be very deep in winter, for the Alders are flattened under it as though a steam roller had been over them, and what looks from below like a slope of dwarf bushes is the most difficult thing to climb among I can imagine ; the long, prostrate stems give under your feet, catch round your ankles, and whip your legs, and the upright portions are no good to catch hold of

My Garden in Spring

for support, as they join on to the long and supple stems
that lie on the ground, but do not root again, and so pull
away with your weight and sway about, and are less help-
ful than a broken reed. But wherever there is a space
among their stems, Cortusa, *Soldanella montana,* and *Saxifraga
rotundifolia* fill it up. I had often purchased Cortusa and
tried it in various positions in the rock garden, and always
failed to make it happy enough to live the round of a year,
but some of those I brought away from this shady grove
have thriven and increased among Hepaticas and Wood
Anemones in a border shaded by Purple-leaved Hazels.

The Spring Primulas wind up with the dumb-waiter-
like whorled flower-heads of *P. japonica* and its family.
Their idea of luxury is mud, and it suits their requirements
as well as those of a cockle-gatherer. The margin of a
pond and the bottom of a not too wet ditch provide a
happy home for them, and failing these the richer and
moister soil you can give them, the better will be the result.
There are some good colour forms of *japonica,* a so-called
salmon, which is much more like anchovy sauce if one must
give it a fishy name, a pure white with large orange eye,
one of the loveliest of Primroses, and a very deep coppery
red one, so there is no need to tolerate the old magenta
forms and still less the speckled and ring-straked abomina-
tions that a bad white strain produces so freely among its
seedlings. Even *P. pulverulenta* is crude and twangy beside
the best deep *japonica.* I planted some seedlings along the
pond edge and grouped *pulverulenta* with the deep red and
white *japonicas,* and directly I had done so was sorry,
believing the Chinese *pulverulenta* would kill the colour of
the Japanese. When they flowered it was the Chinese that

146

Primulas

were defeated, and had to be removed to a separate canton-
ment for sake of peace to the eye.   By itself the Chinese,
mealy-stemmed fellow is not bad, and among wildish grass
on the edge of a small pool at the bottom of the rock garden I thought its crimson tiers quite lovely enough to leave
them to seed if they will, as their own mother did higher
up, by the trickle that overflows from one little pool and
fills another.   From these, poor lady, she was ejected as
she was so cabbage-like in profusion of foliage and so
smothering to choicer neighbours, white Calthas and
Cyananthus lobatus, and this last, like the Princes in the
Tower, died this very stuffy death before I noticed what was
going on.   I could forgive almost any plant's death by
overcrowding if it were done by that lovely new mutation
or sport, or whatever the style of its origin may be described
as, which was shown at the Royal International Show and
named Mrs. Berkeley.   I understand it appeared at Coombe
Wood   without   warning   among   a   batch   of   ordinary
pulverulenta seedlings, and although it has a good sturdy
constitution, so far as I can learn it has refused to bear
seed.   I put two plants out in a sort of ditch we made
across a newly-arranged bed.   This ditch idea is a try-on
to see if its northern facing slope will be cool and accept-
able to ferns and Primulas of thirsty habits.   This one
liked it, and the spikes of flowers were in beauty for a long
period.   I cannot think of any name to describe their colour,
but I believe I could mix Naples yellow and Rose madder
and arrive at something like its creamy flesh tint, and it
shades into apricot and tawny orange in the eye, which
gives the flower a warm glow.   Yes, I hope it will spread
and the ferns be obliged to flee before it.   *P. Cockburniana*

My Garden in Spring

at present has a place in the ditch, but I lose it here after flowering, but mean to try it up in the fish hatchery, where, dry above and wet below, it may behave as luckier folk have found it to do, and grow into a clump.

The lovely hybrid " Unique Improved " did well at first, and allowed me to split it up into a nice colony, then something offended it, and every crown yellowed and decayed, leaving nothing but an orphaned seedling which flowered this year and was little more than a living image of its grandpa, *Cockburniana.*

The Pond—The large Bog Myrtle and the steps. (See p. 228.)

CHAPTER IX

March Winds

A PECK of dust in March, we have all been taught, is worth a king's ransom. The farmer may find it so ; he generally wants it dry when others would like it wet, and then grumbles because some crop has not grown. He is always waiting for dry weather to get on the land himself or to get something off it, so he may put that hateful peck of what the schoolboy defined as mud with the juice squeezed out, on his credit side, but I do not suppose I am alone among gardeners in feeling it is more likely to cost a king's ransom to renew the plants it kills. Those cruel, drying March winds do so much terrible damage, or at least they put a finishing stroke to many a struggling invalid, shaken but not killed by the winter's frosts. If only they could tide over another week or two the warmer ground would help along the growth of their new roots, and enough sap would run up to equalise their loss by transpiration, but with imperfect roots and an east wind they shrivel up and give up the struggle in an hour or two. An aged Cistus bush will often be the first to show the bill is coming in ; Bamboos, Miscanthus, and Choisya jot down fresh items, and you are lucky if the young green shoots of Crown Imperials, Eremuri, and precocious Lilies are not included. It is an anxious and

My Garden in Spring

a trying time, not only because it roughens one's own skin, making shaving a painful bore, and the corners of one's smile less expansive, but it is then one notes day by day some pet plant's failure to put in an appearance, or the flagging and browning of a cherished specimen.

I hate the grey, sapless look of the pastures during this spell of dry cold, and the arrest of progress in the flower beds. They look emptier than a week before, and plants seem to shrink, and the ground turns lighter in colour and shows out more conspicuously. There is no scent of growth or pine trees on the wind, and often a numbing suggestion of snow that seems to paralyse one's nose just below the bridge. Spring has come, but one cannot enjoy it or feel that any plant is safe, for any night the temperature may drop low enough to kill treasures January and February have spared.

Here nothing lies between us and the North Pole to take the teeth out of the north-east wind. By the time it has bitten and shaken our tender things it has lost much venom, and before it reaches the west of England is by comparison a refreshing breeze. Or so it seems to me when I leave my wind-scorched garden and go west of Swindon, and find everything green and smiling, and hear tales of what the east wind has been doing. It suits a few things to get this dry spell, but chiefly those that are lowly and sheltered by higher ground and protecting hedges. Some of the later Crocuses open out wide in the sunny hours, and are successfully fertilised by insect visitors. The Spring Mandrake, *Mandragora officinarum*, often fails to get its earlier February-born flowers set, and now

rushes out the remaining buds. Dingy grey-green things
they are, but some insects see and visit them, and if I
happen along and find them agape, I use my amber or
sealing-wax to transfer some pollen, for though I do not
greatly admire the dull flowers, nor later on the coarse,
floppy leaves, I do like to see a good crop of fruit, like
a clutch of emerald-green pheasant's eggs, or a dish of
unripe tomatoes, closely packed in the heart of each plant.
They are at their best when full grown but still unripe,
for they only lose in brightness of green and take on a
dull yellowish tinge when they begin to scent the air
with a mixed odour of bananas and pineapple, and their
next stage is to roll off and rot, and, unless removed, to
produce a crowd of seedlings where they fall. A very
much finer thing is *Mandragora autumnalis*, but like many
other good things it is as scarce, at any rate in England,
as it is beautiful. Fancy a rosette of handsome deep
green leaves, as it might be those of a mullein, lying flat
on the ground, and clean and vigorous all through the
winter months, and then fill up the centre of this rosette
with a score of purple blossoms, much resembling stemless flowers of *Anemone Pulsatilla*, and you have some idea
of what the Autumnal Mandrake should be. Ever since
last November I had been watching for the reappearance
of two specimens, and though it was not until the middle
of May I rejoiced over their safe return, I write of them
here as they should be in flower at the same time as their
dowdy sister, and I believe should have kept up a succession of their purple blossoms from the late autumn. But
it is an unpunctual creature, and you never know when it
will choose to flower from season to season. Its name

My Garden in Spring

certainly implies an autumnal habit when at home, but don't rely on names—plants are no more bound by them than Irish railway officials by the time-table. " Sure, sorr, and aren't you taking the time-table too seriously ? " was an Irish guard's reply to a query whether it was possible the train could make up for an unauthorised stop of three-quarters of an hour ! *Carlina acaulis* grows a fine, tall stem in English gardens, and *Caltha polypetala* never had a petal, let alone many of them, so never take a name too seriously. The only plant of *M. autumnalis* I have known intimately for any length of time is the magnificent old specimen under the south wall at Bitton, and for many years it has flowered in the early spring, but last autumn it began to justify its name by an autumnal flowering. I had heard of plants in Trinity College Gardens, Dublin, and it is in the *Kew Hand-List*, so I hope flourishes there, though I have never seen it, but beyond that I never met it else-where in England except in extreme youth—yearlings, that I had grown myself or seen at Bitton, raised from the fruits of the venerable specimen. But neither here nor there could these one-year-olds be induced, whatever treatment was offered them, to reappear when once they had disappeared below ground. They formed a fat little white root, but it slept like the Sleeping Beauty, and no prince could be found to wake it. A friend of mine once described a plant he had seen in Sicily, and I recognised my long-desired Mandrake, and railed at him for bringing no roots, so when another good friend told me he was going to Sicily, and asked could he send me any plant, I, imagining that island was paved from end to end with Mandrake rosettes, begged for a couple of middle-aged

Steps at end of Terrace—with London Bridge balusters.   (See p. 235.)

ones, and they came, rather dry in the leaves after their journey, but with rich purple flowers still fresh enough to proclaim them as good forms. Only later I learnt that my friend, having hunted diligently but in vain, consulted a high authority, and was told that they only grew in a limited area near Messina, many miles from his intended wanderings. Such is the kindness of the hearts of good gardeners that in spite of all this, those two good men contrived to get me the plants, and now they have revived from their first and perilous sleep in their new home.

It must have been to get a higher price for the roots, and deter others from collecting them, that the herbalists invented such lies as to the difficulties of digging up the Mandrake. They declared that it screamed so fearfully during the operation that all who heard it died, so the best way to obtain it was to loosen it a little in the ground and tie it to the tail of a hungry dog and set his meal beyond his reach. His struggles to reach it pulled up the root, its screams killed the dog, and you returned later on to collect your prize from the corpse. I have dug up many a one, and though I found the large root took a deal of digging—

"There was silence supreme! Not a shriek, not a scream,
Scarcely even a howl or a groan,"

and I, and moreover my dog who watched the operation, were none the worse. Nor have I ever found one with a root showing more resemblance to the human form than any bifid Parsnip does. The usual run of old drawings represented the human-shaped body as below ground forming the roots, and the leaves and fruits issuing from

My Garden in Spring

the head, but in the wonderful old map of the world which is one of the treasures of Hereford Cathedral may be seen a Mandrake whose body branches up aboveground, the head resting on the surface like a Turnip and the hairs of the head growing down as roots.

The Lesser Celandine, *Ranunculus Ficaria*, often flowers during the windy, leonine blustering of this month. The common wild forms one constantly struggles with but cannot entirely expel from the garden, but the major form from Italy does not increase too quickly, and is a fine thing when well grown, quite three times as large as the undesirable native. I like the white form of our wild one, though ; it has a charming, creamy tint and is as beautifully varnished as any Buttercup. It begins to flower very early in the year, but the later flowers are the larger. The double form is worth growing, and in ordinary seasons I notice it flowers when those of the hedgerow and meadow are almost over. A variegated one I found in a hedge has kept up its character for two seasons, and its leaves are prettily blotched with creamy white.

Blotched leaves suggest the Pulmonarias, and though we need not believe, with those who upheld the Doctrine of Signatures, that the white blotches proclaimed it a sovereign remedy for ulcerated and spotted lungs, because as Robert Turner states, "God hath imprinted upon the Plants, Herbs, and Flowers, as it were in Hieroglyphicks, the very signature of their vertues," yet we may admire the " browne greene leaves sprinkled with divers white spots like drops of milke," as Lyte has described them. I have a great liking for them all, and have collected together all I have met with that show any variation, and the working

March Winds

out of the assemblage is one of the jobs I have in store
for that day when I shall have some spare time. Perhaps a
broken leg might fix the date, but at present it does not
appear on my list of engagements. My first affection
for Lungworts dates from a day when I collected some
very distinct forms of *P. saccharata* from a little wood near
Bayonne, where they grew mingled with *Narcissus pallidus
praecox*. Purple and red-flowered forms were there,
charming with the sulphur of the Daffodil, and also their
leaves varied with larger or smaller mottling, and one form
had almost the whole leaf grey and white save for a narrow
edging of green. *P. saccharata* is one of the earliest to
flower, and the redder forms are very attractive ; they look
happier after a little frost than a frozen and thawed blue
one does, and if you cut away the seed heads and so induce
really strong leaves, the variety of their patterns is good to
see till flowering time comes back again. The best of all
red ones is a species, *P. rubra*, with large, pale green,
unspotted leaves. Its flowers are of a charming soft
scarlet-red, and never die off purple. If frequently
divided, and grown in good soil in sheltered corners, it
will often begin flowering in December and go on im-
proving accordingly as the weather does until May. The
best blue is a mysterious form known by many names, and
as my legs are still both sound I cannot yet hunt it down
accurately. It is generally known as *P. azurea*, which
authorities make but a form of *angustifolia*. I have long
known it as Mawson's Blue, and as it has short, wide, heart-
shaped leaves I hope it is not an *angustifolia* and doomed
to live under so false a name. It is dwarf, free flowering,
early, and easy to grow if divided every third year—in fact

all that a good little plant should be, and its colour is not ashamed to sit close by *Chionodoxa sardensis*. Its leaves are unspotted and do not become coarse, and it will not spread too far, for all who see it and have it not are ready to carry off a portion. The best white is the albino of *saccharata*, but it, like *officinalis alba*, is slow of increase: both are pretty, with really white flowers that go well with the spotted leaves. The only other white I know is a form of *P. arvernensis*, but though there are many flowers to a head they are small and crowded, and I do not care so greatly for it or its typical dark blue form as I do for the larger flowered species.

I have not yet lit upon a really satisfactory Cambridge blue form. One that I first saw at Wisley looks as though it should be a pale edition of Mawson's, but has never grown or flowered freely here. Half way up a mountain side in Tyrol I found a pale form lovely to behold in the shade of its rocks : it disappointed me this Spring, appearing washy, but did not flower very heartily, and may be all I fancied it when it settles down. Of purple-flowered sorts there are many. *P. grandiflora* I have from Glasnevin, a showy thing when fully out, but rather on the coarse side, and not very long in full beauty. A strong-growing, long-leaved one from Spain, variable in depth of colour, is good in its best forms, and very hardy and early, but takes up a great deal of room in summer with its immense, unspotted and therefore rather dull leaves. I have a set of puzzling intermediates, many of them seedlings I expect, from Captain Pinwill's wonderful garden, and still others from Bitton, the like of which I have been quite unable to trace in either of the good monographs by Du Mortier and

Tulipa Kaufmanniana.   (See p. 237.)

March Winds

Kerner, but that leg-mending period may some day reveal them among their pages.

Pulmonarias make a good bold edging to a shrubbery or bed of coarse herbaceous plants : the *saccharata* forms are perhaps best used thus, as their handsome leaves survive ordinary winters so cheerfully. *P. arvernensis* is best in the rock garden, and it and our native *P. angusti-folia*, which I have collected in the New Forest, die down entirely in winter.

Among other brave plants that take the winds of March amicably *Hacquetia* (Dondia) *Epipactis* is a good thing for a shady corner. It looks at first sight like a green Hellebore, but a closer glance shows that the golden centre is an umbel of small yellow flowers set in an involucre of green leaves, and is almost an Astrantia, and only just saved from such a relationship by a very slight difference in the shape of the fruit. It has a very bright and cheerful appearance in these nippy, cold days, when its glossy green leaves and yellow heads take the place of the Winter Aconites, but it increases slowly, and so is never seen in profusion.

Adonis amurensis should also be making a show, but slugs love its fat round flower-buds when they are first through and still a bronze colour, and they often lose their hearts as early in the day as the heroine of a penny novelette. The double forms are quaint and interesting, but always flower later than the far prettier single form. Several Corydalis species join the procession now. *C. angustifolia* is generally first, an ivory white, and too delicate-looking a thing to be out so early ; then follow the more robust creamy white *C. Allenii* and *C. bulbosa* with its dingy, faded-lilac flowers. I have never yet made up my mind as to whether I like *bulbosa* to spread about or no. On the one hand . it is so early and does no harm, but on the other it is not very attractive and takes up a certain amount of space. *C. cava* is brighter in colour and also has a good white form, and both are welcome to spread where they will. *C. Ledebouriana* and *C. Semenowii* did well for some years, but have died, I am sorry to say, for I liked their glaucous leaves and the pink flowers of the one and the orange of the other. They would travel underground in their supposed resting season and come up in most unexpected places, and this made it hard to prevent their being dug into or getting smothered by a neighbour. I have not seen them for some years, but always look out for their reappearance each Spring, hoping they may have returned from their travels. The beauty of the family is *C. nobilis* from Siberia, but it does not produce its light yellow flowers till May. Each blossom has a curious blackish-green tip to it, as though a beetle sat upon it. Except *Adlumia cirrhosa*, a very near relation, and some hateful weeds like *Cardamine hirsuta*, I can remember no plants that ripen seeds so quickly as this Corydalis family. It seems one day the flowers look a little faded and wan, and then the next they fall off, leaving a fat green pod, and if you break it open the seeds are black and shining and look ready for sowing.

Petasites nivea is not common in gardens, but is very much so in subalpine regions : it lacks the delicious scent of *P. fragrans*, the Winter Heliotrope, but then it does not run so violently and become such a nuisance, and its

March Winds

flowers are more attractive to the eye, with bright green bracts and creamy-white blossoms. They generally appear with the New Year, but are dwarf until March, when they run up on long stems among the fresh young leaves. It is a good plant to fill up odd corners among shrubs, especially at the back of borders where tall herbaceous plants are grown in front. *P. japonica gigantea* is not very lavish with its large flower heads, but a few go a long way, as each one in the distance looks like a large clump of Primroses, leaves and all. Its immense leaves are its best part, of course, and are those one sees in Japanese pictures being used as umbrellas. They want a swampy bit of ground and good feeding to grow large over here, and in this dry garden the poor things look tired and finally sit down on hot dry days. *P. palmata* is seldom seen ; its handsome leaves are worth having, especially as they are happy in any rough corner. The variegated form of *Tussilago Farfara* is one of the most beautiful of variegated plants, but is as hard to establish and keep as the common green form is to destroy. It will walk underground quite a yard between dying down and reappearing, which is annoying if you have it among other plants which would not appreciate the cold poultice of a half dozen of its great leaves pressing down on their chests. It has walked along one border until it has reached a triangular corner and the gravel walk, and here it has received a check and huddled itself together to think how to proceed. It got such a snubbing for appearing in the middle of the path that I hope it will not try again and get across to the strawberry beds. Its flowers are quite pretty ; the stems have much red and brown on them, but otherwise they are similar to

My Garden in Spring

the small dandelion affairs that star the railway banks so early in the year and puzzle many travellers as to their identity both when in flower and afterwards in seed, when they are balls of silvery pappus silk. Very few people recognise the flowers of this variegated one in the garden, coming as they do without any leaves, and they do not think of the old Colt's-foot. *Prunus cerasifera atropurpurea*, is the name the authorities command us to use for what we know better as *P. Pissardii*. Both it and the newer form known as Moseri, which has double pink flowers, have flowered marvellously freely here the last two seasons, and have been very beautiful throughout March, and would have been still more so had not the sparrows breakfasted, lunched, dined, and supped, besides taking odd meals such as elevens and five o'clock tea in them, the Plum flowers alone constituting the menu of each meal.

I find it a charming plant to cut before the flower-buds open, for they expand and last well in water. As a rule I dislike mixing different kinds of flowers in vases, and only put their own leaves with them, but the brown of these Plum leaves is really charming with bright yellow Daffodils, such as Henry Irving, and Almond blossom makes a delightful harmony with *Iris unguicularis*. Some seasons the early Chinese Almond, *Prunus Davidiana*, is a beautiful sight in January, but the last two years when other things were so forward they hung back, and only came out a very little before the common Almond. The white and pink are both worth having because of their flowering early, but are not to be compared with the real Almond. I find it is useful to spray them before the buds swell with quassia and soft soap, to discourage the sparrows from holding their feasts in and on them.

CHAPTER X

April Showers

WHAT a blessed time it is for garden and gardener when the wind goes round to the south-west and warm April showers begin to fall. The real thing, of course, not the chilly, wind-driven sorts compounded of sleet, hail, or ice-cold rain that come from the north with slight variation to east, and seem arranged on purpose to destroy the Plum blossoms. They leave the air several degrees colder, and if followed by a clear sky after sunset are the forerunners of a killing frost. This form of April shower belongs to what old country folk call Blackthorn Winter, an annual spell of bad weather that we never escape in the Eastern Counties. The only time I have been in Cornwall in April, my familiar native Blackthorn Winter accompanied me, and I saw the Rhododendrons and Camellias turned brown as leather, young Colt's Foot leaves singed by frost, and thick ice on tanks and pools. Therefore I trembled to think of what Arctic conditions must be prevailing here, but on my return found nothing worse than usual had happened, and the plants, being more backward than the pampered Cornish ones, had not suffered very much.

After a week or more of blizzards and squalls, and just when everybody has decided that it is the most curious

My Garden in Spring

and disagreeable season they remember, round goes the wind, hands can be taken out of pockets and yet no longer turn blue and numb, the dove-coloured flush on the trees of the woodland turns to a varied shimmer of tender greyish yellows and faint greens, even the oaks show raw sienna specklings, somebody hears the cuckoo, it rains for twenty minutes and the sun then hurries out and makes a rainbow on the retreating clouds, every plant glistens with sunlit raindrops, and the air smells all the sweeter and feels all the warmer for the shower.

Then it is that grass turns to the true green of Spring, both on lawn and meadow, and the flower stems grow by inches, leaves fall outwards instead of standing up stiffly at attention, and in a good garden the borders should look full once more, and the bare earth should disappear for the next six months. Then the days are not long enough to enjoy the rush of flowers and to do all the thinning, replanting and tying up, and a hundred other things that always want doing in a garden in full growth.

We always try to anticipate the coming of the April showers by removing the row of lights, a heritage from an ancient dismantled vinery, from the bank of the rock garden devoted to succulent plants hardy enough to stand frost if kept dry, but too tender to battle through damp and cold together. If I could have foreseen the trouble and the ugly effect of this row of lights from November till April, and the pain caused by their wicked little barbed spines, I should never have purchased the first three species of Opuntia that captivated me on the rockwork in Robert Veitch's Exeter Nursery. That trio grew so well that I added a few more, and learning that Mr. Andrews of

April Showers

Colorado issued a list of many other kinds, besides certain Cereus and Mammillaria species that were reputed hardy, I wrote for that list, and then for those Cacti, and by degrees some of the more ordinary plants have been banished from this bank and the soil replaced by a mixture of all the gritty, moisture-scorning materials I could lay hands on, such as plaster from a fallen ceiling, brick and mortar rubble from demolished buildings, well-weathered cinders from the furnaces, road sand and silver sand, until nothing but a Cactus or other xerophytic succulent plant could be expected to live in it. It is an anxious moment that recurs each Spring when the lights are off, and I can once more get at the fat green lumps I have only been able to gaze at through the glass before, and can poke them gently with a bit of stick to discover whether they are hard and healthy or soft and decaying. By being bold enough to try almost any succulent plant that came my way and of which any reasonable hopes of hardiness could be entertained, I have got together a large collection of plants that look as though they have no business to be out in the open air. Sir Thomas Hanbury always took a great interest in this bank when he came to see me, and sent me many baskets of treasures from La Mortola to experiment with, Mr. Lynch helped me from the rich collection grown in front of the houses at Cambridge, and I bought kinds I thought worth trying from the Continental nurseries. It is perhaps as well that about half of them have proved too tender for our winters, or the congestion of prickly things would have been worse than it is now. I greatly enjoy seeing these wrinkled Opuntias swell out in the Spring rains and then show red points where the new growths are budding,

163

My Garden in Spring

and trying to make up my mind which are flower-buds and which new branches, for years of experience have not yet taught me any means of distinguishing them at this initial stage. Then there is *Senecio tropaeolioides* to look at : so far, after clearing off its dead leaves, the tuberous root has contained some sound portions, and these have soon responded to warm moisture and sent up their glaucous leaves, as peltate as those of any Tom Thumb Nasturtium, and quite remarkable even in such a family of mimics as the Groundsel tribe.

A gentle tug at the centres of various Bromeliads, Rhodostachys species mostly, with a Dyckia or two, and most marvellous of all *Bilbergia nutans*, which is usually seen in a greenhouse, will show whether they still adhere to the roots or have rotted off at the collar. *Mesembry-anthemum linguaeforme* and *M. uncinatum* generally show that they have got to work and begun Spring growth before the glass lid came off; *Agave Parryi* and *A. utahensis* I have never yet found affected by a winter. A few of our Cape plants share this protected corner ; a fine old *Gerbera Jamesonii* dies down but regularly reappears soon after the rain reaches it, and *Hypoxis Rooperi* and *Haplocarpa scaposa*, two free-blooming, yellow-flowered plants that are seldom seen thriving in the open, behave in a similar way. We try to remove these overhead lights on the 1st of April each year, to let the rain moisten and wake the plants of course, and not at all because it is All Fools' Day as you might think, dear reader. Perhaps some summer day you will see these Prickly Pears and vegetable sea-urchins with their great yellow, salmon, or white blossoms wide open in the sun, and will be allowed to touch the anthers of the

April Showers

Opuntias and watch them close spirally like the tentacles of a sea anemone on a shelled winkle, and thèn perhaps you will forgive and justify our apparent folly in giving them overhead protection during the dull months ; only *overhead*, remember, for the sides are not closed in at all, so that we feel we grow these fat fleshy things in a way that we can describe as in the open air.

Now comes the rush of the Daffodils, and one can indulge oneself in picking freely, and getting down extra flower vases from the shelves, and feel that from now onwards, till the frosts damage the latest Michaelmas Daisies, there should always be a plentiful supply of flowers to pick from the open ground. Crown Imperials (*Fritillaria imperialis*) now shoot up another foot and take on their full beauty. The two best are those known as *maxima lutea* and *m. rubra*. I prefer the yellow one, but that may be because it does not grow so well here as the red, and one always loves most the delicate child. The old red one does well anywhere I put it, and increases only too fast, necessitating lifting and dividing the clumps oftener than I like, for the right moment to do this comes when one is full of other work, and it is unwise to touch them at all if it cannot be done soon after the leaves turn yellow, as they root very early, and soon deteriorate if kept out of the ground. I have the scentless form here, *Fritillaria imperialis inodora*, but it has never done very well and is always a dwarf plant, very unlike those I have seen in better condition in Holland, where there exists also a glorious plum-coloured form that I long to see in this garden, but cannot induce to cross the water. A good race of scentless Crown Imperials would be worth working for. Surely some student

My Garden in Spring

of Mendelism might investigate the family to see whether tall, scentless, and yellow may not be a possible combination of Mendelian characters. The old forms possess such an awful stink, a mixture of mangy fox, dirty dog-kennel, the small cats' house at the Zoo, and Exeter Railway Station, where for some unknown reason the trains let out their superfluous gas to poison the travellers. The various species of Codonopsis possess a similar odour, but have the decency only to let it loose when broken, and then of course it is fair for them to retaliate, but Crown Imperials waft it abroad on a lovely Spring day without being touched. One can do without the stinking *Phuopsis stylosa* (the Crucianella and Old Foxy of my childhood) in the garden, but I cannot forego Crown Imperials even though I have to hold my nose sometimes when near them. Like most things, however, this is a matter of taste, and hunting folk enjoy this odour in gardens. I love showing children the tears in a Crown Imperial's eyes, and of all the monkish legends, I like best that which tells of the origin of these. How that when Our Saviour entered the Garden of Gethsemane all the flowers bowed their heads, save the Crown Imperial, which was too proud of its green crown and upright circle of milk-white blossoms to show humility, but on the other hand expected admiration. When gently reproved by its Creator, it saw its error and bowed its head, flushing red with shame, and has ever since held this position and carried tears in its eyes. These honey drops are very curious, and though the cavities which distil them and in which they hang are to be found in some degree in other Fritillarias, they reach their highest development in *F. imperialis*, and being lined with white they have a wonderfully

166

April Showers

pearly effect when filled with the honey. What animal in its native Persia looks up into the flowers and is attracted by these glistening drops ? Observers have watched honey-bees alight on the stigma and crawl up to it to reach the honey, and as this flower is protogynous it can only receive pollen from an older flower, thus ensuring cross-fertilisation. These observations were made in gardens in Germany, but surely this tall drink, this pool of nectar, is not so cunningly arranged for nothing larger than honey-bees.

The double flowered forms are not free in flowering nor very pretty when they do overcome their ungenerous habits, and if they die, I shall not buy others. The Crown-upon-crown variety is curious with its second tier of green crown leaves, and like the fasciated form known as *Slagswaard* it is only a very strong, well-grown bulb that produces the abnormal structure, and in most seasons my clumps cannot be recognised from the ordinary form. I am fond of the two variegated forms, both the golden and the silver ; the mingling of burnt sienna, green and cream colour in a young shoot, is very beautiful—especially when backed by a group of the green-leaved forms.

F. persica exists but without happiness, and I should like more of its curiously metallic effect : the glaucous leaves suggest weathered copper, greened with age, and the flowers are like bronze bells wrought by some Japanese artist. *F. pyrenaica* has somewhat similar flowers, but they are parcel-gilt, and also lack the plum-like bloom so suggestive of aged and weathered metal which is the great charm of *persica*. I have a fine tall form with yellow flowers, which is by repute and tradition a form of *pyrenaica*, but quite unlike it in appearance and habit, as here *pyrenaica* increases so freely it requires frequent thinning to get a good flowering, but this yellow beauty is very slow to spread. A single bulb given me by Dr. Lowe, who told me he had it from Miss Hope of Edinburgh, has in twenty years only trebled itself. Very much like it in build, but with a pleasing dull crimson bell, *F. gracilis* is both rare and beautiful. It came to me through a kind friend who travels to strange out-of-the-way places and often sends me unusual plants from distant lands. This one has a very limited range in certain Montenegrin woods, but is making itself happy in this rock garden, and seeds so freely I hope it will soon grace many others. Several forms of our native Snake's Head, in fact as many as I can get, find welcome here— even the curious double form, that looks like a bunch of fragments of the marbled cover of the exercise books we used in our schoolroom days. The pure white is my favourite of all, and I like to see it rising out of *Erica carnea* as well as anywhere, and it appears to like such company too, and seeds freely there. The curious narrow-belled form known as var. *contorta* is worth growing. I only knew of the white until recently, when I saw a good stock of the mottled type in a Dutch nursery, so now I grow both, but the white is the more attractive; the squared shoulders of the type have disappeared, and the long, tubular, white flower is very graceful. This cylindrical aberration has been noted as occurring among the normal form at Wulfshagen, and has been observed to be too narrow to admit the humble bees which are the chief insect visitors of this species, but further evidence is

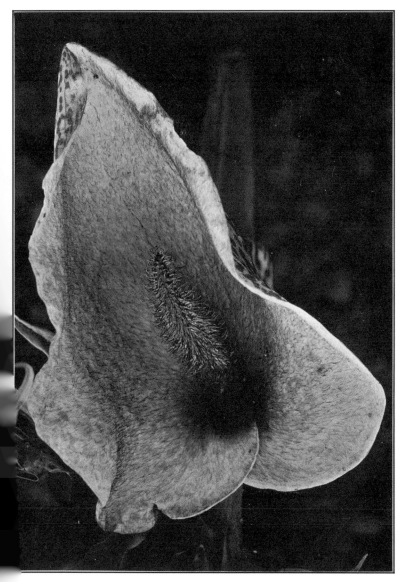

Helicodiceros crinitus.   (See p. 280.)

April Showers

wanted to show whether these flowers are fertile and whether this is a cleistogamous line of development of service to the plant, or a useless variation. One of the best of the family is *F. pallidiflora*, and if it has a fault it lies in the shortness of stem, which seems insufficient for the large bunch of soft yellow flowers. It grows well here in semi-shade, and I wish I could say the same of *pudica, recurva,* and the *latifolia* forms, all of which have left me.

Why does one so seldom see good patches of *Sanguinaria canadensis?* It seems to ask nothing more than planting and leaving alone, but I rather expect suffers from being lifted and stored, as is almost necessary for purposes of sale, and so is difficult to obtain in robust health.

I have found it good-tempered enough if divided when in full growth, and it is one of the plants I am over generous with, as I do so enjoy lifting a piece and seeing the realistic imitation of bleeding given by a broken root. It does this in the manner of a grazed wound, a gradual oozing of blood from several pores, and not a gushing out, which might upset some who watched the process.

A good clump in full flower is one of the joys of April. The thick white petals have a wonderful brilliancy, while the anthers are of a soft yellow, rather unusual with a white flower. It is a very variable plant, and its varieties have borne many names. That known as *grandiflora* is the best, but I see by *Das Pflanzenreich* that it ought to be known as var. *Dilleniana*, a pretty compliment to Dillenius and his beautiful figure of it in the *Hortus Elthamensis*. He also figures the minor form, and one he calls *flore pleno*, but which is hardly worthy of the name, having only

My Garden in Spring

a slightly increased number of petals and all of them about half the proper width. I have such a form here, but do not like it as well as the wide-petalled ones. I also have a rose-coloured form, but I find that only in certain seasons is there any trace of the rose, and only then on newly-opened flowers. I have no wish to see Niagara or New York sky-scrapers, but I should like to stand in a wood full of Bloodroot when the flowers are wide open. The blossoms do not last long, but to catch a clump with fifty or so widely agape is a treat worth lingering over, perhaps even a camp stool and a long visit, for it is only on a really fine warm Spring morning it deigns to open, and if a few days of bad weather follow you may find every petal lying on the ground by the end of them.

Magnolia stellata in full flower is not unlike a magnified Bloodroot growing on a bush. I have only one specimen in the garden, but it is a large one, about 12 feet high by 13 feet through, and being in the rock garden and too near a path I am obliged to cut off large boughs at times. It seems a dreadful thing to do, but if done early in the season, just after the last flowers have gone, the vigour of the new growths resulting from air and space and an extra allowance of sap quite makes up for the removals, and the increase being in more convenient parts of the tree adds to the beauty and size of the specimen. In 1912 I realised for the first time how strongly scented the flowers are ; a delicious whiff of bean fields reached my nose and set me sniffing around to locate its origin, and I tracked it down to the Magnolia. The bruised bark emits quite a different scent; you might shut your eyes and think Homocea was being used to touch some injured spot.

April Showers

One day when sawing off a rather large bough to clear the legs of the bush I was struck by the resemblance of the scent of the wood to that peppery fragrance peculiar to wooden Japanese cabinets, and I can believe it possible that Magnolia wood may be employed in their construction. It usually happens that once or twice during its flowering season the glorious white flowers are browned by frost, but after a few days of mild weather and a good shaking to knock off the browned petals, the show will be almost as good as before the calamity.

Last year I noticed a number of fruits forming, but later on, when I looked hoping for seeds, they had disappeared, and I have never seen this species bearing ripe seed anywhere in England yet. Another bush we are proud of and that is generally in flower in April is the hardy Orange *Aegle sepiaria*, or *Citrus trifoliata* as we once called it. When covered with its large, starry white blossoms on the spiny, leafless, but bright green twigs, it is a goodly sight. I grew mine from pips taken out of an orange given me by Canon Ellacombe, that had ripened in his garden, and two of the resultant youngsters planted side by side in the rock garden have grown wonderfully quickly. They are now 10 feet high and 9 feet through, and I have to cut them in severely or they would be half across the path, and scratch all who pass by. I am gradually trimming away the lower boughs, and hope some day to be able to walk under a crop of Orange blossom and later in the season of oranges themselves. The flowers are interesting because most of those that open first bear stamens only. Later there will generally be a few that are perfect hermaphrodite flowers, and the

My Garden in Spring

latest buds bear only stigmas. Some seasons my plants bear no female flowers until the pollen-bearing ones have fallen, and then of course I get no oranges. They fruited freely in 1911 after the hot summer, and I have raised a nice row of babes from the pips. I should like to make a hedge of them some day, as many of the spines are quite 3 inches long, and so stiff and sharp that the interlacing boughs armed freely with these fierce weapons would be worse than barbed wire, and not even a boy could get through a close hedge of Aegle. Little sprays when cut off are useful to discourage birds and fourfooted beasts. A faithful old dog, who always thought he helped me to garden by lying on cushions of plants, ruined a fine specimen of the white *Erica carnea* until I insinuated a chip or two of Aegle in among its growth. Poor old Taffy! how he jumped the next time he tried that bed, and he never attempted to lie on it again. Aegle has another charm in its beautiful autumnal colouring ; in suitable seasons it takes on a brilliant yellow, and the leaves remain on after many other plants are bare.

Some interesting hybrids were raised in America between Aegle and some edible Oranges, and three of these intermediates have been fairly widely distributed. I have got them here close to the New Wall, and they have passed quite unhurt through the last three winters, but though they have grown into good specimens, there has been no sign of flowers yet, still I hope I may some day eat marmalade made from these home-grown oranges. The handsomest of them is called Colman, and has fine broad leaves that look much like those of an ordinary sweet Orange. Those on the younger growths are not

April Showers

always sufficiently ripened to pass through the winter without scorched tips, but this kind shows no signs of the deciduous habit of its hardy parent. Morton is nearest to Aegle, having long thorns and shedding many of its leaves during winter and the third, named Savage—after a man, not its thorns, as it well might be—is intermediate between these in general appearance. They have acquired the pleasant name of Citrange in America, and the fruits are used for marmalade and what is there called orangeade. I tried the Bitter Orange which grows so well on the hills around Florence, and drops ripe oranges on to the snow in severe winters up there. But although I planted them in the most sheltered position I could afford, they lost their less ripened growth every winter, until precious little was left alive, and I believe the only survivor is at its last gasp this season, and so I must rest content with Aegle and its offspring. I believe Aegle is much hardier than most people think, for I have seen finer plants in places where the winters are severe than in Cornwall or Ireland, where it usually looks yellow and sickly, and refuses to start away upward, but to flower well it needs a hot sun and thorough ripening of the wood. One Spring it had a bad shaking here, and that was because it was in full flower and shooting into leaf-growth, when a severe frost on a Good Friday simply split the sap-laden shoots and every bit of even two-year-old growth was killed; and every bud, whether of leaf or flower, was destroyed, and the trees looked very sad for about a month, then adventitious buds formed on three-year-old wood, and by the end of the summer the young growths had grown out beyond the dead wood.

My Garden in Spring

Azara microphylla has done well here until this Spring, and I had two fine standard specimens, then on one gusty afternoon that in the rock garden was blown down, and all its roots snapped beyond cure, and about half of the other was torn out, yet no other tree in the garden was injured, and these two were a long distance from each other. I missed the Vanilla-ice-cream scent of its funny little blossoms that had always pervaded the rock garden at flowering time, and called my attention to the bloom which is so much hidden under the leaves that it needs a careful scrutiny to notice it. *Xanthorhiza apiifolia* was not blown over, nor ever could be, for it is a lowly shrub, and makes so many suckers that an interlacing mass soon develops. It grows close to the vacant site of the defunct Azara, and I like its quaint beauty. In late March and on through April it bears its tassels of tiny livid flowers, but so freely that when the sunlight catches it, especially the low beams of a setting sun, the whole group appears reddish-purple. It is quite an oddity, for it belongs to the great Ranunculus family, and yet is a woody shrublet, and except in Paeonia and Clematis woody stems are not common in that family. Its leaves do not appear until the flowering is well advanced, and they are prettily divided, but the root is astonishingly yellow, and it is worth pulling up some of the too-widely spreading suckers to see the golden roots which give it its generic name of Golden root in Greek words, while the specific appellation is simply Celery-leaved turned into Latin. I seem to have taken you to the rock garden, for the Magnolia, the largest Aegles, and Xanthorhiza live there, and the poor overturned Azara used to, so now you are there you might

April Showers

as well look at the large bush of Golden-fruited Ivy, by the side of the Magnolia. Just now, when its fruits are turning yellow, and before the birds have given picnics to all their friends to come and eat them, it is worth looking at. It has grown so large and looked so heavy that as you see I have short-coated it, trimmed off its petticoats up to its knees, like the good lady of nursery rhyme fame, and this gives a better chance in life to the *Crocus Tomasinianus* colony of February beauty, and the mass of the orange-coloured Welsh Poppy which glows beneath it in May. I am very fond of these fruiting bush Ivies, and whenever I see Russell's wonderful groups of them at the shows I long to be able to buy and group the whole lot in the garden. They are not separate arboreal varieties but only the fruiting branches of various Ivies cut off and struck, and if really woody flowering portions are chosen for this they very seldom send out any creeping shoots, but grow into wonderfully shapely bushes, good to look at all the year round. This golden-fruited form *Hedera Helix*, var. *chrysocarpa*, is one of the best, and very pretty when in fruit. It has also been called *Hedera poetarum* as it is plentiful in Italy and Greece, and was the Ivy associated with the worship of Bacchus, and much more suitable for garlands with its cheerful golden fruits than our native variety and its dull black berries.

I have an Ivy that was given to me with the reputation of bearing scarlet berries. No book mentions it, and had it been offered me by any ordinary gardener I should not have believed in its refulgent fruit, even if I accepted the plant, but my generous friend its donor knows plants as well as anyone, so I anxiously await the production of berries.

My Garden in Spring

Now come and see the other Magnolias. Having no wall for them, they are grown as standards in the open, and in some seasons this is an advantage, for exposed to all the winds that blow they flower later there than specimens on south walls, and their blossoms escape when the pampered, wall-protected ones are frost-bitten. It is very hard to get a plant of the true *M. conspicua* now, and I was told in Holland that it cannot be layered in the same way as its varieties are. It should be pure white, but even that form known as *speciosa* which comes nearest to it, has a certain amount of rose colour on the outside petals, and my tallest tree is of this second best variety. From the latter half of April and half through May it is generally a beautiful sight, but I am afraid its head has got up into the wind, and it will not go much higher. The best and quickest grower of the *conspicua* forms is that named *Alexandrina*, and it has made a fine shapely tree here, and flowers well, but is an early form, and so sometimes gets cut by frost when at its best. The flowers are rosy-pink on the outside and nearly white inside, and very large. The sensible one of the family is *M. Lennei*, a hybrid between *conspicua* and *obovata discolor*, for it flowers later, and is seldom damaged. The flowers are like immense rose-coloured Tulips, and after the main flowering a constant succession of a few blooms at a time is kept up all through the summer. The habit of growth is rather lax, one might even say sprawling, so it needs careful pruning if one wishes to grow it as a compact specimen, but if it had abundance of room allowed it I expect a naturally-grown sprawling dwarf would be very beautiful after some years. Mine has not very much space allowed it, for it

April Showers

has many neighbours, and grows in the turf in a piece of garden that has come to be known as the Lunatic Asylum, for most of its occupants are cranks or eccentrics, showing some departure from the normal habits or appearance of their genus or species. I suppose this sensible Magnolia is there as a keeper now. It went there at first because I had an idea of collecting Japanese plants in this corner, but it and some Cherries and Bamboos had no sooner got established than the freaks were put under their protection, and they have increased in number sufficiently to demand a chapter to themselves.

CHAPTER XI

The Lunatic Asylum

In the days of my early youth a vast clump, or so it then seemed to me, of evergreens occupied the space which now forms my home for demented plants.   It was the sort of planting one sees at one end of a London square.   Portugal Laurels there were, and the still more objectionable Common Laurel ; Laurustinus bushes, which in showery weather exhale an odour of dirty dog-kennel and an even dirtier dog ; leprously spotted Aucubas and Privet jostled one another round the feet of two Weymouth Pines and a dead Yew covered with Ivy, the whole dismal crew being rendered more awful and uninteresting by having all their attempts to show any beauty that might be inherent in their natural manner of growth nipped in the bud by the garden shears.   This agglomeration consequently bore the semblance of a magnified dish of Spinach with a few trees emerging from the top, where a giant poached Roc's egg or two might have lain.   A thick wall of such snubbed greenery of course had a hollow interior of dead branches, a playground ever desired by the child, and never permitted by the nurses and guardians, who foresaw the black hands and faces, torn clothes, and missing buttons that would result from a scramble in that unknown wilderness.

Most of this has now been cleared away, but the Wey-

The Lunatic Asylum

mouth Pines were left, and also the tower of Ivy that smothered the Yew, a very fine specimen of tree Ivy, rather too much the shape of a gigantic button mushroom perhaps, but a wonderful sight when in full flower, and the resort of a crowd of old pauper wasps and bluebottle and drone flies that, at the end of the honey season, live on its charity.

Some large blocks of Kentish rag were placed to form two rocky mounds round the stems of the trees, an irregularly shaped bed or two left, and the rest of the circular patch where the evergreen clump had stood was first planted with Crocuses and then turfed over. The beds were to have held Japanese plants, and the whole might have developed into a sort of imitation Japanese garden, but before it had got far that sort of thing became fashionable, and bronze cranes and stone lanterns met one in all sorts of unsuitable surroundings, the Temple Show began to bristle with giant toads, and pagodas, and jingling glass bird-scarers frightened the last idea of reproducing a page of Conder right out of my head. Then a home was needed for some trees and shrubs of abnormal characteristics that I had been collecting, and the Lunatic Asylum sprang into existence.

The twisted Hazel was the first crazy occupant, and is perhaps the maddest of all even now. It was first found in a hedge by Lord Ducie, near Tortworth, who moved it into the garden, increased it by layering, and so distributed it to a few friends, my plant being a sucker given me by Canon Ellacombe from his fine specimen. It is a most remarkable form, for it never produces a bit of straight wood ; the stem between each leaf is curved as though one side had grown much faster than the other, and alternating lengths are generally curved in opposite directions; frequently they are twisted spirally as well, so that the whole bush is a collection of various curves and spirals, a tangle of crooks and corkscrews from root to tip. They do not straighten out with age and thickening, and in winter, when leafless, the interlacing twigs are beautiful as well as curious, but when covered with the large crumpled leaves it has a heavy and somewhat diseased look, for each leaf is twisted or a little rolled, and they look as though attacked by leaf-rolling caterpillars. I have not seen catkins or nuts on it, and wonder whether the former would be curly lambs' tails, and the latter coiled like rams' horns. A young plant of a similarly twisted Hawthorn has now come to be a companion to the nut, but has not had time to develop its mania very fully. As a contrast there is the fastigiate form of the common Elder, the wood of which grows as stiff and straight and upright as a grenadier. A good specimen is an attractive object, as the leaves come in congested bunches at intervals on the straight wood, and though the leaflets are large, they are closely packed owing to the shortness of the central leafstalk, and look very much more like those of a Mulberry than an Elder.

Close to its feet grows a pigmy form of Elder that was a discovery of mine. It appeared one Spring in an old tree in the garden as a dark, heavy mass, and at first I watched it to see what strange bird's nest it was, but it constantly increased in size and altered its shape and I never saw a bird near it, so I climbed up to investigate closer, and found it was a Witch's Broom and then about a foot in diameter. When the leaves fell from the rest of the

The Lunatic Asylum

tree they still remained green on this mass until long after Christmas, and had not all fallen when new growth commenced. A year or two after, a violent February gale blew down many trees, and this Elder among them. I was loth to lose my quaint Witch's Broom, and so cut it off with a foot of stem of ordinary Elder wood, and planted it in the Lunatic Asylum, treating the stem as a root, and it has never shown any sign of discontent nor shot up any normally strong Elder shoots from below ground, and the masses of small congested growths have perfectly retained their very original character.

Cuttings struck from them make very interesting, round, bushy plants, and though they increase fairly rapidly in width do not grow more than 8 to 10 inches high in several years, and are practically evergreen, as the old leaves last on until the new ones push them off.

Yet another Elder has been certified insane and admitted to this select company. Its madness consists in the greater portion of the lamina of the leaf blades being reduced to a mere thread, and it looks as though an army of locusts or caterpillars had halted to dine on it, but for all that has rather a soft, ferny look from a distance.

Two Laburnums have developed strange habits, and qualified for admittance: one pretends to be an Oak, and has, so far as it can, imitated its leaves, and the name of *quercifolium* has been added to its own of *Laburnum vulgare.* The flowers are of a good rich yellow, but of course turn to ordinary pods, not acorns. The second is var. *involutum*, and has every leaflet rolled inward, giving the whole tree a heavy, congested appearance, and at close quarters one would think the leaves must be full of green fly to be so much rolled up. I see a self-sown seedling has appeared with the same curious leaves, so evidently this form of madness is hereditary insanity. A Buckthorn, *Rhamnus Frangula*, var. *asplenifolia*, has leaves consisting of little more than the midrib with just a serrated margin of lamina on either side, with a few irregular projections that produce a fern-like outline.

One of the strangest is a little Ash that is quite a dwarf, and has crimped leaves which are nearly black and beautifully polished. It bears the fine name of *Fraxinus excelsior*, var. *atrovirens nana*, which is nearly as long as itself, for it is a very slow grower, and makes but a few inches of wood in a season. It looks very strange even in winter, as the little black buds are set so closely together.

The Viburnum family have sent some inmates. *V. Opulus*, the Guelder Rose, has a curiously Japanese-looking dwarf variety. It makes a beautifully rounded bush, covered with small leaves, but it is a seriously minded lunatic, suffering from melancholy madness, for it never flowers. I have a similarly afflicted form of Philadelphus, but it is not so attractive, and therefore is banished to a private home for incurables under the farmyard wall. *V. lantana foliis punctatis* is a pleasingly silver-spangled form of the Wayfaring Tree, and almost too sane for the company, but its eccentricity appears when it comes to ripening its seeds, for then it cannot make up its mind what colour they shall be, and some turn white while others remain green, and red and black ones may all appear on the same head. The variety called *foliis auriis variegatis* has just arrived, and I like its soft, downy, sulphur-yellow leaves, and am waiting to see what coloured fruit it will produce.

Ring-leaved Laurel and Ring-leaved Willow share the

The Lunatic Asylum

same mania for leaves curled into rings, but are very different in appearance otherwise. A charming little narrow-leaved Laurel, *Prunus Laurocerasus angustifolius,* has been very sick since its arrival, but is settling down and growing a new crop of its tiny leaves. Several Ivies might be moved here, but are quite harmless and look very happy elsewhere, so *Hedera Helix,* vars. *minima* and *congesta,* remain in the rock garden, but var. *Russelliana* has gone here. It is the most distinct in appearance of all these curiously, small-leaved Ivies, of which *minima* is most commonly seen. They are extremely interesting morphologically, for they combine the two-ranked arrangement of leaves of the juvenile, creeping condition with the free woody habit of the fruiting mature state, in which a ⅖ phyllotaxy is normal.

These stiff, free shoots, with the tiny leaves placed very closely one above the other, and in two ranks only, have a very striking appearance.

Russelliana grows taller towers of leafy shoots than any other of them, and makes a curiously upright, narrow plant if carefully kept from falling out by its own weight. As a contrast I have planted the var. *obovata* close to it. This makes a round-headed bush, and has remarkably short and rounded leaves. Where it touched a block of stone my bush put out a climbing shoot which has now nearly covered the rock, and it is interesting to have both the creeping and tree form thus on one little plant.

Two forms of Butcher's Broom make another good contrast ; one is *Ruscus aculeatus,* var. *lanceolatus,* a very elegant form I get from Continental nurseries, but little known in England. Its cladodes are very narrow and

183

sharply pointed and greyer in colouring than other forms, so that it is a light and graceful-looking plant, showing some family resemblance to its not very distant relations, the Asparagus family.

R. hypoglossum, on the other hand, has very broad cladodes and fine, long tongues growing out of them, really the bracts from between which and the cladode the flowers ought to spring forth. This plant is not over hardy here, and so does not flower often, and alas! has never fruited. Close to them are some Docks. *Rumex flexuosus* is as mad as any plant well can be, for it has long, narrow leaves so brown in colour that they look more like a seaweed than a land plant. In early Spring when they first appear they have a most peculiar effect. The same plant has sown itself rather freely among the joints in the paved walks of the Pergola garden, and springing from between the stones looks wonderfully like some Laminaria on rocks between tide marks. Later on they throw up a tangle of slender, straggling flower-stems from which I suppose the specific name is derived, and then they look rather untidy, but if cut down a fresh crop of seaweed soon appears. *R. scutatus* with grey-green, arrow-shaped leaves, grows next to the brown species, and a little further along is the Fiddle Dock, *Rumex pulcher*, a rare British plant from Romney Marsh. This looks very much like an ordinary weed of a Dock, unless the leaves have developed the curious narrowed tuck-in on each side that suggests their musical name. Plantains are strongly represented. There is the Bush Plantain, *Plantago cynops*, a very strange, narrow-leaved slender bush that no one would dream was a Plantain unless they saw its characteristic flower spikes. *P. argentea,*

Hardy Palm in flower.   (See p. 282.)

The Lunatic Asylum

a silver-leaved one, is a really pretty thing, and is also allowed an honoured place in the rock garden, and *P. nivalis*, which is whiter still, and looks very miffy, has been put into the moraine for greater safety, but the grass-leaved Plantain *P. graminifolia,* and *P. asiatica,* a very lanky sort of Ribwort, are weird enough in appearance for the Asylum. I have several times found variegated forms, but they have poor constitutions, and never live long. One gloriously blotched cream and green *P. media* I found on Mt. Cenis was thriving grandly till a bough was blown off the Weymouth Pine overhead, and the end of it pierced the heart of my piebald treasure and it rotted away in a most unromantic fashion. The red-leaved Plantain is a handsome thing when well grown: a form of *P. major*, it grows into a big plant, and has leaves as red as those of a Beetroot, but with a dull surface to them quite unlike the glossy Beet leaves. The most remarkable, though, are the two Rose Plantains, whose flower-spikes are furnished with leaf-like bracts. The neater of the two is a form of *P. media,* and bears pretty green rosettes instead of a flower-spike, and I think neither flowers nor seeds. It must be the fifth kind of Gerard's *Herbal,* of which he writes: "The fifth kinde of Plaintains hath beene a stranger in England, and elsewhere, untill the impression hereof. The cause why I say so is the want of consideration of the beauty which is in this plant, wherein it excelleth all the other. Moreover because that it hath not bin written of or recorded before this present time, though plants of lesser moment have beene very curiously set forth. This plant hath leaves like unto them of the former, and more orderly spread upon the ground like a rose, among which

My Garden in Spring

rise up many small stalks like the other plaintaines, having at the top of every one a fine double Rose altogether unlike the former, of an hoary or rusty greene colour."

Johnson in editing the second edition has given the plate from Clusius' *Rariorum Plantarum Historia*, and interpolates this remark: " I take this set forth by our Auther to be the same with that which Clusius received from James Garret the yonger, from London, and therefore I give you the figure thereof in this place, together with this addition to the history out of Clusius : That some of the heads are like those of the former Rose Plantaine : other some are spike fashion, and some have a spike growing as it were out of the midst of the Rose, and some heads are otherwise shaped, also the whole plant is more hoary than the common Rose Plantaine," which contradicts Gerard's statement that his plant has at the top of every stalk a fine double Rose. The heads that are "otherwise shaped" are in Clusius' figure either spiked or branching, and my plant never produces any but the fine double Roses, so I feel sure it is the plant Gerard praised so highly. It came to me from Glasnevin, and is a much rarer plant than the other Rose Plantain, which is a form of *P. major* and the same thing as that figured in Gerard and Parkinson. This last produces both spiked and rose-shaped flower heads, some of them attractive but others very untidy, shapeless masses of small leaves, in the axils of which a good number of flowers appear and bear seed freely, so that young seedlings are plentiful round the old plants, quite unlike the other, the *P. media* form, which is quite barren, at least here, and must be increased by division. The green and yellow Snowdrops, both double and single, which I have

The Lunatic Asylum

already described, have a place in one of these beds. The viviparous form of *Poa alpina* still bears its crop of young plants instead of flowers just as it did on the banks of the roadside at Lanslebourg. Several Strawberries are sufficiently crazy to come here. First and foremost the Plymouth Strawberry, which is one of the strangest of plants, and has a wonderfully curious history. It is certainly wrong in the head if ever a plant was, for it is just an ordinary wild Strawberry in every way until it blossoms, then every portion of the flower is seen to have been changed into leafy structures; the petals are little green leaves, even the anthers and carpels are replaced by tufts of tubular leaves, but this does not prevent it from ripening a kind of fruit which has a central portion of red flesh studded with the tubular leaves instead of pips, and with two ranks of leaflets round the base which are the sepals and petals. In this state it is a pretty green and red object. It is first mentioned by Parkinson in the *Paradisus* in 1629, and he gives a very rough but quite recognisable figure of it. His description of it is so exact it is worth quoting. He writes: "One Strawberry more I promised to shew you, which although it be a wilde kinde, and of no use for meate, yet I would not let this discourse passe without giving you the knowledge of it. It is in leafe much like unto the ordinary, but differeth in that the flower, if it have any, is greene, or rather it beareth a small head of greene leaves, many set thicke together like unto a double ruffe, in the midst whereof standeth the fruit, which when it is ripe, sheweth to be soft and somewhat reddish, like unto a Strawberry, but with many small harmlesse prickles on them, which may be eaten and

My Garden in Spring

chewed in the mouth without any maner of offence, and is somewhat pleasant like a Strawberry: it is no great bearer, but those it doth beare, are set at the toppes of the stalks close together pleasant to behold, and fit for a gentlewoman to weare on her arme etc as a raritie instead of a flower." Johnson adds a paragraph about it in the 1633 edition of Gerard, and tells us its history thus : " Mr John Tradescant hath told me that he was the first that tooke notice of this Strawberry, and that in a woman's garden at Plimouth, whose daughter had gathered and set the roots in her garden in stead of the common Straw-berry : but she finding the fruit not to answer her expectation, intended to throw it away : which labour he spared her, in taking it and bestowing it among the lovers of such varieties, in whose gardens it is yet preserved." Then Marret in his *Pinax* published in 1667, declares he found it growing in woods in Hyde Park and Hampstead. Ray mentions that it was in cultivation in the Cambridge Garden for many years, and then it disappeared so entirely that Dr. Hogg, as quoted by Dr. Masters, wrote of it as a " botanical Dodo," saying that " though a century and a half have passed since there was any evidence of its existence, it serves still as an illustration for students in morphology of one of those strange abnormal structures with which the vegetable kingdom abounds." In 1766 M. Duchesne informed the world of the generosity of M. Monti of Bologna, who divided with him a dried specimen in his herbarium. Some time after the publication of his *Vegetable Teratology,* from which I have quoted these facts, Dr. Masters came across his botanical Dodo alive and happy in Canon Ellacombe's garden, and carried

188

The Lunatic Asylum

off plants of it to grow in his own. From these came my original stock, for Dr. Masters gave me some plants and at the same time told me the account of his re-discovering them. I had the pleasure of sending some to Cambridge this year, for they had disappeared there, and I am quite willing to send others to Plymouth if the descendants of that good woman's daughter want them.

The double-flowered Strawberry is really pretty ; the first flowers of the season are like little white Roses, but later on they come only semi-double, and these turn into small fruits. The one-leaved Strawberry is not often seen. It is only a variety of the wild *Fargaria vesca,* and known as var. *monophylla.* Now and then the normal number of three leaflets are produced on a leaf stalk, but as a rule only the central and terminal one is developed, so that the plant hardly looks like a Strawberry until it flowers and fruits. This variety has appeared in several places ; Linnaeus found it in his travels in Lapland, it is to be seen in a picture by Holbein now at Munich, and Duchesne, the author of the *Historie des Fraisiers,* raised it from seed of the wild Strawberry. A handsomely variegated Strawberry which bears large white fruits is the last of that family in this plot of ground, for I have lost a white-fruited Alpine form that ought to be here.

I cannot describe all my maniacs so fully as these, and will only mention a white-flowered *Ajuga reptans,* and that strange form *A. metallica crispa* a Hen-and-chicken form of the common Daisy, the Green Primrose, Parsley-leaved *Anemone japonica,* the dwarf form of *Daphne Laureola* known as *Philippiana,* and a form of *Campanula lactiflora,* that instead of growing 6 feet is content with one, and has

My Garden in Spring

narrow lanceolate leaves from its childhood instead of the ample ovate leaves of its brother seedlings, and constantly correlated with these peculiarities is a curious dialysis of the coralla similar to that seen in *Campanula rotundifolia*, var. *soldanalliflora*, in which the bell is divided into five narrow petals. I can always recognise a *C. lactiflora* that inherits these oddities even when its first leaves appear above the cotyledons, by their singularly narrow outline.

Does my Lunatic Asylum appeal to you or appal you? I cannot tear some visitors away from it, and others who do not care about the demented inmates are pleased with the effect of the surroundings. When the Cherries and Magnolias are out, and later when some standard Wistarias, both *sinensis* and *multijuga*, in both lilac and white varieties, and the white *brachybotrys* are in flower, I sometimes think it looks rather like a Japanese garden after all.

CHAPTER XII

Tom Tiddler's Ground

I HAVE never felt the disgust for variegated foliage evinced by so many good gardeners, and in many cases I warmly admire it. For instance *Iris pallida, Astrantia major* (as seen at Bitton, for it does little more than just exist here), *Acer Negundo,* and *A. californica aurea, Hypericum Moserianum tricolor* and *Polemonium coeruleum* in their widely different lines of variegation are to my idea delightfully delicate in colour harmonies. The cream and soft yellow alternating with grey-green in *Iris pallida,* and forming endless intermediate shades of colour where one overlays the other, make a leaf worth examining closely, while a good clump of it is a strikingly beautiful thing among other Iris foliage.

Towards the end of summer, and before the autumnal tints begin to brighten them up, most of our shrubs and trees become very heavy in their tone of green, and we miss the contrasting shades of Spring vegetation. Then the value of a Silver Elm or *Acer Negundo,* the Ghost Tree, and of golden-leaved shrubs is apparent, and even in the borders variegated herbaceous plants seen in fine specimens and bold groups give relief from the uniformly heavy greens of late summer and the glaring brilliancy of crowded flowers. But even if a plant is not improved in beauty by varie-

191

My Garden in Spring

gation, there are the scientific sides of the question, and how very little we know of the causes of variegation, or the answers to such questions as, " Why should golden forms do best in full sunlight and most silver ones in shade ?   Why does variegation sometimes appear on one half of a stem only, and is it generally true that the variegation in such cases occurs in a self-sown plant towards the magnetic north as has been solemnly averred ?   Is it a disease, and if so is it communicable ? "   Mr. Wollaston of Chislehurst, of fern-growing fame, believed it was, and used to associate plants of which he desired to obtain variegated forms with the piebald or skewbald representatives of others more plastic than they, and showed many results of what those who deprecate variegation would call corruption of good greenery by evil company.

I have given a hearty welcome to all forms that have come my way.   Some few are only fit for the Lunatic Asylum, but I have for the last three years been trying to group the really beautiful forms of variegated plants in an irregularly-shaped parcel of ground that was available for planting after the downfall of sundry Horse-chestnuts and Portugal Laurels.   I thought it might be effective as well as interesting to group them according to the nature and colour of their variegation, and so it began with a planting of purple-leaved things at one end and golden forms at the other, and a witty friend christened it Sennacherib's corner. But since then much silver has been added, in grey-leaved things at one corner and as an edging stretching both ways from it and reaching on one side to the commencement of the golden plants, and a central planting of white variegation forms a wedge-shaped group with the narrow

Tom Tiddler's Ground

end of the wedge running between the purple and gold groups. As purple-leaved plants are not very numerous, and many of them lose their depth of colouring somewhat in late summer, the general effect is rather of gold and silver, and therefore Tom Tiddler's ground is now a fitter name. Some of the colour effects persist throughout the seasons, especially in the grey corner where *Centaurea Clementei*, perhaps the most silvery of all white-leaved things, has come through the last two winters with a brave show. The leaves of *Cineraria maritima*, though dulled by damp, soon dry up and look white and fresh in Spring sunshine. *Santolina incana* is best cut down annually, but I like to leave a few of the plants unshorn till the scissor-snubbed ones have reclothed themselves, to carry on the grey tradition of their clump. The powdered stems of *Rubus tibetanus* and *Rosa Willmottiae* rise up among the lowlier plants, and are very effective in Winter and early Spring, but *Rubus biflorus* is the most startlingly white-stemmed of all, and I am frequently asked why I have whitewashed it. It puts the others so completely out of court that I have it among the variegated silver plants rather than the greys, and there, when most of its neighbours are leafless, it stands out in its coat of paint. Except for *Osmanthus ilicifolius fol. purpureis* and some dark-leaved Antirrhinums the purple end retires from business in Winter. *Cornus Spaethii* in the golden end has bright red bark to its young shoots, but Golden Thyme, and a grass or two, with the golden *Juniperus sinensis*, and the old, old golden Feverfew, keep up the reputation of the golden corner, while *Ajuga reptans fol. var.*, white-flowered *Lamium maculatum*, *Barbarea vulgaris*, and this last year a fine specimen of Jack-

My Garden in Spring

by-the-Hedge (*Sisymbrium Alliaria*), half of whose leaves were white, from a neighbouring hedge, perform the same good work in the central silver portion. But as the best Spring effect is to be seen when the Tulips are in flower, it is then that I shall lead you forth to see Tom Tiddler's ground. We will approach it over the old bowling green lawn, and so arrive at the grey corner where *Artemisia Halleri*, *bicolor*, and a good form of *Absynthium* I found plentiful at Lanslebourg are all showing up in the front. *A. borealis*, a lovely lacy and silvery edition of Old Man which might well be called Old Lady, backs a patch of the brilliantly white *A. stelleriana*, which is allowed to sprawl on to the gravel walk. *Æthiopappus* or *Centaurea pulcherrima* is newly arisen, and also wonderfully white. The *Centaurea*, *Cineraria*, and *Santolina* before mentioned form higher mounds behind, and *Cerastium tomentosum* makes a mat before the entrance, for, as the ground was too wide to reach over comfortably, I ran an irregularly curved line of stepping-stones across it to give access to the central portions, and they start from among the *Cerastium*, and various dwarf plants are planted between the stones. *Ajuga reptans* with silver leaves is very effective used thus. The tall, silvery-grey leaves of two giant Onions rise up among the silver plants ; *Allium Rosenbachianum* has the more gracefully recurved ones, but those of *A. Babingtonii* are taller. Both plants send up large round heads of mauve flowers ; those of Rosenbach's are very handsome and come in May, but Babington's not till July, and they think nothing of reaching a height of six feet, but quite half the buds are transformed into bulbils, and

Tom Tiddler's Ground

unless one wishes for a large crop of this rare British plant, the heads must be cut off before these bulbs drop and plant themselves. Among large subjects *Atriplex Halimus* has made a big bush of itself in spite of constant applications of my secateurs, and now is very silvery and charming, so much so that one wonders why it is so seldom to be seen except on gardens on sea fronts. *Eucalyptus Gunnii*, I believe the true thing and therefore the hardiest of all, is shooting up above everybody else, and these with the Rose and Bramble and a young *Picea pungens glauca* form the tall centre of the grey corner ; the lawn front contains other Artemisias, *Salvia argentea* with its immense leaves like grey plush, *Anthemis Cupananii*, a plant too little known, for besides feathery grey leaves it has white daisies that are singularly well shaped and brilliant. *Suaeda fruticosa* and *Artemisia maritima* from the Norfolk coast are here, but *Diotis maritima* refuses their company, and will only live in the rock garden. *Onopordon bracteatum* comes for a short stay, and flowers and dies when at its best, in its silly biennial way. *Anemone Pulsatilla* does well here, and thrusts up fluffy, lilac flowers with Chinchilla fur boas round their necks among the steely blue-grey leaves of *Cerinthe alpina.* *Seseli gummiferum*, a strange, stiff-habited, glaucous, umbelliferous biennial, is very effective just before it starts flowering, but *Festuca glauca*, the grass with imitation hoar frost eternally on its leaves, is the best of the whole lot, and finishes the grey plants by running as a wedge into the beginning of the golden things. Golden Thyme is the first plant in the golden edging, and then comes a fine striped form of Foxtail Grass that

My Garden in Spring

is very brilliant in its young growth, and remains good till late in summer if the flowering stalks are kept pulled out. Golden Ling, a *Viola cornuta* with white flowers and golden leaves, the Feverfew (*Pyrethrum Parthenium*), the beautiful, golden-leaved *Veronica Teucrium* that originated in Captain Pinwill's garden, and a corner clump of *Cornus Spaethii* are the main features of the front rank. Laburnum, Lilac, Mountain Ash, *Robinia Pseudacacia*, *Ptelia trifoliata*, *Ribes sanguineum*, the Common and the Cut-leaved Elders, have all provided golden-leaved forms, and are represented here. *Acer californica aurea* is perhaps the most brilliantly yellow of all, though *Sambucus racemosa plumosa aurea*, runs it very close, but ought to be ashamed of its pre-Linnean length of name. The Ptelea does not come out golden, but the leaves become spangled and afterwards almost suffused with gold as they age, and therefore it stands out as the best when the others are losing their brilliancy. The Laburnum's gold vanishes as soon as that of a spendthrift, while the Ribes is a good colour throughout the season. I have derived great pleasure from this golden group, and am trying to extend their effect by planting more golden forms in a line with it to carry the colour on until the Bamboos and Yews by the river are reached. Two Alders have come into this, and *Alnus incana aurea* is a very beautiful thing, the colour of the winter bark is so brilliant, like red coral. Golden *Acer campestre* also pleased me much this year. But to come back to Tom Tiddler's ground and the undergrowth of the golden grove, there is Creeping Jenny and Meadow Sweet, pure gold both of them, and another form of the latter with gold blotches. *Thalictrum glaucum* "Illuminator" is very effective when in young growth, but afterwards turns glaucous, though if beheaded it soon springs up golden again. *Iris Pseud-acorus*, with striped leaves, and forms of *I. versicolor* and *I. spuria*, with the young growth brilliantly yellow, grow up among a wonderful grass I first saw in the Birmingham Botanic Garden, instantly asked for, and shortly after gratefully received. I have not found a name for it yet, but it is the lightest, clearest yellow of any leaf I know, and seeds freely, and comes true from seed—a veritable treasure. I planted a clump of the Early Tulip, Yellow Prince, with golden variegated leaves, and they looked so well when in flower that Daffodils were introduced to help the early golden glow, and yellow Tulips to carry it on. Of Daffodils, Olympia, Duke of Bedford, Hamlet, Lord Roberts, Butterfly—a pretty light double—Whitewell, and Henry Irving have all done well, and join on to the planting of cooler-coloured ones that I have mentioned in an earlier chapter. But the supreme moment is reached when the late Tulips are out. Yellow Rose, the fine old double, is at the corner by the Cornus, and if a few short twiggy branches are put among the buds as they rise, they get enough support, and the full-blown flowers hang gracefully from among them instead of fainting on to the walk. Ellen Willmott, Solfatare, and Mrs. Moon are good tall yellows, and are planted in the middle distance. Ixioides, with its rich black base, is very effective, and a great favourite of mine. Moonlight is the best pale yellow, a lovely colour, and in front of the others shows up well. Inglescombe Yellow, Jaune d'œuf, Golden Spire, Primrose Beauty,

My Garden in Spring

and other yellow Tulips are there, but those I have named I consider the best. Starting at the grey corner, I planted pale lavender-coloured Darwin Tulips, working into lilac and mauve sorts, and then carried them down either side of the stepping-stones in small patches of eight or a dozen, dotted here and there among the variegated plants, and as they approach the purple-leaved things at the end the shades of the Tulips grow darker, until we end with the deepest purple ones we can find. Erguste, Bleu Aimable, Rev. H. Ewbank are in fairly large clumps to represent the lilac shades, and then come Franz Hals, Greuze, The Bishop, Vespuccio, and Velvet King, which are fine rich purples. Purple Perfection, Fra Angelico, Grand Monarque are rather deeper, and of redder or browner shades, and Faust is the finest and darkest of all. I have not planted anything nearer black in this bed, such as Sultan, Zulu, and La Noire, as they would not be effective against the *Prunus cerasifera atropurpurea*, Purple Barberry, and Hazel that form the background. The most beautiful of all purple-leaved things is certainly the Purple-leaved Peach. It keeps its colour to the end, and constantly sends out young crimson growths through the whole summer. Its flowers are as rosy and large as those of the Almond, and in 1911 it bore a crop of hard, purple Peaches.

We sowed some of their stones and got a purple-leaved plant from each of them. A good specimen occupies the post of honour in the foreground here where the shaded lines of Tulips end, and the newer form of purple Plum (I cannot write its long but correct Latin name again) which I bought as *Pissardii nigra* is certainly very deep in colour.

198

Tom Tiddler's Ground

The purple Sloe looks rather dingy beside these two, and the purple *Euonymus europaeus atropurpureus* is best in its autumn coloration, and so far I have been rather disappointed with a purple *Acer campestre* that has been so only in name.   The central gathering of silver variegation is becoming very interesting to me as the collection grows, and I can begin to reckon what main lines variegation follows.   It seems that but few plants have leaves naturally and always marked with white in their typical form.   Of course there are the Lungworts, *Lamium maculatum*, and the well-known Milk Thistle, and I have here, too, a smaller Thistle with white markings which are evidently permanently specific characters.   It was sent to me by a good friend who found it wild in Italy, and kindly remembered my collection of such things.   It is only an annual, but sows itself most obligingly, and its autumn rosettes are very charming.   I have been trying to think of other hardy plants with a regular design of white or grey marks on their leaves as usual specific characters, and either my memory is bad or their number is small.   I recall Red Clover, several Buttercups, all Crocuses, except such as have struck out a line for themselves, and I hope you will believe me when I say that until I had written that last sentence I was quite unconscious of its punning sense, but leave it as it is so absolutely true, for the two species with semi-cylindrical leaves, *Crocus carpetanus* and *C. nevadensis*, and the four-winged leaf of *Scharojanii* have dispensed with the usual conspicuous white line of the rest of the family. *Scolymus hispanicus*, Echium and Cerinthe in several species have small, white spots.   Cyclamen leaves, except those of true *Coum*, vary from small spots to zones of great

My Garden in Spring

beauty, *Richardia albo-maculata*, which is quite hardy here in warm corners, but once caused my herbaceous exhibit to be disqualified at a local show, has along with its near relations the many white transparencies on the leaves that provide its specific name. It has been said that no plain green form is known of *Pachysandra terminalis*, that strange Euphorbiaceous plant from Japan. So many of the older introductions from that country were garden forms, as witness *Anemone japonica*, first known as a semi-double red form, then by the white, and it is only lately that the var. *hupehensis* has arrived, which is clearly the wild rose-coloured form. Again, *Rosa rugosa*, and from China the Chrysanthemum, all came to us first in garden forms, so that I suspect *Pachysandra* has been treated in the same way, for I have lately seen the green form in the Cambridge Botanic Garden, and hope it will soon be in this one too. And the figure in *Somoku-Dzuzetsu*, the Sowerby of Japan, shows no trace of variegation. The variegated form we now possess is an attractive plant with narrow white margins to its leaves. In greenhouse and stove natural marbling is common enough, and I need not make lists of Begonias, Caladiums, &c.

Variegated leaved shrubs are numerous, and cannot all be squeezed into Tom's silver mine. Cornus varieties number three, and the best is *C. sibirica elegantissima*, a free grower with large leaves, the major portion of each being white. *C. brachypoda variegata* is slow to grow tall ; most likely it starts life as a layered shoot, and like all such is loth to shoot up strongly, but a sharp knife and a hard heart and patience are training my specimen in the path of uprightness—and it begins to show the whorled char-

Eremurus Elwesianus.   (See p. 283.)

acter of branching, a dumb-waiter effect, that this species
is noted for. *C. Mas aureus elegans* is very soft and pretty,
with a creamy-white variegation. *Elegans* may pass, but
aureus is an untruthful epithet ; it is weaker in golden
glow than an Australian sovereign, and so has been placed
among the silver plants. *Weigela rosea* and *Philadelphus
coronaria* have good silver forms. The variegated *Ruta
graveolens*, if kept sheared over twice in the season, makes
a wonderfully beautiful, hoary-headed specimen, looking
more like a plant in full flower than mere variegation when
seen from a distance. *Euonymus europaeus aucubaefolius*
has up to the present only come out in spots towards the
end of summer, but an older specimen may be more effective earlier. Of herbaceous plants also only a few of the
best forms of variegation have been planted here as yet.
Scrophularia aquatica is one of the most effective, broadly
blotched with cream colour and good at most times
of the year. *Mentha rotundifolia, fol. var.*, requires looking after. It runs and spreads with marvellous rapidity,
and is inclined to go back green, but makes up for
it by giving a large number of wholly white shoots ; so it
is wise to keep on replanting from the most variegated
portions. *Acorus Calamus* has a very effective variegated
form, with a certain amount of burnt sienna and rich red
about the bases of the leaves. It is best in a bog, but
consents to live in a not too dry border. *Artemisia vulgaris*
[the Mugwort], *Lychnis dioica*, a Chrysanthemum, several
Funkias, Crown Imperial, and Sweet Violet all have good
green and white forms, and grasses provide *Phalaris
arundinacea* or Gardeners' Garters, but in the better form
with the centre of each leaf broadly white. *Arrhenatherum*

My Garden in Spring

bulbosum is a very good variegated grass, but the whitest and most effective of all dwarf ones is *Molinia coerulea, fol. var.;* it grows near the stepping-stones with *Funkia undulata* (also *fol. var.*) for a neighbour, and the two are about as pretty as any variegated plants I know. In earliest Spring I get an effect of blue among these silver things from Hepaticas, *Pulmonaria* Mawson's variety, *Scilla bifolia, Chionodoxa sardensis,* and a few other things of lowly habits, and later in the season these are replaced by Violas, especially forms of *V. gracilis,* and deep purple bedding Violas, as of course the blue groundwork has to disappear before the lilac Tulips claim the field. To take their places later still there are other flowering plants hiding among them, but that is another story, or rather a chapter of another volume, for this book must end with the commencement of Summer.

CHAPTER XIII

Anemones

THERE is a charm in the simple form of a single Anemone that goes straight to my heart. The central boss of carpels, and the surrounding ring so rich in innumerable stamens, start the flower on pleasantly concentric curves ; then the segments of the coloured floral whorl are generally so ample and delightfully hollowed that their outlines are always bold and good.

It is botanically correct to deny petals to an Anemone, but I never feel quite happy about considering all the coloured segments as sepals, as it often happens in certain species that the outer ones have a slightly more woolly texture, especially on the outer side, and the inner are rather more perfect in shape and coloration, and look more like petals. On the other hand, I must own that when doubling occurs by the anthers becoming petaloid they as a rule take a narrow lanceolate form quite different from the ample coloured sepals.

It is rather curious that this particular form of double flower should bear the name of "Anemone-flowered," and be used for any family in which there are double flowers with a ring of large regular outside segments, and the central portion is filled with quilled or narrow rays. The term "Anemone-flowered" surely ought to bring to

My Garden in Spring

one's mind the original simply beautiful design of the single Wind flowers and not the double freaks of garden origin.

I lately saw some huge China Asters with an outside fringe of ray florets of extra length and narrowness, and the disc a mass of large quilled florets. Anything more unlike an ordinary Anemone could hardly be imagined, yet everyone who saw them at once dubbed them "Anemone-flowered," having in mind the race of Chrysanthemums so called, I suppose.

Analogous instances may be noticed in the way fully doubled flowers are called Rose-flowered, and thus when a double Rose is more than usually rich in petals it has to borrow an epithet from the Cabbage, and the most solid of Cabbages from a drumhead. Let us hope that the limit has been reached there.

Certain double-flowered Anemones are by no means to be despised : that known as Chapeau de Cardinal, a pure scarlet *A. coronaria* with the regular centre so well be-loved by the old Dutch painters, is a very glorious thing. It and its brethren the other *coronarias* are never happy here for long, and their cultivation must be pursued on the buy-and-die system, which I dislike as wasteful and unkind to the plants. But their price is so low that I occasionally invest in a hundred or so to get at least one season's fun out of them. I will not go into raptures over their well-known beauty, nor describe the way we struggle with plants that others can grow with ease, but in spite of their resemblance to stale fruit of *Castanea sativa* I must indulge myself by retelling tales about *coronaria* that I myself enjoy. The first is of good Umberto, Bishop of Pisa, who arriving in the Holy Land just too late to be of

Anemones

any use when the Crusaders were returning home defeated, determined some good should come of his enterprise and so filled his ships with earth from Palestine, carried it to Italy, and filled the Campo Santo at Pisa with it that the dead might lie in the holy soil. There within those lovely cloisters the scarlet *A. coronaria* was seen for the first time in Italy, having been imported with the soil no doubt, but its appearance there was regarded as the result of a miracle, and to typify anything the fertile fancy of medieval monks might suggest about the blood of holy martyrs shed on that soil. It is more pleasing to think of the certain pleasure thus given to the living than of the advantages that were imagined for the dead. The other story has a villain for hero, a Dutch burgomaster who coveted a magnificent strain of Anemones possessed and jealously guarded by a burgher. Seed was refused to the great man, so he plotted, arranged a visit to Mynheer's garden at Anemone seed-time but before the harvest ; he arrived in state and clad in his civic robes, and by cunningly allowing his furred mantle to brush over the seed heads went home with a plentiful supply of the fluffy seeds caught in the fur. Now that I have written it out I perceive a second villain in the tale, and cannot decide which was the worse, the thief or the miserly gardener who refused to share his plants.

I try to keep a little colony on the rock garden of the Palestine *A. coronaria*, known as var. *syriaca*. Like other Palestine members of the family, Adonis and Ranunculus, the type form is pure scarlet, and lacks the usual white eye. I have had white forms, though, among collected roots. It is a fine thing for a sunny rock bank, and especially glowing if backed by grey stones and silvery-leaved things as I

My Garden in Spring

had it this Spring. *A. hortensis* has been mentioned in an early chapter as having typified and announced the Spring in Greece to me, a wanderer on its hillsides. I wish this race might have borne some other name, for it is one of the most magnificently coloured of all wild plants : its varieties, *fulgens* of the Pau district and *graeca* from Greece, have never been improved upon by garden-raised seedlings. Sutton's Strain, or the Aldboro' lot, fall far short of those I saw on a bank edging the Olive gardens on the road to Kephissia, outside Athens. There grow the true broad-sepalled *graeca* form, and not only scarlet forms but of every shade of cerise, salmon, and some pure white all over, others with broad, white rings in the centre of the rosy flowers. I had seen a few of these mixed with the normal scarlet being sold in tight little bunches in the market-place, but could not learn whence they came. Daily excursions from Athens did not reveal the secret until, chasing a magnificent *Lacerta ocellata* (the great-eyed lizard), I crossed this bank, forgot the Saurian and dug the plants.

The first Anemone of the season here is another Greek plant, *A. blanda*. I have seen it in flower before Christmas at Bitton, but never before mid-January here. Our earliest form is in a broad edging at a corner of the large herbaceous bed, and resulted from a planting of some collected tubers. They are mostly of rather a pale blue, and have well-marked, white eyes, and are not so good, in spite of their early appearance, as the deep blue form sometimes known as var. *Ingramii*. This band has been lengthened by a patch of that darker variety, and in the end of February and onwards the two are

Anemones

generally out together, and make a fine display in the sunshine.

The pure white is pretty if a really good form is procured, but the variety *scythinica*, at one time misnamed *cypriana*, is particularly lovely, as it is rich sapphire blue outside but pure glistening white within, and a half expanded flower showing the contrasting colouring is a sight worth looking at. Both in this band, and in the rock garden, this form not only thrives but seeds freely, and the greater number of the babes are as handsome as their parents: a few washy ones have appeared, but I suspect them of being bastards, and should say if grown isolated from other *blanda* forms the seedlings would all come true *scythinica*. It comes into flower rather later than the blue forms here, and lasts on longer than any. There is a lovely rose-coloured form, but rather scarce, and it is wise only to buy var. *rosea* when seen in flower, for some shades of mauvy pink and pinky mauve are quite unnecessary in a plant with good blue and pink forms. I complained to a friend that I could no longer obtain the best pink form from a certain nursery, and he owned up that he had overhauled their stock one Spring and left them none to send to me. In reparation he most kindly gave me the best form I have ever seen.

A few years ago Bishop Umberto's miraculous Anemone was surpassed, for the bed under the south wall of Bitton garden presented its scholarly chronicler and venerable master with a tribute of its affection in return for his wise and kindly rule of over half a century, in the shape of a set of seedling *A. blanda* beautifully double and ranging in colour from pale lavender blue to deep ultramarine.

My Garden in Spring

A note from the Canon brought me to gaze and wonder at their beauty. The doubling is interesting and of a two-fold nature, for not only is there an increased number of sepals, but the anthers are transformed into short petaloid bodies set among the whorls of sepals, and are in some forms deeper in colour than they, reminding one of the doubling of a Narcissus such as Butter and Eggs, where the pale perianth segments are repeated mingled with the smaller and deeper-coloured sections of the corona. It must by this time be quite apparent to my readers that half of my choicest treasures are due to visits to Bitton and the generosity of Canon Ellacombe, and they will not be surprised to learn that both a pale and dark form of this glorious miracle are now thriving in a bay of my rock garden and annually remind me of his kindness. *A. appenina* everybody should know—it ranges from Italy to Turkey ; but save a pure white form, one of Dr. Lowe's many valued gifts to me, I have not seen any other that I could think of as approaching *blanda* or an intermediate between the two species. This white one is earlier than any other *appenina*, and rather dwarfer too, and is a true albino, with no trace of pale Prussian blue on the backs of its sepals as there is in most white varieties of *appenina*, and the leaves are of quite a yellow shade of green. A rose-coloured form has been offered, but has very little claim to the title. One clump that I bought as var. *rosea* is tinged with pale lilac outside instead of the Prussian blue of the common white ones. A lilac form that originated with Messrs. Van Tubergen forms a pleasant contrast, and is prettily irregular and starry in shape, but the double form also sent out by them is a poor, thin thing

Anemones

compared with the double *blanda*, but is interesting in spite of its rather washy colour.

The typical blue form is one of the best plants for naturalising in semi-wild parts of the garden. I have planted some among rough grass at the edge of the pond and running back into the border among deciduous shrubs, and those among the grass do quite as well as those in the border soil, and like most flowers rising out of grass look all the prettier for it. The Anemones that thrive best here and so give most pleasure and effect are those of the *nemorosa* section, with running, stoloniferous growths that ask to be kept plump and cool or even moist throughout the season. It puzzles me why they should do so much better than those with tubers that can stand any amount of baking and drying off. You can keep *A. coronaria* and *hortensis* dry for weeks or months without injuring them otherwise than causing them to grow out of their chosen season, but try the same treatment on any *nemorosa* and you will find it as dead as Rameses the Great, and in this dry garden one would think I could give a happy home to the sun-lovers on grilling ledges of the rock garden more easily than I could imitate the cool woodland home of the *nemorosa* section. Of course I do what I can for them by finding western or northern exposures for them, and tucking up their little naked brown limbs with a new leaf-soil quilt when I see they have worn a way through the old one, and most of them have spread into good-sized carpets and are among my greatest joys of Spring. Two round beds cut in the turf, and full of dwarf shrubs and herbaceous plants, are almost carpeted by them in April. Shaded, low-lying parts of the rock

My Garden in Spring

garden hold some of the rarer varieties, and most beds of permanently planted, mixed plants are annually receiving the overflow from the crowded patches, as I do love to carpet bare spots under deciduous shrubs and round tall-growing things with such plants. The ordinary wild *nemorosa* is worth collecting from different districts, as it varies greatly in shape, tint of colour, and time of flowering, and keeps up its old customs in the new home. I have a very early form and a very late one, and the common type of the Cotswolds, which has the outside, especially of the buds, more or less pink, and of a charming creamy-rosy tint. It is so noticeable in the bud stage, when the flowers still hang their heads, that one of the most noted botanists, when first shown them in a Gloucestershire wood, mistook them for a Cyclamen.

Two varieties are listed as *rubra* and *rubra fl. pl.*, but though they are worth growing they open quite white, and only flush to a red as they age. The red, it must be confessed, is rather too cold, and suggestive of that little devil whose name is Legion as well as Magenta who too often possesses and ruins pink flowers. They are both effective when contrasted with white and blue forms, and seem to linger on longer than the white ones, loth to shed the flowers that have gradually deepened to such a fine colour. The so-called fl. pl. is not much more than semi-double, having at its fullest no more than a second row of sepals.

There is a dainty little pure white one called Vestal which Herr Max Leichtlin sent out into the world, but I do not know where it originated. The anthers are nearly as white as the sepals, and make the flowers look like *A. trifolia*, but the leaves are those of *nemorosa* right enough.

Anemones

Two very fine forms are listed under the one name of grandiflora ; one is a tall grower with long and narrow leaflets, and the flower also is rather starry and slightly doubled and faintly flushed with pink, and I believe it was found in Ireland some years ago by Lady Doneraile. I do not like it so much as the other form, which I have always called Leeds' variety, as Dr. Lowe gave it to me under that name, and told me he had it from Leeds himself, but I do not know whether he was the finder of it.

There is a good figure of it in the *Garden* for October 15, 1887, and Burbridge wrote about it later as " a large, pure-white form, very distinct and beautiful. I first saw it at Munstead, and I think it was there called Dr. Lowe's Variety. In general size and stature it resembles the lovely pale or lavender-blue *Robinsoniana* which may possibly be a form of it, varying mainly in colour." I have always felt the same about it, and have tried to find out where both of them grow wild, and hope that at last I am on the right scent, for a year ago I saw in a Herefordshire garden a form of blue Anemone evidently *Robinsoniana*, but with a redder tint on the stalks and young leaves, and learnt that it came from a wood in Norway. I am now the happy possessor of some of this stock, and am watching its behaviour beside the older form. But I want very much to see what Norwegian white Wood Anemones are like, as I hope they may prove to be Leeds' Variety. I have never seen any wild forms from Britain or Ireland that approach these in the width of segments and good form. Leeds' is perhaps even more perfectly shaped and formed like a single Rose than is *Robinsoniana*, and its bright green, ample leaves make a fine background

My Garden in Spring

for the large flowers, which when doing well are nearly two inches in diameter.

I do not believe *A. Robinsoniana* originated in Ireland, as I have several wild blue forms sent me from Irish woods, and they have all been of ordinary *nemorosa* type. Mr. Robinson has told me that he first saw his blue Anemone at the foot of a wall in the Oxford Botanic Garden. Baxter, who was then the curator, told him it had been sent to him by a lady in Ireland.

I think this started the idea of its Irish origin, but of course she may have had it from Norway. I am quite convinced Leeds' Variety is the best of the white forms, but will not say that *Robinsoniana* is peerless among the blues. For I can never forgive it for closing so readily on dull days and towards evening in a rather sulky, short-tempered way, and then displaying what I can only call a cotton back, a poor greyish-tinted outside not much better than a dirty white. When open its soft, glowing, rosy-lilac flowers are certainly very lovely and a large patch of it glistening with April raindrops in its leaves, but its flowers open to the sunshine, makes one want to cease worrying about weeds and just enjoy the Spring scents and flowers. But *A. Allenii* has eclipsed it in beauty, being larger in all its parts yet beautifully proportioned, and of a slightly deeper shade of lilac within and flushed with rosy purple on the outside, so that a bud and closed flower are warm, glowing things like snow mountains flushed with a sunset glow, while a closed *Robinsoniana* is like the effect of death pallor that follows when the light leaves the peaks.

How Mr. Allen must have enjoyed his first sight of

Anemones

this, the largest and loveliest of blue Wood Anemones, when he first saw it among his seedlings.

It is still rather a rare plant, and is one of those that all who see long for so passionately that it has not spread into a very large clump here yet, but it seems a good grower, and so I hope soon to get broader effects from it. The most effective blue form I have is known as *A. nemorosa*, var. *purpurea*, because the closed flowers are quite rosy-purple even in the bud stage, but the open flowers are of a good soft blue. It grows very freely, and I have been able to make several colonies of it. It will grow well in sun or shade, but the flowers are taller and larger and last longer in the shade. It has been found wild more than once in the neighbourhood of Pau, and was mainly distributed by Herr Max Leichtlin.

Much like it, but of varying shades, are some beautiful forms sent to me from Lismore woods by Miss Currey, who told me that those growing along the banks of the streams were mostly blue, but in the rest of the woods only the ordinary white form occurred. Mr. Allen also raised a beautiful seedling he named Blue Queen and which is the brightest blue of any, quite a Forget-me-not blue and a pretty early flowering form, but on the small side. Celestial is much the same but paler, and I believe another of his seedlings. Then there is the form known as var. *coerulea*, which is plentiful in certain districts of Wales where the slate crops out. It varies from rosy tinted forms almost as deep as purpurea, to others only flushed with blue in very young blossoms, and the pale forms flower earlier than the deeper ones—at least so I find here.

My Garden in Spring

A late flowering and distinct form from Co. Wicklow I owe to The O'Mahony, who found it wild in wet land close to the river. It has some likeness to the one known as Blue Bonnet, which was found in Wales and taken to Daisy Hill, Newry, where Mr. Smith's magic wand makes everything grow. Blue Bonnet is the latest of all the *nemorosa* section to flower, and is very distinct in appearance, being more waxy in texture than the others, and of such good substance that it lasts on till the middle of May in shady nooks, and I have never noticed it flag with the warmer temperature.

There is yet another called *Robinsoniana cornubiensis*, but I have never seen it doing really well anywhere or looking very much like *Robinsoniana* : it strikes me as a lanky form of *nemorosa purpurea*, but if it were really strong and vigorous it might improve. I think much might be done by collecting these blue forms and sowing all the seed they give. Besides the so-called double rose-coloured one mentioned above, there are two distinct double white ones commonly grown : the best is a very old inhabitant of gardens, with six well-formed and regular sepals, and then the whole centre filled up with a rosette of petaloid bodies, beautifully neat and regular, looking like a small double Daisy. It is well figured in Maund's *Botanic Garden* and in Wooster's *Alpine Plants*, but without any hint in the text of either as to its origin. I like to think it was the plant that Gerard grew, and of which he writes : " There is in some choice gardens one of this kinde with white flowers very double as is that of the scarlet anemone, and I had one of them given me by a Worshipfull Merchant of London called Mr. John Franqueville my very good friend." There is no figure of it in the original 1597 edition, and Johnson has used Clusius' figure, and in his additional note mentions that, unlike the single form, it has leaves in two places on its stalk, which, together with the beautiful old woodcut, show that it is not the neat double form that he is referring to but the one we now know as *A. nemorosa bracteata, fl. pl.*, a ragged, untidy thing that never comes two seasons alike.

Now Clusius tells us the history of this and a double purple form which seems to have been lost, how that they had only recently been discovered, and had not been described elsewhere. He had not seen their flowers until the April of 1593, though one John Boisot had sent him the plants two years previously, directing that they should be kept in pots and somewhat starved, for with excessive luxury they would degenerate and bear single flowers. Both had bracteate leaves under the flowers as well as the usual involucre of three leaves, and had been found by chance a few years previously in two woods, of which he gives the names, in Belgium. It is very unlikely, then, that Gerard knew of them prior to the publication in 1601 of Clusius' *Historia*, and I am sure if he had seen one with the two sets of involucral leaves he would have mentioned that peculiarity.

I much prefer the neat, double form to that eccentric Mad Hatter and March Hare in one, the variable *bracteata*, which in some seasons may be nearly single, then in another the green bracts will be mixed among the white sepals, or they may be striped with green, or at other times stained with a dull purple. There is a mild excitement to be obtained from growing such an unreliable

My Garden in Spring

plant and watching its vagaries, and those people who enjoy statistics might like to tabulate the periodical reappearances of any particular form.

The yellow Wood Anemones are not so effective in the borders as the white and blue, but are pleasing in contrast with them. *A. ranunculoides* in its typical form is rather small flowered, but makes up for that defect when in good health and vigour, by producing two blossoms on each scape, and as the second one does not open until the first has fallen, the flowering period of a clump is lengthened. There is a larger flowered form of it which I believe is found in Italy, and is a good thing, but not plentiful as yet, nor does it spread so quickly here as the older one, which has made wide carpets in some borders. Quite lately a semi-double form has been introduced, and is pretty and well worth growing, as it is not too double to interfere with the central fringe of stamens. My favourite form is one known as var. *pallida*, with fairly large primrose yellow flowers, but it increases very slowly, and does not form so dense a clump as the others. There is a very interesting hybrid between *ranunculoides* and *nemorosa* that is found growing among its parents in Silesia, Saxony, Baden, and Alsace-Lorraine, and is named *A. intermedia*. It is small in flower, rather thin in texture, and a pale sulphur colour, but is quite worthy of a place in the rock garden, as it is always the first of the *nemorosa* section to flower, and often breaks through the ground in February, and opens its blossoms a few days after the arched stems have lifted them through the soil. The Italian and Austrian *A. trifolia* differs from *nemorosa* chiefly in the curious deep green of

Eremurus bed. (See p. 283.)

its leaves, that look as though they should be evergreen, they are so dark and of such firm texture : the flowers are of a very cold white, and perhaps rather small for the important-looking leaves. I have brought home a blue-flowered form of singular beauty from the Dolomites, but it has not yet grown strong enough to show its beauty here, and whether or no in changing its sky it will not change its sky colour also. The Japanese *A. flaccida* is good for a moist position, but gets thirsty and tired and then faints on warm days in an ordinary border. The leaves are very attractive, as they vary in colour from youth to age. At first they are a golden bronze, then turn a bright green spotted with white, and end by being dark green marbled with grey, and a good-sized clump will bear many shades of green at one time. They suggest the leaves of a Buttercup in shape and general appearance, but are seen to be too glossy for any common one when looked at carefully. The flowers are about the size of Wood Ane-mones, but more creamy in colour. The various forms and near relatives of *A. Pulsatilla* are delightful plants for edgings to borders or grouping among other plants in good, broad masses. I find the best way to establish them is to sow seed as soon as ripe, either where you want them or in a reserve ground, and pricking out the resulting plants when about a year old. Sown as soon as gathered they germinate freely in a few weeks, and look wonder-fully like small Buttercups for their first season, and not till the following Spring will they produce the finely-cut leaves they bear ever after. They dislike disturbance and interference with their long tap-root, so are rather difficult

My Garden in Spring

to transplant when elderly. The large, pale-flowered form is the most effective to plant freely, but there is a good one often sold as *A. Halleri*, with even finer cut leaves than the common form and deep purple flowers. It looks well mixed among the others, but is not *Halleri*, which may be easily recognised by its silky pinnatifid leaves. I have lately got as *A. rubra* a deep chocolate-red form of *Pulsatilla* that is very distinct, but some sad fate has always decreed the destruction of the white form just as it was settling down here. The most frequent cause of failure here among the Pulsatilla family is some evil but undetermined underground animal that eats holes in the collar of that plant which are followed by decay and a sudden flagging of leaves, and if the injured part is not at once removed the whole plant is liable to rot off. A very fine old clump of the form called *A. pratensis montana* has lost more than three-quarters of its many crowns in this way this season. This is a very tall growing variety with nodding flowers of very deep purple: unfortunately they do not open widely enough to be as beautiful as they seem to promise, but the seed heads are very fine, great balls of grey-green feathers borne on stems two feet in height.

I struggled for years with *A. sylvestris*, and got for my pains thin carpets of rather unattractive leaves, and after a season or two a bare centre and an ever-widening circle of the flowerless tufts. Then the var. *baicalensis* came, and I thought was better, as though rather stingy in the way of bloom it generally produced a half dozen or so that were pretty with their rosy purple exterior. Then some ten years ago I got the var. *grandiflora* from a Con-

Anemones

tinental nursery, and I could soon see the other forms
might be allowed to die out for want of replanting, for the
newcomer gives abundance of larger and purer white
flowers, does not travel too rapidly, as every one who sees
it wants it and carries off the outliers, and best of all it
does not die out in the centre when it has occupied the
ground for more than two seasons, so the crevice in the
rock garden in which it was first planted is still full of it,
and the large, white flowers come in Spring, then the ripe
seeds like lumps of cotton wool follow, and are very white
and ornamental, and till late in the autumn the plant is
continually throwing up a fresh flower-stem or two. I still
keep the double-flowered form because I like its wonderfully full flowers when they appear, and also because it
has taken possession of the slate bank of the rock garden
and would be hard to dislodge.

Some day I hope *A. alpina* and *A. sulphurea* will be worth
writing about here ; at present they are mostly playing the
rôle of foliage plants, which any Carrot or Parsley could
do as effectively. Some are only seedlings, and so cannot
be blamed, but others I brought from Mt. Cenis, where
one walks for miles among knee-high tufts, and now and
then is obliged to stop and admire the extra light turquoise
back of one, the soft sulphur tint or pure dazzling white of
another, the semi-double or extra wide sepalled flowers of
more, and wonder which is the most beautiful. Unless
Ranunculus Lyallii covers the Alps of New Zealand with
a wonderfully lavish profusion of flowers I feel sure *A.
alpina* on Mt. Cenis must afford the most beautiful floral
display of the world. It looks so hardy and easy to

My Garden in Spring

manage when seen springing up in the mountain turf that I am rather disappointed that so far only one of my carefully-nursed plants has recovered its spirits enough to flower ; but the one splendid white flower it gave me this Spring makes me feel no trouble is too great that will help them to grow strong.

CHAPTER XIV

The Iris Walk in May

THE northern bank of the New River provides us with a long grass path and one of the most sheltered walks in the garden. For it is protected from the cold winds by the row of fine old Yews I have chronicled in an earlier chapter, and the southern side is bounded by the river, and so is open to catch all the sunlight, and the first Daisy of the season always appears close to the water's edge on the slope of the bank. The long beds that flank this path were at one time monopolised by a dreary collection of Laurels, Laurustinus, and the other dull things that former generations planted so largely and called shrubbery, but they have all disappeared to make way for my principal collection of Irises, especially those of the Bearded section. This group suffers much at the hands of catalogue makers, and members of it are often dubbed German Irises, though very few of those included under the heading have any affinity with *I. germanica*. I have seen and heard them called Rhizotomous—a travesty of rhizomatous—and all the while the pleasant title of Bearded Flags is good English and faithfully descriptive.

Three of these borders are very much overhung by the old Yews, and of course the roots fill and drain them very effectually, and though they lie so close to the river,

My Garden in Spring

not one drop of its water soaks through to them, for to begin with Sir Hugh Myddelton saw to the proper construction of its clay banks three hundred years ago, and vigilant officials, first of the New River Company and now of the Metropolitan Water Board, have ever since been on the watch for weak spots and ready to apply fresh clay when needed. So that in spite of the nearness of so much water, these beds are about as dry and starved as any in the world, and very few plants will grow in them so happily as the Flag Irises.

Where the row of Yews ceases, the beds are wider and more open at the back, and there is one between river and pond that runs back a good way, and holds two fine old Scots Pines, and a group or two of flowering trees. The Chinese Almond, *Prunus Davidiana*, in both its pink and white forms opens the season, often flowering in early February, but sometimes in late January, when the Witch Hazels race it for first place. *Hamamelis arborea* is always the first of these, and its rich orange threads catch the sunlight on bright days and make a brave show. Then the newer *H. mollis* opens its rather larger blossoms, and is followed by *japonica* and its variety *Zuccariniana*, which have paler yellow flowers and show up well from a distance. These grow towards the pond side, but at that period of leaflessness can be seen from the river bank across the Iris bed and through the central group of Crabs which later on completely hides them. A Siberian Crab behind and two *Pyrus Malus floribunda* in front make a lovely picture when full of flower, especially while the *floribunda's* buds are still round and crimson. Three purple-leaved Birches rise just behind them and form the

Iris florentina in May.   (See p. 223.)

The Iris Walk in May

background. A Judas tree, *Cercis Siliquastrum,* leans out over the Irises, but not a very large specimen, as my forbears forgot to plant one, and it is one of the trees that a thoughtful great-grandfather should plant for his descendants. So this is of my planting, but has grown quickly and flowered well in some seasons, and seems to be an especially brightly coloured variety, approaching a crimson, though not of so deep a shade as the flowers of a glorious row I saw in full bloom in the chief square of Corfu one Spring. The whole front of this bed is planted with a band some 8 feet deep and 20 yards long of *Iris florentina,* with every now and then a clump of *I. germanica* among them. At first it was all *florentina,* but a purple *germanica* got in by accident, and I saw how greatly its presence improved the general effect, which was rather too cold before, so I planted others at regular intervals. When this bed is in full glory in the middle of May it is as beautiful as anything in the garden, whether viewed end on to get the solid mass of blossoms or from the opposite bank to see the line of grey and purple flowers reflected in the water. Looking eastward you get the bend of the river as background, and the terrace with its beds of Darwin Tulips reflected in it, and the other way looking down westward, the view is blocked by a fine old Weeping Willow, growing on the pond bank and hanging right over the grass path, so that we have to keep an arch cut in it to make a way through. Next to the Willow is a good specimen of the Weeping Ash which carries on the series of arches, and makes when in leaf a very pleasing colour-contrast with the paler green Willow. The Weeping Willow is a tree that is full of interesting associations, so we will sit on the

My Garden in Spring

seat under this one to review some of them. The use of the Willow as an emblem of grief is older than the introduction of the weeping variety, for most of our older English poets have connected the ordinary Willow with sorrow, and especially that of forsaken lovers. Shakespeare writes of it in connection with grief at least eight times ; and Ophelia fell into the stream when endeavouring to hang her garland on a Willow. Was it then on account of the wailing sound of the English name, or, as some think, did the literary association arise from the Bible translation of the hundred and thirty-seventh Psalm : " By the waters of Babylon we sat down ; yea, we wept when we remembered Zion. We hanged our harps upon the Willows in the midst thereof " ? This latter seems the most likely explanation I have met with. It has frequently been asserted that the Willow growing along the banks of the Euphrates is actually this Weeping Willow, and on that account its scientific name is *Salix babylonica*. Linnaeus certainly gave it the name under this impression, and I must own to a feeling of disappointment in having to bow to such great authorities as Messrs. Elwes and Henry, who declare in their great joint work that the trees of that Psalm are *Populus euphratica*, and that this Willow does not occur now in Babylonia, and its original home is Central and Southern China. But if this fond old belief has to be abandoned, it is pleasant to have this tree thus surely connected with the familiar one on the Willow Pattern plates that has provided the name for that celebrated Chinese landscape design, in spite of the fact that the acrobatic pair of forky-tailed birds and the wonderfully fertile apple tree that bears such a crop of fruit without

The Iris Walk in May

a single leaf, are far more remarkable than the moribund, sparsely-branched Willow. The date of its introduction to England is doubtful, but it was before 1730, for it was included as " S. orientalis, the weeping Willow vulgo " in a catalogue of trees and shrubs of that date, and from Dillwyn's *Hortus Collinsonianus* we learn " Mr Vernon, Turkey merchant at Aleppo, transplanted the Weeping Willow from the River Euphrates and brought it with him to England and planted it at his seat at Twickenham Park, where I saw it growing anno 1748. This is the original of all the Willows in our gardens. In July 1765 I measured a Weeping Willow at Mr. Snelling's at Godalming, Surrey, of about fifteen years' standing ; it measured six feet in girth, or two feet in diameter, and the height in proportion," and therefore we must not credit Pope with its introduction, though we may still believe the tale that he was visiting Lady Suffolk when she received a present from Turkey which was bound round by Willow twigs, and he noticed that some of them were alive, and took them to plant, saying, " Perhaps these may produce something which we have not in England." One of them grew in the garden of his villa at Twickenham into the Weeping Willow afterwards so celebrated, and which was cut down in the year 1801, by the then owner of the villa, because he was so much annoyed by the numbers of people who came and asked to see it. Shortly after this the Weeping Willow became associated with Napoleon. When General Beatson was Governor of St. Helena, he had some trees sent out from England to plant in the island, and a Weeping Willow was among them, and had grown into a fine tree by the time of

My Garden in Spring

Napoleon's imprisonment on the island. He had a seat placed under it, and frequently sat there, as it was close to a spring, the water of which he liked to drink. About the time of the Emperor's death, a storm shattered the tree, and Mme. Bertrand planted some cuttings of it round Napoleon's grave. Before the opening of the Suez Canal, ships touched at St. Helena on their way home from the East round the Cape of Good Hope, and the passengers generally visited Napoleon's tomb and brought away cuttings of the Willow, which quickly rooted in a bottle of water, and were ready to be planted by the time they reached England. Several trees in this neighbourhood are known to have been brought in this way from St. Helena, and I believe the tree here was a cutting from one of them. An Arabian legend tells that the Weeping Willow sprang from the tears David wept when he repented of the murder of Uriah.

It is a favourite plant throughout the temperate regions for planting in cemeteries. The pendant branches I suppose are thought to resemble the hanging head of a mourner, and so we term such forms of trees weeping varieties, but it always strikes me as unfair to associate the Weeping Willow with grief. The grey-leaved Willows are sombre and sad-looking in summer among green-leaved trees, but *S. babylonica* is always the first of deciduous trees to look green in Spring, remains a tender light green all through the summer, and is often one of the latest to shed its leaves, and has the appearance of a flourishing, happy, and gaily-clad tree for a longer period than most others. It is a curious fact that, unlike the other weeping trees, Ash, Beech, Elm and so forth, of

The Iris Walk in May

which the upright forms are the commoner, the supposed upright form of *S. babylonica* known as var. *pekinensis* is exceedingly rare, and has been but lately introduced to Kew.

Now, then after this rest on the seat under the Willow, let us cease our musings over dead poets and emperors and get back to the flowers. Either end of the *Iris florentina* bed is rounded off by one of the two bays formed by the pond ; the Willow benefits by rooting into one of these, and the other helps a clump of *Gunnera chilensis,* as we nowadays must call *G. manicata,* the finest of its family, for though its leaves are not so much indented as those of *G. scabra,* its longer petioles raise them some foot or two higher. In May these leaves are not fully developed, but, unless sharp frosts have been worrying them, should be large enough to be worth looking at and yet not too large to hide the huge cone-shaped heads of insignificant little flowers which show up more then than at any other time. I like to leave one or two of these heads to show what sort of flower these plants think fit to produce, each floret about the size of a housefly's head, while a leaf is five feet across and on a stalk six feet or more high. But I cut off the remainder of the dozen or so flower-heads that my clump produces, as I think their loss encourages it to put its strength into the leaves.

A round bed in the turf comes between the pond and river here, and a fastigiate Hawthorn grows in its centre and makes a good contrast to the Weeping Ash of the other bay of the pond. Now we will turn to the left and follow the pond edge until we get a view right

My Garden in Spring

across its width to the stone steps. I built them out of the debris of an old house that was pulled down on an outlying part of the estate. The old doorsteps, copings, and window-sills and some black and white hall flooring have met again here, and look as though they had· been quarried for the purpose, and that some centuries ago, now that various plants have sprung up in the cracks and holes. They make a convenient place to stand a collection of Agaves, Aloes, and other specimen succulent plants during the summer; the first arrivals, Agaves and Agapanthus in tubs had just been placed there when the photograph facing p. 148 was taken. The large Bog Myrtle on the left bank behind the clump of *Scirpus lacustris* is a fine specimen of which I am very proud. Round its feet I grow a collection of various forms of *Caltha palustris*, and one of the best is var. *semi-plena*, not quite so heavy as the other doubles. But all of them look well from the windows of the house as seen growing on the water's edge and reflected in it. It is astonishing how many forms there are of this plant. *Monstrosa, fl. pl.*, is the earliest to flower here, and makes a compact mass of glowing yellow bloom very wonderful when doubled by reflection in water : var. *purpurascens* is a deeply coloured single form with purple stems, very rich and effective. Tyerman's var., a large pale but clear yellow form, has the most perfectly formed flowers : var. *sibirica* has small flowers and a habit of rooting at the ends of the long stalks that bear them, so that it soon founds a colony, and seems to prefer to grow in shallow water, and so carries out the golden effect further from the bank. A minor form I found in the New Forest keeps its character here, and flowers late.

The Iris Walk in May

A somewhat similar one from Ingleborough, that Mr. Farrer led me up to see and advised me to collect, is interesting in that it has the appearance of the rare northern *C. radicans*, with sagittate leaves, but it does no *radic-ing* as do the true species and var. *sibirica* and the emperor of the whole family, *C. polypetala*. I do so greatly regret that the introducer to Britain of this last noble plant denies the lovely legend that was invented about it, and declares that the Vatican gardener willingly presented portions of it to Miss Hanbury, and of course once it had reached La Mortola everyone knows how generously it would be distributed. It was such a good lie that I still try to believe it. I dare not grow this giant among the others, or it would soon be all giant and no others, so it has a corner of the pond to itself. The white species of Caltha, *C. biflora*, *C. leptosepala*, and *C. rotundifolia*, are in a choice corner of the rock garden as they are such neat growers, but alas! very stingy in giving me any of their Grass of Parnassus-like flowers. Right about turn and back to the river bank, please, and on our left we find the Iris borders again. It is too early for their great show of bloom, but the race of Intermediate Irises raised and distributed by Mr. Caparne of Guernsey come out in late May. Those I like best are Golden Fleece, a large-flowered free form like a soft yellow *florentina;* Edith, a starch blue with darker shadings, and Ivorine, creamy white. All of these have very showy orange-coloured beards. The beds are mostly edged with dwarf Irises, which keep up a succession of flowers from the beginning of April to the end of May. These dwarf forms have been known as *pumila* varieties, but except

229

for the two pale blue forms that open the season for bearded Irises, there is not a true *pumila* among them.

Chamaeiris has provided several purple and yellow forms, and *I. Reichenbachii* others, all of which have unbranched flower stems. *I. aphylla* gives us innumerable shades with many flowered stems, and under this name are now included the rich purple, blue-bearded plant we used to call *I. Benacensis*, and that strange, dingy-flowered thing formerly known as *I. pumila gracilis*. The colour is about as lovely as the waistcoat of a defunct toad, being a pale buff bun-bag shade, mottled irregularly with smoky grey, but it flowers with such freedom that one can hardly see leaves for flowers, and in the afternoon sunlight a length of it planted as an edging lights up in such a charming way that I always enjoy the effect thus produced, especially where the flower-stems fall out over the grass path. It is also good for cutting, for even the youngest buds will open in water, and they are much lighter and more pleasing in colour when opened in a room. The best of this section is a garden-raised plant known as Leander, a really good yellow, and very floriferous ; Bluebeard and Blanche announce their colours in their names, and are good companions for Leander. The old blue *germanica* is a wonderfully useful plant, quite the best tempered and most generous I ever met for dry, overhung, or starved positions, therefore it appears in large bands and masses at the back of these borders round the old Yew trunks, and is a grand bit of colour when in full flower. The purple form known as Kharput does almost as well under this studied neglect, but its flower-stems being taller it is inclined to drive forward towards the light and then to fall over.

The Iris Walk in May

It has the longest fall of any Iris I know. Here and there among the broad-leaved flag Irises appear the long, narrow leaves of the Little Widow, La Vedorina of Italian gardens, no longer allowed to be an Iris, and obliged even to change her sex and reappear as *Hermodactylus tuberosus*. What a pity it is that the question of votes for women cannot be as easily settled by allowing Mary and Jane to appear on the register as Tom and Harry. I love this weird little flower, made up of the best imitation I have ever seen in vegetable tissues of dull green silk and black velvet—in fact it looks as if it had been plucked from the bonnet of some elderly lady of quiet tastes in headgear. I am fond of picking just enough for a vaseful to stand among other vases holding Daffodils ; both the sombre Little Widow and the gay bachelor Daffs gain by the contrast.

A portion of one of the Iris beds was taken out to a depth of three feet and then treated as nearly as we could arrange it in imitation of the wonderful hollow of shell-sand among the sand-hills outside Haarlem where the celebrated Regelio-cyclus Irises have their happy home under the protection of Mynheer van Tubergen. I have no shell-sand and no dunes, but my favourite birdcage variety of sand and the screening Yew trees are used as substitutes. We, as well as the Dutch, have cows, so we can provide the same form of nutrition for the Irises here as that which agrees so well with them in Holland. The lower portion of this hole we fill with manure collected directly from the meadows where the cows are browsing, and then cover it with about six inches of the yellow sand in which lie the rhizomes of the precious Irises, while their roots can wander down and feed fatly. Artemis,

My Garden in Spring

Hera, Charon, and Isis were very beautiful this May after two years in the sand, and *Gladiolus atroviolaceus*, a dainty Spring-flowering species of lovely amethyst colouring, shares their bed and seems to enjoy the same treatment.

I think more could be made of this layered mixture of sand and manure for voracious but easily-rotted plants. I am now trying a few of the Oncocyclus species here, and in this, their first year, we rejoiced in fine blooms of susiana, &c., but I can hardly hope to solve the difficulty of their cultivation so easily.

Of course Irises are to be found in other parts of the garden, but these beds are so well suited for those that love drought and heat, such as the Bearded Flags, that they contain the main collection, and those that prefer a cooler root-run find it elsewhere. *I. longipetala* and its near relations, for instance, are planted among herbaceous plants, and are very useful for flowering in late May, and good for cutting. The Crocus frame has been found to be the only satisfactory home for *I. Sisyrinchium*, the most widely distributed species of the whole family. I have collected it in Egypt, where it is so abundant on the lower flats of desert round Cairo that it colours the landscape with a purple haze for miles from noon to teatime, just while the fugacious flowers are open. It has been said that it is the flower a business man never sees, except on Sundays and Whit Monday, for when brought to England it still adheres to its hours of opening and closing as punctually as a public-house. The little flowers are very lovely when you do see them, and so many are produced on one scape that a good succession is kept up. I found some charming white-flowered ones in the desert,

Eucalyptus cordata.   (See p. 285.)

The Iris Walk in May

but they have long since disappeared, and only the purple type with its conspicuous white-spotted falls now appears in the frame. I have had it sent to me from Spain, Malta, and Afghanistan, but can see no difference among them. *Iris mellita* flowered well this year in the rock garden in early May. It is very dwarf, with large, well-formed flowers of a dull rosy plum colour, but very distinct and pleasing, quite welcome to its sunny ledge, and too small in stature to be trusted even in the very front of the Iris beds.

I hope in another volume to lead you along these beds on a June day among the pallidas and other summer glories, but now we will pass by them, and try not to tread on the Fantail pigeons that will walk under our feet, leave the Lunatic Asylum on our left, gaze for a minute or two at the fine bole of the isolated Yew, the last of the row in this direction, a pillar of clustered columns that I am never tired of admiring, and so past the first of the leaden ostriches that guard the bridge over the river, and then looking through the ivy-clad arch into the kitchen garden I hope the stretch of May-flowering Tulips under the wall will hold your attention long enough to let me turn over a page and begin a new chapter.

CHAPTER XV

Tulips

BEFORE I can permit you to go through the archway and down by the Tulip beds I want to air some of my views about Tulips in general, so let us lean on the iron rail of the bridge for a while. It is a very good resting-place in mid-May, for just then it commands the two best views of Tulips in the garden. To our left we can see the long line of choicer sorts growing in a narrow bed under the fruit wall. We look all down this long bed, in which several hundreds of varieties are grown, and seen through the archway the mass of colour is a fine sight on a sunny day. We try to group them in their classes and then again by colours, so that those nearest to us are all Darwins and pink or rose coloured, next come purple and then crimson Darwins, and following them, further away still, are Cottage Tulips, and then the English to finish with. Turning our heads to look straight along the course of the river, we see a stretch of old Yew hedge on our immediate left running parallel with the river bank and starting from the right-hand side of the arch that leads to the kitchen garden and the Tulip beds. The river takes a long curve here, and about half-way along this bend the Yew hedge divides, turning down at a right angle to the path and river, and making room for a terraced garden before the correspond-

Tulips

ing second portion of Yew hedge, with a similarly down-turned end, is reached. In my childhood's days the space between these two hedges was filled by a steep grass slope very suitable for rolling down when no nurse was on guard. Then a wall was built at the foot of the slope and filled in behind with soil and the Terrace formed. It is backed by a low parapet with a wide stone coping, on which a row of stone vases stands all the year and a large collection of succulent plants in pots during the summer months. Stone steps lead down to the kitchen garden at both ends, and between them are fifteen box-edged beds and several stone vases. A stone seat in the centre is made out of portions of the balustrade of Old London Bridge, and three of the balusters stand at the heads of the flights of steps and bear stone vases. I found them hidden away among the shrubs here, but could only find three, so one has for its fellow a stone group of The Three Graces with a stone vase on their lovely heads. These beds are filled with Tulips for Spring, and when at their best look very well viewed from the bridge, and reflected in the river. They are backed by flowering fruit trees below the wall, and then the trees of the park rise up behind on the side of the hill. So rest here and gaze while I tell you that in this garden the word *Tulip* stands only for true species and the May-flowering garden varieties, for I have long ago lost every scrap of affection for the early-flowering garden varieties that are still the most conspicuous Tulips in most public parks and many gardens. I cannot afford them here—space is too valuable, and though of low price they are costly in the end, because very few of them find a sufficiently congenial home in an English garden to think

My Garden in Spring

it worth their while to settle down and produce a good flowering bulb for a second year. They are dumpy, easily destroyed by the bad weather they are almost certain to meet with in April, and need to be renewed or largely reinforced annually from Dutch-grown stocks to give a really good effect. I make an exception in favour of a few of intermediate season of flowering combined with good constitution that are neither dumpy nor difficult to keep, and these I should not like to be without. They flower about the last week of April and the first in May. The variegated form of Yellow Prince that lives in Tom Tiddler's ground is one. White Swan is fairly tall, and bears a beautiful white flower good for borders or cutting. Thomas Moore is an old favourite and a charming shade of soft orange, and Couleur Cardinal is a fiery scarlet when fully open, but in bud and when half expanded has a wonderful plum-like bloom on its crimson external ground-colour. Mr. Van Waveren once told me that he bought the stock of this Tulip when it was first offered. It was one of his earliest purchases, and he gave rather a high price for it. His father, who was present at the sale, asked, "What fool has bought that?" and was very angry when he learnt that it was his son. It proved to be a wise investment, however, and has been for many years the best of all red Early Tulips.

When I can speak of a plant as the Tulipa something-or-other it is of course more precious to my botanical mind, and I should like to grow every species of Tulipa, even the starry green and white early flowering ones such as *biflora* and its near relations, one of which tries to make a floral display in December, but has been so severely snubbed by the Clerk of the Weather that I fear its courage is

236

Tulips

evaporating and it will end the struggle by dying of a broken heart. These look more like some Star-of-Bethlehem than a Tulip, so I feel the real Tulip season commences with the appearance of *T. Kaufmanniana*. Plant it six inches deep at least, and leave it alone, and every March its large, water-lily-shaped flowers should herald in the Tulip days. It varies from white to crimson, and on the way can be pure rich yellow flushed outside with red. Many varieties have been selected and named ; *aurea* and *coccinea* the two finest are very dazzling and wonderful when fully open in the sunshine. I believe in all its forms it has the deep yellow base that helps to make it look like a water-lily on land. *T. dasystemon* has a somewhat similar appearance on a smaller scale. It is dwarf, and a good bulb will bear several flowers which are pure glistening white when open, with a very bright yellow centre, but when closed they are dull and green and still look like some small Nymphaea bud.

It is a charming plant for the rock garden, and is easy to grow. *T. linifolia* and *T. Maximowiczii* are so much alike that it is very hard to distinguish them, but one need not grumble at whichever comes under either name, for both are brilliant scarlet with a black base, of beautiful salver shape when open, and have the neatest possible habit and narrow leaves with waved margins. They do not increase much, but keep in health for many years if occasionally lifted and cleaned by the removal of some of their old jackets. A very curious tuft of woolly hairs ornaments the top of the bulb, and is worth noticing. *Batalinii* is very closely related to these two, and differs chiefly in the colour of its flowers, which are of a lovely soft butter-yellow, but also in increasing well by offsets. Seedlings vary in colour a good deal : I have had buff, salmon, and orange-coloured forms, and one almost as scarlet as *linifolia,* but the base was a light slate grey, not nearly so deep in colour as in *linifolia.* It is quite possible, though, that these colour varieties may be hybrids. One of them was selected some years ago and named Sunset, and received an award at a Temple Show, and I was delighted when I found its exact counterpart among some of my seedlings. *T. Batalinii* is one of the few Tulips that will sow itself in the rock garden. *T. praestans* is a great beauty of pure scarlet, and when robust bears two or more flowers on a stem. Two varieties of it are known, and the earliest and best is called var. *Tubergeniana.* It makes such an early appearance above-ground that it is best planted in a sheltered position facing west or south-west, where it will not be tempted into growth too soon, and the morning sunshine will not fall on its downy leaves while they are still frozen. I have a clump in the rock garden sheltered by some dwarf conifers that in most seasons flares out in its glowing vermilion before one has such a Pomegranate-blossom colouring elsewhere in the open. *T. primulina* is a refined little many-flowered species, and very charming when open in sunshine, but is rather shy about showing off its charms, and too green outside to make much show when closed. *T. stellata* is the Himalayan representative of the well-known *T. Clusiana,* the Lady Tulip, and like it runs about too much at the root making small bulbs, and therefore seldom sends up enough flowers. When they do appear they are very lovely, star-shaped and of a soft sulphur shade, with a deep red base and rosy tints on the outside of the segments,

Tulips

T. oculus solis is rare in English gardens, but grows plenti-
fully round Florence, and it was from thence I obtained it.
It appears to be impossible to buy the true plant from
nurserymen, as *T. praecox* is so largely grown under the
other's name. *Praecox* is a good thing, but is almost
always damaged in our gardens by the frosts that worry
its large, early flowers. It is taller than *oculus solis*, and
has lighter red flowers, which are greenish on the outside
of the three outer segments and wider than they are long.
The true *oculus solis* is deep crimson, and has long, pointed
segments ; the basal eye is composed of a greater proportion of black and less of yellow than that of *praecox*, and
it is also wise enough to wait for finer weather to open
its flowers in.

I must not attempt to describe all the species of
Tulipa I tuck away in the rock garden and choice corners
of sheltered beds, but cannot leave out two which are
special favourites. *T. Fosteriana* is one, and so brilliantly
coloured that at times I think it almost too gorgeous.
The vivid scarlet, with the pure yellow or black and
yellow of the eye, is absolutely dazzling in the sunlight,
and the flowers are so very large for their height ; but
a long bed of it in Zwanenburg Nursery at Haarlem
is one of the most marvellous floral displays I have ever
seen. It is none too vigorous here, and has to be carefully nursed in the peach-house border, where only rare
or tender treasures are admitted. I will close the list of
species with the latest of all, *Tulipa Sprengeri*, an elegant
and tall species with crimson-scarlet flowers ; but it is
always rather sad to see the first one open, for it means
the close of the Tulip season, and that a day or two onward

My Garden in Spring

the hot sun and old age will tell on the Darwin and English Tulips that still remain, and it will be time to go round snapping off the fat green seedpods. It is rather fascinating to place a forefinger on the stalk, and then, pressing it towards you, bend over the seed head with your thumb in the opposite direction, until you feel the sudden snap with which the juicy stalk breaks, and it is good to think that you are thereby aiding the ripening of a fat bulb for next season, but I much prefer gently opening the segments of a half-expanded new variety to see what sort of eye it has, and feeling that its full beauty is still to come. Well, "them's my sentiments" about earlies and species, and now we had better move on and look at the May flowerers before snapping-off time comes upon us. First, then, to the Terrace beds. The shape of the first one we come to is a semicircle, and it is bounded on the straight side by a dry wall built up by the side of the flight of steps and which has a cascade of *Rosa Wichuraiana* hanging down over the stones and mingling with *Othonnopsis cheirifolia*, a good, grey-leaved, succulent plant that thrives in this dry garden in a way that often astonishes people from warmer but moister climates. It is a large bed, and takes a good deal of filling, so we use three kinds of Tulips of orange shades, La Merveille, *Billietiana* "Sunset," and *Gesneriana aurantiaca*, but, excepting this and the two central beds, all the others are filled with one variety only. Thus the next contains Mr. Farncombe Sanders. Tall, and of dazzling rose-scarlet with immense blooms, I do not know a better Tulip for distant effect, and can only charge him with one fault, and that is, he loses his head in sudden danger, for a heavy shower coming quickly after sunshine

240

Tulips

catches the immense flowers half open and weights them with water till they bend over and snap, and I have seen a bed decimated in this manner in a few minutes. A bed of Clara Butt comes next, and her lovely, soft, warm pink blends well with the scarlet on one side and the deep rich maroon-crimson of King Harold in the next bed. The fine old scarlet *Gesneriana*, with its wonderful blue eye, is one of the most effective of all Tulips, and so fills two beds on this terrace, and looks very well between King Harold and a bed of the still deeper brown-purple of Philippe de Comines, described in bulb lists as velvety-black. Next we come to the two circular central beds on either side of a fine tripodal stone vase, and these are filled with two yellow varieties in alternating rings. *Retro-flexa* flowers first and goes over rather too soon, so Parisian Beauty, which is a later bloomer, then takes up its duties and keeps the yellow beds bright to the end. We have generally had a bed of *La Noire* for the next, but although it looks well next to the yellow, it is too dark to be effective from a distance, and most likely will be replaced by something lighter next season. Europe is my favourite of the glowing orange-salmon shades ; it is one of the few Darwins with a pure white base, and the bed devoted to it is a lovely sight when full of its flowers. The next bed we thought rather a bold venture when we first planned it, for we were half in doubt whether the cool lilac tint of Erguste would look well between the two salmon scarlets, Europe of the last bed and Laurentia of the next, which are very similar in general outside appearance, but Laurentia differs in possessing a rim of pale blue round the white of the base. However, we were delighted

241   Q

My Garden in Spring

with the effect both when standing among the beds and also from a distance. I have long preached that Erguste is the best of the lilac Darwins, but many people think otherwise and cry up The Rev. Ewbank. I must confess that I am rather particular, and I dislike any Darwin that has a paler edge to the segments, and a dingy grey look about the central darker portion, and I find both of these unpleasing features in Ewbank. To my mind they make it look faded and weary even when young, whereas Erguste is as nearly self-coloured throughout as one could expect, and looks as clean and fresh as a newly washed and starched lilac sunbonnet, until the segments are ready to drop. All these lilac Darwins seem to inherit one fault with their colour, they are more open to flattery than their red brethren, and the west winds of Spring can persuade them that they are indispensable and the world is waiting for them, and that they must hurry up at once, and they generally push out leaves sooner than they should.

The flowers of purple and lilac Darwins, as a rule, open before those of other colours, but that could be forgiven them, and their particular foolishness and unforgiveable sin lies in starting into growth too soon. Last winter was very bad for them in that respect. The west wind roused them in their beds before Christmas, and in a lying spirit declared it was half past winter and time to get up ; their hot water was provided by warm showers, and they popped their noses out of the curtains and found it was so pleasant and muggy that they grew away as fast as they could, and so had large, tender leaves and exposed buds by the end of March that would have done them credit a month later ; all those bitter winds

Tulips

and cold hail-showers of last April bruised and worried them, and large patches of decay began to show themselves, and then the dreadful ravages of the disease that Tulip-growers call "fire" spread through the bed, and ate into the flower-stems, and robbed us of the fine effect we had enjoyed the season before. Another bed of *Gesneriana* follows Laurentia, and then one of *elegans alba*, one of the most lovely of Spring flowers. I love the pointed shape of this and its sisters, *elegans*, *fulgens*, and *retroflexa*. They have been named as though they were wild specific forms, but I was told by a Dutch grower that he had spoken to an old man who remembered the first appearance of all four of them in one seed-bed in Holland. It is supposed that they are crosses between *T. acuminata* and some other form of *Gesneriana*, the pointed reflexing character of the flowers coming from *acuminata*, which from its curious, long, slender segments has gained the name of the Chinese Tulip—I imagine because they suggest the finger-nails of a mandarin. *Elegans alba* is much more like a white form of *fulgens* than of *elegans* in its greater height, later time of flowering, and less recurved segments. These are pure white, beautifully edged with the finest imaginable wire-edge line of crimson. It is very effective in this bed, but equally good for planting in borders among herbaceous plants. The last of the Terrace beds has for many years been filled with the white-eyed *Gesneriana* that has two names, *Gesneriana albo oculata* and Rosalind. It is rather later than the others on the Terrace, and I must confess of too blue a rose colour to go anywhere but at the end, and I expect you can guess that the white bed is placed next to it on purpose to cut it off from the

My Garden in Spring

scarlet and salmon shades. Everybody admires it when thus isolated, especially with the evening sunlight shining through it, but in all lights the purity of its white base, with a wee touch of ivory in its very eye, is wonderfully satisfying against the vivid rose segments. It appears to have one of the best constitutions of all, and once purchased should never fail to fill its allotted space and provide offsets for growing on as well. All these beds have to be lifted annually to make way for summer bedding plants, and it is therefore necessary to get the Tulips ripened off as early as possible. So as soon as the segments fall I snap off the seed-heads, and it is wonderful how soon one can lift after the loss of their seedpods has removed all inducement to keep their roots actively at work. We apply the old test of Tulip-growers of bygone days, and as soon as we can curl a flower-stem round a finger without its snapping feel it safe to lift the bulbs and lay them in a dry bed of light soil to ripen off. With this treatment we can generally rely on sound, large bulbs for another season, but we keep a certain number of offsets planted up in the kitchen garden to draw upon should one of our Terrace varieties fail in size or number. So let us turn down the steps at this end of the Terrace and go past these beds of offsets. Many varieties we shall see are flowering freely from the small bulbs, but though as a matter of course the blossoms are not so fine as those from full-sized ones, they are very useful for cutting. Turning to the left, we pass the Strawberry beds, and then the range of vineries and the Crocus frames we visited in February, and so reach the wall and the long bed of Tulips. I have generally planted it in alternate rows of Tulips and Carnations for

244

Tulips

economy's sake, on the same principle as the excuse of the child rebuked for extravagance in eating butter and jam on one piece of bread, that it was economical to make the same slice do for both. But this year we tried separating the quondam partners, and were rather pleased at being able to harvest the Tulips earlier than Carnation-layering time, and to manure and crop the vacant ground to get it ready for next season's bulbs. By this route we come first to the English varieties, the very élite of the Tulip world, for after the Dutch, Flemish, and French florists had developed the Tulip to a certain standard, the English florists took it in hand, and became much more exacting in their requirements, and succeeded in producing a strain of more symmetrical, cup-shaped flowers with purer bases and ground colours than had been known before.

The love of the English Tulip may be an acquired taste, but I am sure it is really good taste, and just as an art connoisseur will turn away from showy, meretricious objects to a really fine piece of work even though it may need looking into and handling to appreciate its best points, so will anyone who compares many Tulips, and has access to really well-grown English florists' varieties, grow to love the beautiful proportions and delicate featherings or rich contrasts of the best of them more than any gorgeous display of Darwins. Not that I wish in any way to disparage Darwin Tulips for garden display, or even for cutting for large vases in halls and large rooms. But one could not hang the walls of a picture gallery with Limoges enamels instead of pictures, nor banish the Apollo Belvedere from his pedestal in the Vatican to make room for a Japanese netsuke, and so there are no English Tulips on the Terrace,

but here they are at the end of the Tulip beds to linger
over and enjoy, and to cut for some small, good old
glass vases for the dinner-table, or the writing-table in
my own sanctum, and for these purposes nothing liliaceous can vie with them. I am sorry to say they are
not easy to grow in their best form here ; the Breeders
break too easily, and some of the finer Roses or
Bybloemen become flushed or coarse, but a few good
flowers appear each year among them and make us hope
to do better next time. Let us examine one or two carefully, that in case you need conversion to a true love for
them I may have a chance of effecting it. I wonder how
deeply you are steeped in Tulip lore ? If you prefer a
Rose fr. to a Rose fld. please skip the next page, but if
you do not understand those mystic words pray read on.
Now I will pick this exquisitely soft-rose coloured one. It
is labelled Annie McGregor, Breeder. Notice first the
proportions : in outline it is a sphere with the upper one-
third removed : see how smoothly rounded the edges of the
segments are, how clean and white the base is, and how
distinctly it ends and the rose colour commences. This
is the form in which this beautiful Tulip first appeared
when it flowered in the seed-bed many years ago, and it
and one called Mabel are still the best Rose Breeders
known. You think Breeder is an ugly name for such a
lovely flower ? Perhaps it is, but it has a meaning, and
tells us how that at one time these self-coloured Tulips
were not valued at all for their pure self-colour, but only
because they were the possible parents of striped forms.
For all seedling florists' Tulips are self-coloured as seedlings,
and remain so for a number of years, seldom less than six

Tulips

but sometimes many more, then a few bulbs of the stock are liable to suddenly change ("break" is the technical term for it), and the old ground-colour then appears as stripes on whichever colour, white or yellow, was most prevalent in the eye or base of the self-coloured Breeder. Now look at the next row ; it is labelled Annie McGregor Rose fld., and you will see that though exactly similar in shape and size, and with the same white eye, this form is practically a white Tulip with finely-pencilled, rose-coloured featherings round the edges of the segments, and up the centre of each there is a broad band, called a flame, of the same rose shade.   This is the broken form of the same Tulip, Annie McGregor, and would be shown in the class for Flamed Roses : now you know what fld. means.   The next row is labelled similarly, but has " fr. " instead of " fld." at the end, and you can see at a glance that the flowers are much the same as the last, but the segments are pure white except for the featherings of rose-colour round their edges, and so are Feathered Roses this time, and I may tell you that you are very lucky if you do find this last one as I describe it, for it is precious seldom I can manage to grow a perfect feather in this garden.   Higher up the bed you will find Byb. fld. on labels, and will notice that here again we may have the same variety as a lilac self with a white base or as a white flower feathered, or feathered and flamed, with some shade of lilac or purple instead of rose, and these bear the old Dutch name of Bybloemen. Further on we have some selfs, purple, chocolate, or rich red and almost scarlet, but in all of these the bases are bright yellow instead of white, and when they break the ground-colour becomes yellow with marvellous, rich tones of copper,

My Garden in Spring

bronze, black, brown, or crimson, mixing or lying alongside, to form the feathers and flames. This group bears the name Bizarre, and they also can be Breeders or fr. or fld. Sir Joseph Paxton is one of the best, and a good instance of a flower that can appear in all three forms of a Bizarre. The flamed Sir Joseph is one of my greatest favourites, and the colouring is like some grand old piece of buhl, and I keep on turning such a flower round and round to try and settle which of its segments is the most perfectly coloured and the best to place towards me as I dine or write. I believe the love for the English Tulip will some day revive and perhaps grow into a rage, and that the noble little band who keep up its cultivation and the Royal National Tulip Society are doing a great work for future gardeners. How many conversions has this sermon produced ? The outward and visible sign of one is the posting of a letter to the Secretary of the Society (W. Peters, Farcet House, Cambridge) asking for full particulars and election as a member, and help in the shape of a few bulbs to start your collection. After the rows of English end we come to Cottage Tulips, a very elastic term, for it includes all the late kinds that are not true species, Darwins or florists' forms. I have too large a collection to be fully described here.

The beautiful illustration (facing p. 176) shows two of my favourites, but it is hard to pick out any and leave out others in such a wonderful range of colours and forms. Walter T. Ware is certainly the best deep yellow, Louis XIV is a wonderful combination of rich plum-purple and golden bronze, and looks as though shot with the two colours. Don Pedro is a rich brown, John Ruskin long and egg-shaped and apricot-orange shaded with rose and lilac, and as if that

248

A happy accident in grouping. (See p. 285.)

Tulips

were not enough has an edge of yellow just the shade of a beaten-up egg. Sir Harry is a lovely mauve-pink, and breaks into a still more wonderful thing known as Striped Beauty, in which the original rosy-lilac shade has crimson and cerise stripes added to it. There are many kinds of various shades of yellow, reckoned as cottage varieties, and some of them have been already mentioned as forming part of the golden store of Tom Tiddler's ground, but a reserve fund of some of the best is kept here. Pure whites are scarce; Albion and L'Innocence are the best, but Picotee with a rose-coloured edge, and Carnation with more and deeper rose colour, are exquisite pale flowers, and this class includes the two varieties of the Green Tulip, *T. viridiflora praecox* and *tardiva ;* the former and earlier one is the best with a larger flower, and of a better and softer green ; the other has a wide yellow edge to its segments and is not so pleasing. The early one is very pretty when cut and grouped with rose-coloured Tulips. Then we reach the Darwins, and the first few rows here are like the horrid child's sweet and were pink once, but have broken and so become what the Dutch nurserymen have christened Rembrandt Tulips. Some of them are very beautiful with bold splashes of crimson and scarlet on a white ground, but when they break they always lose a few inches of their stature, and I am afraid some of their grand sturdy constitution goes too, for they never seem as healthy as their breeder forms, the Darwins. Among the red Darwins Isis stands out as the very brightest and best. La Noire is the nearest to black I grow, and quite as near as one wants a flower to be. Margaret is the palest pink I care about. Nigrette is a curious and beautiful brown red, the Bishop the best bright purple and Faust the best dark purple. In among these various kinds, and always in what we consider the choicest, cosiest place, irrespective of what are its neighbours, we plant my best beloved of all Tulips, a wonderful old Dutch variety called Zomerschoon. It has a groundwork of old ivory or softest primrose heavily striped and flamed with a glorious, glowing salmon-red; the base is sulphur yellow, and in the sunlight casts a primrose glow over the whole interior of the flower, especially in a newly-opened blossom. It is seen at its best in the morning sunlight, and when the first blossoms open I find it hard to tear myself away from them, so intensely do I enjoy the glow of the blend of salmon and primrose tints in their cups. As the flowers age the sulphur fades to ivory white and the red markings deepen a good deal: they are still beautiful, but not so marvellously glowing and subtle as in the day-old blossoms. It is a very old Tulip, and I have a rather poor figure of it in a Dutch book dated 1794, but it has always been scarce, as it does not increase so fast as others, and so has always been rather high in price, but the last two years have seen a change, and now eighteen pence will buy a good bulb of it.

The tallest of all Tulips is *T. fulgens*, one of the pointed-petalled set I have already mentioned. Three feet of stem I should say would be its average height. It is a glowing pure crimson, and its beautiful, soft-yellow base is too pale to be open to an accusation of gaudiness even when seen by the side of so bright a crimson. Some years ago I planted a clump among some patches of *Iris ochroleuca*, and the effect of the great, sword-shaped leaves of the Iris among the tall Tulips was very good, but the group had to be removed to make way for a new Yew hedge, and I have

Tulips

always meant to make another similar planting, but time
and space have not allowed it as yet.   This grand Tulip is
good almost anywhere, and very suitable in a bed of tall
herbaceous plants, as it produces a grand mass of colour in
May, and is well out of the way before Delphiniums and
other tall plants are clamouring for head-room.

Like other Tulips planted in groups in the permanent
borders, it requires lifting and thinning every second or
third year, or the bulbs scrouge each other, and grow
smaller and weaker until nothing but leaves appear, and
Tulips are not worth space as foliage plants.

CHAPTER XVI

My Rock Garden

MY rock garden is a home-made affair, that is to say I planned, built, and planted it, and have had the chief hand in caring for it for twenty years. When I say built I mean I chose out the stone for each position, helped to move it and generally gave it the final lift or shove, or jumped up and down on the top of it, to fix it in place just as I wanted it, but, of course, several heads and hands helped me, especially with the large blocks and the excavating and shovelling up of soil. It was formed a bit at a time, and always under the belief that the present piece of work was to be the very utmost extent that was likely to be undertaken, and so of necessity it possesses many faults. I can see that had it been planned as a whole I could have greatly improved it, and as the oldest portion, which dates from 1893, was my first piece of work of the kind, I have learnt something since then. It is a rock garden but by no means an alpine garden, for though alpine plants have a first choice of places I have always been ready to plant any bush or even tree in it, that I think will grow better for the advantages of drainage and protection the chosen site will afford it. I often say that I must reserve a new wing for choice alpines only or clear out an older range for them, then I come along with a choice young Eucalyptus in a pot, or one of the giants of the Eryngium family such as *E. serra* or *E. Lasseauxii,* or some other

My Rock Garden

son of Anak; a suitable cosy nook is given to the poor homeless waif, and so long as plants flourish I cannot bring myself to destroy their happiness. So do not expect the orthodox grouping of dwarf alpines, or even carefully-stratified stones, for I have never hesitated to stand a large, flat block up on end to form a miniature south wall for tender sun-lovers, but I have always had the sense to fill in the back of such an one with soil and continue the rise above the stone, and so treated the bank looks natural enough. I have used Kentish rag throughout, and until my ship comes home with a cargo of more guineas than I know what to do with I shall not change it for mountain limestone. The rag weathers well here, grows as much moss as I care about, and tones to a good soft grey colour; it has enough sandstone facing on some blocks to make a little crumbling surface for some of the plants to root into, and yet is solid enough to resist the weather. It may flake a little its first winter, but not sufficiently to do any harm.

Much of the rock garden is built on a steep clay bank that Sir Hugh Myddelton constructed three hundred years ago to support this loop of the New River and so carry it round the valley instead of, as now, across it in pipes: that means the upper edge of my rock garden must be a straight line bounded by the walk along the riverside. A second straight walk had been made along the foot of the bank, and this also has had to be respected, but a triangular portion of the meadow was cut off, in two bites and with several years between each mouthful, and forms the main expanse of rock garden and saves it from the stiff outline that

My Garden in Spring

would have been the result of only using the bank. We reach the newest portion first, a good long stretch of bank between the river above and the meadow below. In the centre of this is the fish-hatchery moraine bed I have described in a former chapter, and as the whole bank faces due south such a sheltered home for new plants has filled up with marvellous rapidity. I was obliged to plant a screen of Hollies and other evergreens at the top by the river-walk, as otherwise there would be no intervening protection between the rock garden and the North Pole. This bank has had a year to get covered, and this May morning is full of flowers.

From a long way off one sees a glowing orange patch that at close quarters turns out to be *Meconopsis heterophylla*, the only member of the family that comes from America. It is hard to beat when well grown, but an annual, and unless self-sown is difficult to induce to grow into a strong tuft. The plants we are looking at appeared last autumn, and though they looked very sad during cold and wet spells of winter weather, they battled through, keeping a few of their many-patterned leaves green in spite of frosts and slugs, and starting off into rapid growth in Spring. Now they bear a thick crop of orange coloured flowers of a particularly beautiful shade that is greatly improved by the deep chocolate-red eye. Above them *Linum arboreum* is a solid sheet of the clearest Daffodil yellow, very effective wedged between two large blocks of grey stone. *Helianthemum umbellatum* is full of its dainty white flowers, and one of the most refined and beautiful members of this sun-loving family, and very different in

My Rock Garden

its very neat, narrow leaves and upright growth from the sprawling, coarser-growing kinds. Its near relation, *H. libanoticum*, which is practically a yellow-flowered counterpart of it, and the still more dwarf *lunulatum*, are equally neat growers.

At the foot of the steps that lead up to the moraines *Aquilegia viridiflora* is in full bloom. It is a very unusual-looking flower, for its petals are dark purplish-brown, and its sepals a curious dull green that harmonises beautifully with the dark circular petticoat. The spurs are long and without hooks at their ends, and the anthers protrude and add to the grace of the flower. There is a charming figure of it in Jacquin's *Icones Plantarum Rariorum*. It is not an easy plant to please, but in this spot it is as happy as I ever saw it.

One seldom sees *Lotus Tetragonolobus* in England, but it is well worth a place at the foot of the rock garden, where it makes a cheerful green carpet for many months, and now and then gives out a scent so much like cow's breath that the first time I got a whiff of it I turned round to look for the cow, and finding none traced the milky odour to the plant. I do not understand the conditions under which this scent is produced, for I often try to smell it myself or present it to the noses of others and fail, and then occasionally it is quite strong on the air even without touching the plant. The large, solitary, pea-shaped flowers are of a delightfully soft yellow, and in a garden specimen are much more freely produced than those one sees scattered here and there in the Alpine pasture. The seeds are four-sided and bear prominent wings on each

255

My Garden in Spring

angle, and so have provided it with the majestically sonorous word once its generic but now reduced to its specific name. When it was followed by *siliquosus* it was mightily filling for a label, but sounded as though it might be an efficacious spell against witches if pronounced impressively.

Viola bosniaca is a mass of bloom up among the higher rocks, and has sown itself so freely that a dozen or so large plants are staring at us with their friendly rosy faces. I wish I could say the same of *V. calcarata*, which was planted close by it and has grown into a yard-wide bed of leaves of a Watercress appearance, and is bearing three blooms and no promise of more. Yet these very plants were solid bunches of flowers when I dug them up on Mt. Cenis two years ago. *Helichrysum bellidioides* has lived here through three winters, but was so badly cut that it had all it could do to try and look green again during summer, and found no time to waste on flowers until I planted a bit at the foot of a stone facing due south and gave it a lean-to of glass. The mild winter has favoured it, and it is now thickly covered with pure white Daisies and well repays the little extra trouble. A fine specimen of *Muehlehbeckia varians* stands as the boundary post between this newly-built rock bank and the older portion, mainly devoted to succulent plants. I find it hardier than *M. complexa*, and though it looks a bit shabby by the end of the winter, after I have cut its hair and the warm rains come and shampoo its head it is soon covered with its characteristic fiddle-shaped leaves, and later in the season produces heart-shaped ones as well, and bunches of minute greenish flowers, but I have not yet had berries on it. It

256

is trained up poles and is now about nine feet high. Here I grow a good many of the giant Eryngiums, such as *serra* with rosettes of green, two-edged saws, *agavifolium* with sword-fish snouts for leaves, *Sanguisorba* with glaucous grassy leaves and flower heads, anyone might be forgiven for believing to be a true Sanguisorba ; *Lasseauxii*, the giant of the family, with narrow leaves six feet long, looking like some great Pandanus, and a set of queer hybrids that defy classification and have taken up positions where I could permit them to remain and develop. A few good Yuccas share the bank with these, and lead one's mind gently on to the Prickly Pears and other Cacti, Bromeliads, Dasylirions, Agaves, and other succulents for which the rest of this bank is reserved. We must stop to admire two Oxalis species that grow among the Eryngiums. *Oxalis purpurea* is full of flowers which are large and crimson by courtesy, but rather close to magenta I fear in fact, a colour I can forgive in an Oxalis though not in a zonal Pelargonium. Just above it *O. brasiliensis* is only commencing to flower, and is a better shade of crimson. These two have lived amicably in this nook for many years, and are very brilliant in Spring, and look well among the subtropical foliage around them, though neither would be pleasing near scarlet flowers. *Cereus paucispinus* is full of fat flower-buds promising a gorgeous patch of scarlet for next month, and several of the Echinopsis section of Cereus show grey tufts of wool where their large white or pink flowers are to come. The young growths of the Opuntias have not yet taken on the round outline that means flowers or flattened out to show they are only fresh branches.

My Garden in Spring

It is too early in the year to fully enjoy this bank of prickly things, so turn and look at the opposite side of the path, for here one of the corners of the triangular main portion of this rock garden has its commencement. A northern slope is crowned with tall growing plants to give more shade lower down. A fine specimen of silver-leaved Rue is now very effective, the young leaves as white as ivory. A fine purple effect is given by *Clematis Pallasii fol. purpureis.* It has the habit and flowers, later on of course, of *C. recta,* but is as rich in colour as a Copper Beech while its leaves are young. The large spherical heads of *Allium Rosenbachianum* rise up beside it, and their mauve colouring is charming against its purple leaves. The double Welsh Poppy *Meconopsis cambrica fl. pl.* is rather inclined to play the weed on the lower slope, and tries to smother *Saxifraga sarmentosa,* which is as happy here round the feet of the stones as it is in cottage windows, where it is known as "Mother of Thousands." *Ranunculus nyssanus* runs about freely, and its large varnished Buttercup flowers are good with the deeper orange of the Poppy. *Orchis sambucina* from Mt. Cenis is giving me half a dozen lovely sulphur spikes charming in contrast with a colony of a good blue-lilac form of *Phlox divaricata,* var. *canadensis.* Of course my usual space-grudging views have led me to pack a hundred and one other plants among these, so that the ground is full of bulbs, Dianthus species, *Primula marginata, P. Auricula* and several others, Saxifrages, Potentillas, and too long a list to remember, let alone to write out, but at this moment the effect is produced by those I have named as being in flower. Such totally different styles of shrubs as

My Rock Garden

two Caraganas, a fine specimen of the mop-headed Bladder Senna, *Colutea arborescens*, var. *bullata*, *Viburnum bullatum*, *Hedera conglomerata*, and a spreading tree of the pink double Cherry J. H. Veitch, form the forest of the slopes and ridge, and in their shade Ramondias have made some fine rosettes. *Anemone nemorosa* forms are happy in a level bay, and other woodland things like *Trillium grandiflorum* and Snowdrops as well as a clump of *Lilium Marhan* find a home.

We are now opposite an old ivy-covered summer-house, that was here long before the rock garden was begun, and tucked away under a fine old Thorn it is not too incongruous to be left and utilised as a tool-shed and a refuge in sudden storms. Opposite its door the main path turns down the slope to the south, runs through the centre of the triangle of rock garden and leads at the lower end to a wooden bridge over a pool, and then through a meadow and into the park, and as it forms the short cut between us and my brother's house on the other side of the park it is a rather wider path than is necessary in a rock garden. Branch paths run right and left from it, and lead down into two excavated hollows with high mounds to flank each of them on all their sides, which mounds form the four somewhat parallel ranges of mountains that are the main portion of the rock garden. We will take the left-hand path, and so find a bank facing due south and a level bay at its feet full of treasures, but we must only stop to notice a few of those which are in flower now in May. *Viola gracilis* was first revealed to me here. I got it from Sprenger of Naples several years before it was generally discovered by English nursery-

259

men, and it soon wedded with *V. Munbyana* and produced
several seedlings of hybrid origin.   One of these caught
the critical eye of Mr. George Paul, and I gave it into his
hands, and he has sent it forth as strong young plants, and
named it Mrs. Bowles in memory of my mother.   I still
keep a little colony of it here, as it flowers for just as wonderfully long a period as *Munbyana*, and is a good purple
blue.   The variety known as *V. gracilis* Purple Robe is much
like it, but neither so blue a shade nor quite so good a shape,
I think.

Erodiums are much to the fore among the rocks here.
E. amanum has begun its long flowering season, and looks
very pretty now with its silvery grey leaves and white
blossoms.   It is a dioecious species, and the pistil-bearing
form is pure white, while the pollen-bearing male has pink
anthers and a few rosy lines in the throat and so is the
prettier flower, but one needs both to get seed and the
self-sown seedlings that I like to see it produce.   Next to
it is a planting of young plants of *E. chrysanthum*, one of
the rarest and loveliest of this family.   It closely resembles
the last species, but its leaves are more silky and more
finely cut, and its flowers are a most beautiful sulphur that
looks rather unusual on such silver foliage.   In *chrysanthum* the sexes are as rigidly divided as in some Lutheran
churches, and here again the male or pollen plant has pink
anthers which greatly add to his beauty.   I believe that the
hybrid between these two, *E. lindavicum* Sundermann, is
not uncommon in gardens where *chrysanthum* and *amanum*
are grown near one another, but it is not to be desired, being
intermediate in colour of flower, a dull yellowish-white, and

One of the slopes in the Rock Garden. (See p. 270.)

representing the spoiling of two good plants. Above these Storks' Bills and in a crevice is one of the best of all Houseleeks, *Sempervivum rubicundum*, which reverses the general order of family colouring and has rich red leaves with green tips. It is just now at its best for Spring colouring and wonderfully bright, but is one of the plants that suffers from too many friends, for all who come fall in love with it and carry off a rosette, so that it spreads slowly in the crevice but rapidly into distant gardens. On the level below are some huge rosettes of *S. Comollei,* another really good one. It makes rosettes as large as those of any Houseleek when generously treated, five inches or more across and of wonderfully beautiful colouring, glaucous green shot with blue and purple, more like an Echeveria than a mere Houseleek. Canon Ellacombe noticed this fine thing in the Jardin des Plantes in Paris, received a rosette from there, and after a few seasons was able to distribute it, and so it came back with me after one of my visits to Bitton.

A curious plant grows at the corner here, *Allium Dioscoridis,* often called *Nectaroscordum siculum,* a tall, strange-looking thing to be one of the Garlicks. It possesses the most pungent and evil smell of any plant I know, and I enjoy breaking a leaf in half and getting my friends to help in deciding whether it most resembles an escape of gas or a new mackintosh. It is already throwing up its curious heads of flowers ; at present they are enclosed in a leafy bag looking like the bud.of some very tall Narcissus. Later on they emerge, and the buds hang down and open a few at a time, but after flowering stand upright. The flowers are a shrimp pink marked with green and dull red,

My Garden in Spring

and are very interesting because it regularly happens that the first to open has eight perianth segments and anthers to match, the next few have the normal six of a liliaceous plant, but towards the end of the flowering it can only afford the last few flowers four each. The true *Linaria hepaticaefolia* is pretty running all about the level bed; its tiny leaves are those of *Cyclamen ibericum* in miniature, and are similarly banded with white zones; the little white flowers are scattered among them very close to the ground. Climbing about on the shady side of a rocky slope close by is *L. aequitriloba*, which in many lists bears the name of the other. It has purple flowers, and leaves, as the name implies, of three distinct equal divisions like those of the Ivy-leaved Toad-flax *L. Cymbalaria*, which it closely resembles but on a much smaller scale. Now on our right we get a brilliant mass of mixed Aubrietias, the result of self-sown seedlings. Originally I planted Dr. Mules and Bridesmaid here, and they both exist, but as grandparents now among their descendants ; any objectionably violent in colour were pulled up, and the rest left to fight it out or agree amicably as they chose. Behind them *Erysimum Allionii* sows itself freely among various dwarf Cytisus bushes on the ridge, and its vivid orange is very good here among several dark-leaved plants and against a flowering mass of the pale lilac *Veronica circaeoides.* Near these are the wonderful leaves of *Allium karataviense,* var. *Ellisii;* their wonder consists in the extraordinary metallic colouring they show when young, purple-violet on the under side and steel-blue above with a deep red edge. They are especially lovely when a few raindrops are caught in their

My Rock Garden

pleated folds, but the head of flowers is not worthy of this early promise, and a very dingy affair, much too large for its short stem.   The other side of the walk calls for a glance ; a group of the two heaths, *Erica carnea* and *hybrida*, crowns the mound, and white Fritillarias have been making a pretty contrast with its red flowers : both are passing over by now, but some very good Camassia seedlings are taking their place.   The first I planted here were some named seedlings of *C. Leichtlinii*, a pure white, and a very deep purple called Purple Robe ; now seedlings have appeared in all directions, and some are of very good deep blue and purple shades.

There are several large clumps of *C. Leichtlinii* in the rock garden, both the typical cream-coloured one and the lilac-blue variety, and if one sees them on an afternoon when they have freshly opened a series of flowers they are a fine sight, but sometimes I wish to impress a visitor with their beauty and find never a bloom open ; yesterday's have all faded and they make the plant look untidy, and the next four or five buds on each stem will not open until the late afternoon.   A good-sized bush of *Berberis Fremontii* astonishes many people who think it needs a wall to do well.   It grows in a very exposed position here, and is exquisite when the crimson of the young growth contrasts with the steely blue of its prickly little leaves.   *Corylopsis pauciflora* grows in a sheltered nook with *Olearia nummulariaefolia*, a Bush Ivy and a prostrate Juniper to keep it company.   The Corylopsis gives bunches of flowers like Cowslips on fine twigs in early Spring, and then for the next four months bears imitation Hornbeam leaves of delightful shades of pink and red and tawny brown, more

263

My Garden in Spring

like Autumn than Spring tints, but in late Summer they turn green and cease to be remarkable. Lower down is a remarkably fine Dead Nettle not often seen, *Lamium Orvala*, with handsome, deep-green leaves and flesh-pink flowers. On the other side of the path is a plant of *Orvala lamioides*, by some authorities considered the same as the Lamium, but it has a very different habit and appearance, and leaves that are tinged with red and much like those of a Coleus and that colour finely in Autumn. Hereabouts grow many Violas; there are three forms of *V. cucullata*, a deep blue, a white, and a pied, besides *V. sorora*, another American species with light-blue flowers of great size, *V. pubescens*, the largest flowered of the yellow Violets, and *sagittata*, a pretty blue one. These are all tuberous rooted and die down each Winter, after the manner of *V. biflora*, the wee yellow Violet of the Alps, and its American representative, *V. scabriuscala*, which scarcely differs from it except in having markedly pointed instead of round leaves. I have one little tuft of *V. biflora* with pale sulphur flowers that I brought from the St. Gothard district, the only variant I have ever found among the thousands of normal ones I have met with. Much of the right-hand slope is carpeted with two forms of *V. canina*, both given me by Mr. Wolley-Dod, one a pure white and of very neat habit, which though it seeds all over the place comes quite true from seed, the other a pretty blue and white pied form, but which spreads much less than the white. Another and larger white Violet I believe to be of American origin, and either white *Riviniana* or very near it. Dr. Lowe gave it to me many years ago, and bade me remember that it was *not* the white

Sundial in the Pergola Garden.   (See p. 288.)

My Rock Garden

Dog Violet, whatever people might say to the contrary. I have also a starch-blue one from Wisley that is either a form of it or some closely allied one. These banks are packed with plants, but it would take a whole volume to mention half of them, so we must move on and by turning to the right can avoid walking into the pool, and rejoin the main path.

We pass a collection of naturally dwarf trees and shrubs, such as the pygmy forms of the Scots Pine and Spruce, several *Euonymous japonicus*, and a Box or two of dwarf habits. *Ligustrum japonicum*, var. *coriaceum*, and its subvariety *involutum* have grown into fine specimens, and look wonderfully like dwarf Camellias. But the gems of this corner are a dwarf Cedar of Lebanon, a variety known as Comte de Dijon, and two of the small form of Irish Juniper that I have seen in a catalogue as *J. communis hibernica compressa nana*. The dwarf Willows, *Salix reticulata, S. herbacea*, and the larger *S. lanata* are also here, and each has a decided character of its own. The two first are the lowliest of British shrubs, for although *reticulata's* leaves are large and round, and with their footstalks stand up two inches or more from the ground and the curious brownish catkins, which closely resemble the Plantain-heads that children play the game of Soldiers with, over-top the leaves, yet the woody trunk of this minute tree lies flat upon the ground, however aged and thick it may be. *Herbacea* has very small leaves and thin twigs that never rise up for more than an inch or two, while the stem prefers to bury itself in the ground after the manner of a root. *Lanata* should make a handsome bush of

My Garden in Spring

several feet in height, but seldom finds life in a garden sufficiently worth living to stay there long enough to exceed one foot. Its large, round, woolly leaves are very striking, as they are of an unusual shade of grey-green, but the male catkins are its chief glory, from the moment they burst their bud-scales and appear as white as snow till they have successively imitated blue Persian kittens and yellow hairy caterpillars and, their pollen shed, they fall to the ground. Several almost microscopic plants, such as *Arenaria balearica, Epilobium nummularifolium, Mentha Requienii* smelling so strongly of Peppermint, *Erodium Reichardii,* and *Veronica repens* make carpets under the small trees. At the corner of this bank Saxifrages behave better than in most parts of this dry garden, and *S. Burseriana, Salomonii, Elizabethae, oppositifolia,* and *sancta* are here, also *taÿgetea* looking like Soldanella in leaf, and *tenella,* which I was told by its donor I should not be able to keep long, but has been happy in this, the original site I allotted it, for at least twelve years, an instance of the inevitable happening of the unexpected. I wish *S. oppositifolia* would do a little better here; it occasionally flowers well and encourages me to plant more, and then for a season or two may look brown and bedraggled, in fact "a positive failure" as a lady once called it. I sat down on a carpet of it to eat my sandwich luncheon up in the Cottian Alps, last June, and looked at the rosy cushions and longed to see a slope of the rock garden similarly furnished, but though *S. retusa* has settled down most amicably in the piped sand bed, and flowered well this Spring, *oppositifolia* by its side is slowly dying.

My Rock Garden

Look at *Allium paradoxum* on your left: the little transparent yellowish bulbils struck here and there among the flowers look like Mistletoe berries. *Spirea Thunbergii* at the opposite corner has been flowering ever since Christmas, and is still full of blossom. It has grown into a fine specimen, I believe chiefly due to the fact that I give it a good clearing out of old wood each season just after flowering. Did you catch a whiff of an unpleasant smell like fish frying? I often wondered how it was possible to smell kitchen operations down here so far from any house until I discovered it was the scent of *Cotoneaster multiflora,* the umbrella-shaped specimen growing on the top of the high mound. It is something like the scent of Hawthorn, but much more unpleasant. The tree is graceful, though, and of course the scent passes away with the flowers, and they atone for their wickedness by turning to good red berries in autumn. Among these large cordate leaves you can find the weird blossoms of *Asarum Bealei,* livid red with three tails, each one of which is nearly three inches long, and close beside it grows *A. grandiflorum* with very similar flowers, both of them so uncanny and evil-looking that they would make a suitable button-hole for the Devil. *Claytonia siberica,* both pink and white, seeds about freely in this semi-shady corner, and is comely and welcome now, but later on it becomes aggressive, sprawls out in a chickweedy way that proclaims its rather plebeian lineage, and reminds us of its poor relation *C. perfoliata,* whose only beauty is the green carpet it provides in hopelessly shady places during the winter months.

My Garden in Spring

Hyacinthus amethystinus, both blue and white, lives and seeds about on the sunny side of the main path, and reminds me of a glorious day on Acro-Corinth when I saw it peeping out among fallen blocks of marble.

Now the path passes between two sheets of water, or so they might appear if carefully brought into the foreground of a photograph. One is in an old circular lead tank sunk in the ground and about six feet in diameter, another heritage from the dismantled house. It grows the major form of *Ranunculus Lingua* very well, three of Marliac's Water-lilies, and *Riccia fluitans,* a curious water Liverwort that floats about in tufts looking like green isinglass. It also supports a family of rudd that a fish-loving friend caught for me in Norfolk, and the largest of our water snails, *Limnaea stagnalis,* which devours confervae and respects phanerogamic plants, and so can be admitted where our more plentiful *L. auriculata* must be excluded. A huge French Edible Frog, one of several brought home from foreign rambles, has settled down here, and generally sits on the edge of the tank sunning himself, and can be watched if cautiously approached, and his metallic eyes and green striped back are good to see, but at any sudden movement he takes a header into the pool in a moment. We hoped great things of the other pool, and cemented rocks together to form its sides, but it suffers from unaccountable low tides occasionally, and is now full of *Cyperus longus* and other grassy things. It is fed by a drip that is the overflow from three other small pools further up in the rock garden, and where this splashes down off an overhanging stone I have planted a few moisture-loving treasures. A maidenhair fern, *Adiantum Capillus-Veneris,*

My Rock Garden

from the Cornish cliffs is one, and has thriven amazingly for some fifteen years, though often encrusted with icicles in winter. The mountains rise high at the back of this pool of disappointment, for here again I planned wonderful things, and spent money and muscle on some very large blocks and built up a right noble cliff. In spite of its cost it is one of the least interesting bits of the garden —too much stone and too little room for plants, in fact. I was foolish enough to plant *Lactuca* (*Mulgedium*) *alpina* on it, and have spent years trying to get rid of it, and but for the concrete I believe it would have filled the whole garden and pushed up through the floors of the house and into the road to stop the traffic, for Atalanta and Charley's Aunt are tortoises compared with such a runner.

Euphorbia Wulfenii makes a handsome bush and a fine dark mass when out of flower, but now with the great yellow green heads rising up out of the almost indigo blue foliage it is a very fine object. The stems turn over at the tips in autumn if they mean to flower next year, and then the heart leaves of these shoots take on red stripes, and the display gradually unfolds all through the winter until it ends in the immense heads of bloom. This is a Euphorbia corner, and *E. pilosa major*, which I cannot distinguish from *E. polychroma* growing next it, almost vies with the Daffodils in yellowness, but certainly beats them in having a second season, for in some autumns it turns a dazzling scarlet. *E. corollata* is only springing up at this season, and will not get its curious, corolla-like, white bracts before June. *E. Cyparissias* and even *Lathyris* the Caper-spurge are here, and several poorer relations less worthy of notice,

My Garden in Spring

but *E. Characias* has always grown on the older range, and so is not represented again here. I like its curious dull green heads of flowers with their conspicuous black spots, and like to call it by a name I learnt from Mr. Burbidge. He overheard a garden-boy at Trinity College, Dublin, showing some people round and answering their questions, and when asked the name of this Spurge he said, "Sure an' I do not rightly know what it is designated, but we boys call it the Frog Spawn bush." *E. melifera* crowns the next mound, but is often severely punished in winter here, so has never reached to eight feet in height as I have seen it at Fota, where I gathered the seed that produced my plant.

Now we turn up a little path of steps to the left and cross a flat stone that serves as a bridge over the overflow channel from the pools. The photograph facing page 164 will show you better than my pen can describe the view from the bridge in the last week of May when Columbines and Thalictrums and pink *Geranium sylvaticum* run riot on the left-hand bank. Only an edge is shown, though, of the Trollius and Sedges that fringe the pools on the opposite side of the path. The big Golden-fruited Ivy stands out well at the end, and the outermost boughs of the large *Magnolia stellata* can be seen at the extreme right, but the flowers of the orange-coloured Welsh Poppies that cover all the bank between them are almost invisible even with a lens, though their seed heads are discernible just under the Ivy, and *Rosa altaica* and *R. hispida* show up well behind. If we go up the path shown we can turn to the right at the head of the largest pool, and after passing the

My Rock Garden

Magnolia, we must stop and wonder at the rose-like beauty of a large bush of *Rubus deliciosus,* that arches out every which way as Huck Finn would say, and bears its snow-white flowers all down the arching branches. It is prettier thus than as one generally sees it crucified flat on a wall, and as it is quite happy in a very draughty spot here must be hardier than people think. One thing is essential to success, and that is to cut out all old wood after flowering, in order to give plenty of room for the yellow-skinned new shoots to spring out into air and light. Mandrakes and Crocuses share the next bank with *Oenothera speciosa,* now just appearing with its red shoots, and a queer little black *Viola tricolor* that starting from this point has gone about the world a good deal lately under the name of Bowles' Black. It is an old garden form of *V. tricolor,* authorities say, and I got it from Dr. Lowe, who told me it always bred true, and so it does if kept to itself, and I rather think its own seedlings decline to be influenced by foreign pollen, though I have made no decisive tests, but I know that it readily influences other Violas, and its dusky charms appear in Mulattoes, Quadroons, and Octaroons all over the place. I am not responsible for its new name, though I know of no old one. (I see that Kew calls it *V. tricolor nigra* now, but it does not appear in the 1902 *Hand-List.*) Canon Ellacombe saw it here, and having lost it at Bitton, carried it back again, where it was seen, admired and coveted by the stream of visitors that ever flows to view the perennial display of good plants in that garden. They were told that Bowles was throwing it away, and many a begging

271

My Garden in Spring

letter came here asking for *my* black Pansy, and most of those to whom I sent it labelled it Bowles' Black, and soon after sent it on to other gardens under that hideous name. Not so bad, though, as one I saw at the last Chelsea Show, for there it was labelled Viola Black Bowles! I am not so black as I was painted on that label, so I altered it. It is a very charming little weed, sowing itself freely, and when in full bloom it has a wonderfully friendly and cheerful look in the yellow Cyclopian eye in the middle of its almost black face. Where we rejoin the main path just opposite the *Erodium chrysanthum* and *amanum* corner we stopped at on our downward way, the path is overspread by *Acaena Buchananii*, a light, glaucous-green species that behaved so badly and greedily in the border that I turned it out, as I have also done with *inermis* and *argentea*, to spread as much as they like on the path, where they are quite a success, and do not mind being walked on. The only trouble is that all stray seeds anchor in them and germinate and provide perpetual labour for the garden-boy. A forest that looks as if it were primaeval spreads over the left-hand corner, and it is entirely composed of *Prunus Amygdalus nanus*, and when one rosy glow of blossom and bud is really lovely.

Mr. Farrer always lingers lovingly over this corner, and declares it to be his idea of good gardening, and I suppose it really is good, and I may say so, for it is not mine but Nature's work, the Almond having walked all over the ground in its own wild way, and the Crocuses and Muscaris, Camassias and Narcissi, Snowdrops and Campanulas that

Old Cross from Enfield Market-place.   (See p. 291.)

My Rock Garden

live among its stems have not been disturbed for certainly sixteen years, and have done much seeding and rearrangement on their own account in that period. So all the credit I can claim is for having wit enough to leave it alone. To the left of the old summer-house lies the oldest bank of the rock garden. It is hard to deal with now, for though many portions are rather exhausted and need remodelling, it contains many good old specimen plants on it that it would be sacrilege to interfere with ; a large *Cytisus cinereus* is one, and now is one mass of the most dazzlingly clear yellow that the garden yields in the whole season. A large bush of *Rosa indica*, the real crimson form, known as Miss Lowe's from her beautiful drawing of it, given me by Dr. Lowe, is opening its first flowers, and will, all being well, continue to do so until close on Christmas. It is the parent of the Monthly Roses ; its flowers are single and purest crimson. *Olearia virgata*, var. *lineata*, above it is a wonderfully light bush with its wand-like growth and tiny, linear leaves, very unlike any other *Olearia* in habit. It bears dull little flowers like those of Groundsel, only white instead of yellow, but its graceful habit makes it good to look at all the year round. Large bushes of *Rosa rubrifolia* and *sericea* crown the top, and going up the main steps we come to a flat hollow filled with peat that I sometimes flatter by calling a bog. Sanguinaria and Podophyllum, *Caltha radicans, Andromeda polifolia*, Trilliums and other peat-loving things live here, and the fern *Hypolepis millefolium* runs about all through it. I started *Saxifraga peltata* in one corner, and it wanted to walk over everybody with its enormous caterpillars of

My Garden in Spring

rhizomes, but this could not be allowed, and so it got cut back, and then took to climbing up the dry wall that holds up the river bank at the back. It has now reached the top, and looks so happy clinging to the stones that I have cleared it out altogether from the peat bed. Just now, before its huge, Lotus-shaped leaves have grown up, the fat marbled rhizomes and tall naked scapes bearing the flat heads of pretty pink flowers look very strange clinging to and springing from the wall.

They may be seen in the right-hand corner of the illustration of the fine old *Tamarix tetrandra* that now, in late May, is the glory of the whole garden. It is one soft cloud of Strawberry-ice pink, as fluffy and light as Marabou feathers, not a green leaf as yet visible ; and against the background of oaks it stands out like a bush in a pantomime scene of the Fairy Princess' Garden, and one almost expects to see it suddenly lit up with electric lights, and then divided asunder to reveal the Princess reclining on a gilded couch, &c., &c. It does look most astonishingly unreal out here in the open air, and what surprises me is that it is so seldom seen in gardens. It is perfectly hardy, easy to strike from cuttings, grows rapidly, is graceful in outline, truly marvellous when in flower in May, and beautifully feathery when in leaf from June to November. Yet you rarely see it, while Dorothy Perkins scratches your nose and claws your hat off in every garden you go into. *Cotoneaster horizontalis* tries its best to block the path up here, and would manage to do so were it not for me and my secateurs. *Hedera conglomerata* has monopolised the top

My Rock Garden

corner by the river, but is very beautiful, and I have sown *Orobanche hederae* among it, and every season increasing numbers of its quaint brown flower-spikes push through the tangle of Ivy stems. Here steps lead us down again, and under the shade of the Oaks which hang out from the meadow not much will grow, but the Alexandrian Laurel, *Danae Laurus* (*Ruscus racemosus* as we used to call it) and Epimediums manage to be cheerful in spite of the canopy of oak boughs. The former has never fruited here yet, though it has grown well, and plenty of victors might be crowned with its wreaths of neat, glistening laurels. " Happy Medium ! what a funny name ! " said an American lady, and I am sure you will not blame me from refraining from correcting her, and so allowing her to collect the imagined name as her latest-found curio. They *are* happy, too, on this slope, and very beautiful when in flower and young leaf, and as I have collected them rather assiduously and seldom bought the same plant twice under the same name, and never found leisure to work them out, you must not take my names too seriously. *E. pinnatum* is so large and distinct and brilliant in its tone of yellow, that it is beyond dispute the finest of them. I can never make up my mind which is the better plan to follow, whether to cut down the leathery green leaves in winter, and so see the shepherd's crooks of flower-spikes from their first appearance and enjoy the yellow bouquet until a sharp frost burns the tallest of them, or to leave the handsome foliage on, and part it with one's hand to see the flowers below, that thus protected are safe

My Garden in Spring

from cold snaps. *E. rubrum*, with crimson and yellow flowers and beautifully mottled red and raw-sienna leaves, is my next favourite, and a pale yellow-flowered form with somewhat similar colouring in the young leaves is better than the pale and small form of *pinnatum* whose flowers are a pretty sulphur yellow, but takes no pains with the painting of its leaves. *E. macranthum* has lilac flowers with four long horns like those of a snail in shape, and is supposed to be closely related to the lilac and snow-white forms that are known by many catalogue names, but are all lovely and not quite so easy to grow as the yellow and red-flowered species. Our British *E. alpinum* has the dullest flowers, but I consider the most effective leaves of all, especially for forming a carpet among shrubs. An occasional treat in the way of a mulch of leaf mould will keep these Barrenworts happy for years in many an overhung corner that would be hard to furnish pleasantly with other plants.

We have almost completed our Spring tour of the rock garden; the only portions that remain to be explored are the path between the oldest bank and the top of the triangle, and the moraines. This path we have now reached by descending the steps and passing the Epimediums. It is wide, and many things sow themselves in it that I like to see there, so please do not tread on *Erodium romanum's* rosettes of ferny leaves and slender stems of dainty rosy flowers just now commencing to open, for if you do not crush them they will continue blooming all through the season. It grows wild on the walls of the Coliseum at Rome, and my plants are descendants of some brought from thence, and the hard gravel path may remind them of their former home, for they grow much better in it than in the border, keeping a neater habit and resisting winter wet better. *Geranium atlanticum* is making a brave show of blue flowers shot with red ; it does not grow in the Atlantic Ocean as an ingenious friend imagined its name implied, but on Mount Atlas. It is not sufficiently well-known, as the beautiful, finely-cut leaves appear with the autumn rains and make a charming carpet to otherwise bare spots, and Crocuses, especially autumnal species, seem quite happy growing among the leaves. The moraines were described in a former chapter, but I must show you how charming *Dianthus microlepis* and *Freynei* are in the edge of the Farrer moraine. *Microlepis* is a flat tuft of grey set all over with stemless flowers of a rosy-salmon colour, reminding one of *Silene acaulis* in the Alps, whose green pincushions are here among the granite chips but refuse to wear any pinheads of flower buds in this lowland garden. *D. Freynei* is a white-flowered counterpart of *microlepis* as I know it, but I have some doubts as to their distinction, and should never be surprised to find that both my plants were but colour forms of one and the same. *Linaria alpina* sows itself amiably among its betters, and most of the plants are the self-coloured lilac form called v. *concolor*, descendants of some collected on Mt. Cenis, and they vary a good deal in the shade of lilac and the white or grey of the spots that decorate their rabbit-shaped noses instead of the glowing orange ones of the type. *Lewisia parviflora* is flowering in a dry overhung corner, and but for belonging to so renowned a family would not be

My Garden in Spring

thought much of. But look at *Ranunculus amplexicaulis major* in the piped bed opposite bearing on several tall, branching stems the largest white Buttercups I have ever seen. Here indeed it is a glorious thing. Another plant in ordinary border soil is not so fine, so I feel my lead pipe and sandy mixtures are worth fussing over to produce such a thing as this. There are sixteen of the glistening white flowers open and a few are over, but many buds are preparing to carrying on the display: even *R. pyrenaeus*, which is very beautiful in other parts of the garden, takes second place to this. Under it the ground is carpeted with the Blue Daisy, *Bellis rotundifolia coerulescens*, a crop of self-sown seedlings, which found this bed just what they wanted, and the grey-lilac flowers are very pretty in a good mass like this, but blue is only a courtesy title I fear. *Androsace Henryi* likes its home too, and has sent up a score of its round heads of small, white flowers above the crenate and cordate leaves that look so unlike those of ordinary members of the family. *A. carnea* in several forms, all from Mt. Cenis, whether white or rosy, are pretty among the *Gentiana verna*. *Primula integrifolia*, who lives in a marsh in her native Pyrenees, grows and flowers under the shade of a stone just behind the colony of *P. pedemontana*. *Senecio incanus* makes tufts of lovely silver fern leaves, but refuses to flower when starved in the granite chips or to live at all if planted in fatter soil.

These are a few of the plants that catch my eye on this May day, but a week hence others will have taken their places and the face of the rock garden be changed, but this chapter must not go on for another week.

CHAPTER XVII

The Culmination of Spring

IF a fairy godmother or a talking fish offered me three wishes I think one would be to have the clock stopped for six months on a fine morning towards the end of May. Then, perhaps, I might have time to enjoy the supreme moment of the garden. And I am not at all sure the second wish would not be used to extend the period. It must be after those plaguey Ice Saints have finished playing the fool with the weather, and when there comes a spell that is neither too hot nor too cold, but just the climate one would expect to meet with in Heaven, and in England sometimes comes to us in late May and September. The tall Tulips would be at their best, *Iris florentina* and its early companions in full glory, Lilacs and Apple-blossom, Hawthorn and Laburnum, all masses of flower. Trees full of tender green, yet not too densely clad to prevent our seeing the architecture of the boughs. The Mulberry would be in leaf and showing that frosts have ceased, for it is the wisest of all trees, and always waits till it is quite safe before it opens its buds. I like to get all my gardening friends to visit me in May ; they respect me and my gardening then, whereas later on they are apt to be critical, seeing how some plants begin to burn up, and noting the poverty of our soil, as shown by

My Garden in Spring

stunted herbaceous plants and gaps where early flowering things have retired below, and we dare not attempt annuals, as might be done in better soils. I grudge no plotting and planning, no preparation and waiting, that will bear full fruit at this period. I was born in the middle of May, and perhaps some mystic influence crept into me from those first weeks of my life. Most of the scents of this time are delicious. Wistaria one can never sniff up too much of ; Azaleas are pleasant if kept out-of-doors, and even Hawthorn is good blown from a distance, while Irises, Lilacs, Double Gorse, Pansies, Lily of the Valley, and Cowslips are all things to bring close to one's nose. Later in the year come heavy *stuffing* scents, as the sixteenth-century writers called them—Elder, Syringa, Lime, and such far-reaching, Hay-fever producers ; but now it is good to open one's nostrils wide. There is one exception, and that is the most fiendish plant I know of, the sort of thing Beelzebub might pluck to make a bouquet for his mother-in-law —the Hairy Arum, *Helicodiceros crinitus*, which looks as if it had been made out of a sow's ear for spathe, and the tail of a rat that died of Elephantiasis for the spadix. The whole thing is a mingling of unwholesome greens, livid purples, and pallid pinks, the livery of putrescence in fact, and it possesses an odour to match the colouring. I once entrapped the vicar of a poor parish into smelling it, and when he had recovered his breath he said it reminded him of a pauper funeral. It only exhales this stench for a few hours after opening, and during that time it is better to stand afar off and look at it through a telescope. It attracts all the Green Bottle-flies of the district, who think there

Solanum crispum in May. (See p. 291.)

The Culmination of Spring

must be some extra gamey carrion down in its bristly throat, and hurry in to the feast, passing easily over the stiff bristles that point inwards in the narrowed portion of the passage. But once in they find these fleshy hairs prevent their getting out again, and on a sunny day the large chamber soon gets filled with flies, chiefly the burnished, green-tailed Lucilia Cæsar. The females lay quantities of eggs on the walls, and in a few days the interior is a putrid mass of dead flies and crawling maggots, and the desired ends of both fly and flower are defeated. For the maggots soon starve for want of more food than is supplied by the bodies of their defunct parents, and the ovaries of the flower are rotted by the damp mass. I suppose in its native Corsican home things happen differently. Probably it is visited by some more strongly built insect—perhaps even carrion-feeding beetles, whose strength helps them to struggle out more easily when the pollen is shed and the stiff bristles begin to grow flaccid ; or again a larger number of plants in flower at one time would mean more accommodation for carrion-loving visitors, and the suffocating crowding of the inner chamber would be avoided. In English gardens there are seldom more than two of the flowers open on the same day, and there is no lack of flies at their period of flowering. I like astonishing people who have not seen this flower before by cutting away a portion of the wall of the lower chamber and allowing the entrapped flies to escape. After a fine morning there will generally be enough of them inside to make a good swarm and to take a minute or two to buzz out of an opening an inch square. I have never seen it set any seed, even after I have liberated the flies. The commoner black Arum, *Dracunculus vulgaris*, never gets choked up in the same way, and occasionally bears a few red berries in September, showing that some visitors have effected its fertilisation. The leaves of *Helicodiceros* are very curious, and worth examining carefully. They are of the general arrow-head plan so frequent among aroids, but are divided into several lobes, and the barbs of the arrow-heads are twisted until they stand upright and form two horns, which peculiarity has furnished the generic name *Helicodiceros*— that is, the spirally twisted two-horned.

It was on a glorious day in late May that many of the photographs that illustrate this book were taken, and I want to lead you round in the track of the photographer to describe some of the results.

The Chusan Fan Palm outside the morning-room window was within a few days of opening its large bunches of flowers. At this early stage they look somewhat like yellow cauliflower, but when open are more spread out and lighter in effect. They are particularly interesting, as this specimen appears to be a peculiar one, and though in most seasons its flowers are wholly male, bearing only pollen, now and then a few of the last flowers to open on the spikes are furnished with ovaries, and twice I have known it to set fruits which swelled to a fair size before severe winter frosts destroyed them. I have shown specimens of the two kinds of flowers and also immature fruit at the Scientific Committee of the Royal Horticultural Society, and have not as yet heard of another instance of a monoecious specimen of *Trachycarpus excelsus*. This

The Culmination of Spring

one has stood here about fifteen years, and was when I first planted it quite a small plant, and I used to water it overhead its first summer from an ordinary waterpot; now its stem is about seven feet high. It has a very good position, sheltered from the north-east by the end of the house and from the north-west by the conservatory, so that our worst winds never touch it, though it has to stand the rough and tumble of a sou'-wester now and then which tears its leaves. Wind is the worst enemy of this hardy palm. It smiles at snow, for as the leaves get weighted with it, they slope gently down until an avalanche slides off and up they go again to collect another load. I cut off, the lowest ring of leaves twice in each season, as I like to see the clean outline of the stem. The photograph was taken before I had operated on it this Spring, and it looks rather clumsy on account of the hanging lower leaves. I have several other specimens of the same palm in the garden, but this is the largest and oldest. We call one border the Eremurus bed, because it contains groups of those stately plants from its commencement under the old Cedar down to the portion that is shaded by a venerable Portugal Laurel shaped like a large umbrella, under which they would refuse to grow. *E. Elwesianus*, a group of which is shown facing page 200, is the handsomest of the family, and that means a great deal, and its white form grows quite as tall as the pink one. They have not been very happy this season, as the unusually mild January tempted them through, and they were soon as forward as they should have been in mid-March, only to learn that the air was not ready for them, so that the spikes got checked and did not reach their usual height. We find they like to have their crowns only just beneath the surface, and a little raised, so that the long, fleshy roots, radiating from the crown like spokes from the hub of a wheel, or the legs of a Brittle Starfish from its circular body, may slope downwards into the soil. When planting we lay them out in the hole dug for them, pour a potful of sand over the crown, and then gently raise it two or three inches so that the sand runs beneath it and supports it. They are greedy feeders, and enjoy a mulch of good manure; Wellson's, which is practically dried sheep manure, seems to agree with them. So we spread a layer of it on the soil as soon as the great crown has pushed through, and in a very short time the yellow, feeding rootlets will have found it and pushed up thickly to gather the nutriment. *E. himalaicus* likes a cooler position than others, but its hybrid *him-rob*, like *robustus*, is happiest in full sun and on well-drained soil. It is one of the most vigorous, and falls little short of *Elwesianus* in size, but is at its best rather later in the season. The yellow and tawny ones mostly belong to next month, and so to another volume.

E. Tubergenii, however, a hybrid between *himalaicus* and *Bungei*, flowers with its white parent, and *Bungei praecox* should be opening the lowest blossoms of its spike before May has gone. We do not believe in covering the young growths unless something especially arctic in the weather line catches them when the young flower-spikes are visible in the open cups formed by the leaves. If the crowns are covered when first through they are hurried

The Culmination of Spring

along too fast, and the leaves are sure to be nipped and disfigured. I like to plant autumn-flowering Crocuses among them and deeper than the Eremuri, so that they may come spearing through between their spokes and make a show in the necessarily large space occupied by the giants, and which would be bare and uninteresting after their resting season commences. I also plant *Gypsophila paniculata* behind the Eremurus clumps, and keep it staked till they die down and then remove the ties and let it fall over the space. The next long border is backed by a Holly hedge that gives protection to some rather delicate shrubs, and among them are some of my beloved Eucalypts, and one of them is in flower, as the illustration facing p. 232 shows. The buds were formed last autumn, and have been opening a few at a time ever since last November. I am rather proud of this specimen, because it was raised from seed I gathered on a large one that lived many years in the rock garden and was quite a timber tree. The fluffy yellow flowers are very pretty among the wonderfully blue leaves. It is *E. cordata*, a Tasmanian species, and one of the hardiest, but very difficult to get true to name. It is very similar in appearance to *E. pulverulenta* from Victoria, which is even more brilliant in its colouring, as the young leaves are shot with pink and the whole plant is very mealy and blue, but is not so hardy as *cordata*, and has more than once been killed outright by a winter that spared the Tasmanian species.

Crossing the old bowling-green lawn we get a charming picture of beautiful foliage and soft colouring which is shown facing p. 248. It is at the back of Tom Tiddler's

My Garden in Spring

ground behind the purple-leaved plants, some of which form the background to this picture. The bed is edged with a broad band of Hellebores. The Christmas Rose, *H. niger*, nearest to us, and various named forms of Lenten Roses at the further end, are planted in a bold group and running right up to the stem of the Yew tree seen at the back. The foreground is part of a band of various species of Geranium which runs for some distance along the lawn front of this bed and contains many treasures, results of my own foreign wanderings and gleanings from other gardens, for I always keep an open eye for a Geranium I have not got. The leaves and buds shown here are of a fine blue-purple form of *G. ibericum ;* then, as all can see, there is a grouping of *Dicentra spectabilis*, chiefly of the old pink form, as it is still the best. One plant is the white, or speaking more truthfully, flesh-coloured variety, and the dumpy one, the second counting from the right-hand side, is the newer form *erecta*, interesting to grow with the others but without the graceful beauty of the old form. The rounded bush rising out of this is *Conium maculatum*, the Hemlock, one of the most poisonous of plants, and generally considered to have furnished the bowl of poison by which Socrates was put to death. Gerard denounces it root and branch, saying : " The greate Hemlock doubtlesse is not possessed with any one good facultie, as appeareth by his lothsome smell, and other apparant signes and therefore not to be used in physicke." But both leaves and seeds are still used to yield the alkaloid Conine, which has a peculiar sedative action on the motor nerves, and therefore is occasionally prescribed.

The Culmination of Spring

An old man used to supply a great firm of druggists with the dried plant at a much lower rate than they could obtain it from any other source. When through age he announced that he must give up the business he was asked how he had always managed to undersell others, and he told a delightful tale of a cunning practice. He used to wander about in the Eastern Counties sowing Hemlock seeds in any waste corner near cultivated lands, then when the plant was fully grown he called upon the farmer and told him that a dreadfully poisonous plant grew on his land, and would kill beasts if eaten by them, and that for a small sum he would clear it away. He was generally paid for collecting his harvest, grown rent free on other folks' land, and therefore could afford to sell it so cheaply. Besides its medicinal value it is a very beautiful garden plant, so in spite of Gerard I grow it. It is unfortunately biennial or at any rate monocarpic, but makes the most of its short life by keeping brilliantly green through the winter. The leaves are as exquisitely cut as any I know of, and wonderfully glossy. All through last winter these large leaves and the already developing central shoot were as beautiful as anything in the garden, and then from early Spring till the seeds were ripe in July the fine specimen shown in the photograph was always a thing of beauty, although it was growing under the shade of an old Scots Pine, and not the least of the Hemlock's virtues is this amiable habit of growing and looking happy in any waste shady corner. Beyond the Pine stem a good group of *Thalictrum aquilegiaefolium* was delightfully effective against the purple of *Prunus Pissardii* and Barbery. It is composed of some

My Garden in Spring

picked forms with extra rich purple and red colouring in the filaments, some from Mt. Cenis meadows, other seedlings I have raised here from good forms, but the last one towards the Yew is the pure white form that occurs in sub-alpine woods and came home with me one year from Airolo. These are very ordinary plants, but growing in this grouping they gave me great pleasure. The path shown leads straight away to the river bank, and when viewed from its centre shows as a finish, one of the beds of the Terrace. At this moment it was aglow with Clara Butt Tulip, and through the summer months we keep it flaming away with *Salvia splendens,* Pride of Zurich.

The Pergola Garden and its warm, well-sheltered borders are full of interest just now. *Erysimum pumilum* from Mt. Cenis is happier here than anywhere in the rock garden, and one of the most brilliant, clear-yellow flowers imaginable. I was astounded at its beauty the first time I saw it growing on the rough, rocky shore of the lake among *Gentiana angulosa* and sheets of Globularia and Dryas, almost dazzling in its brilliancy. It looked so good-tempered and even aged there, that I marvelled why I had never seen it in English gardens. It flowers here as well as there, one solid mass only three inches high of Wall-flower blossoms of purest yellow, but I must own that it has a way of dying off after flowering here, that its woody stock and antique appearance on the Cenis show to be due to something lacking in this lowland situation, and so we have to look out carefully for seeds or self-sown seedlings. *Ribes speciosus* is a sprawling octopus whose tentacles are covered with brown spines and crimson Fuchsia blossoms.

Symphytum asperrimum.   (See p. 294.)

The Culmination of Spring

Olearia myrsinites, a good evergreen for the dull months, is now smothered in its white flowers, that make up in their quantity for their rather small size. Round its feet are some clumps of Wild Hyacinths, Dutch-raised seedlings of wonderful charm. I first saw them at the great Jubilee Haarlem Show. The most distinct appears in lists as *Scilla nutans delicata,* and is of the true *nutans* type with its pendant bells and long bracts, very nearly white but with a delightful pale blue edge to each segment. Robin Hood is flesh colour and not quite a pure *nutans,* having just a touch of the open bells of *hispanica,* as it appears we must now call the *Scilla companulata* of lists and one's early days. The correct scientific name for the common Bluebell is changed so often, and the highest authorities disagree so endlessly, that I never know what to use for it. The *Kew Index* and *Kew Hand-List* and the 1895 edition of the *London Catalogue* all agree that it is *Scilla festalis* of Salisbury ; but the 1908 edition of the *London Catalogue* makes it *Scilla nonscripta* Hoffmgg and Link ; while the British Museum favours *Endymion non-scriptum* Garcke Fl. Deutschl. and the Abbé Coste, the latest French authority, prefers *Endymion nutans* Dumont, and it seems high time that a sort of Esperanto name compounded of the lot was made for it. Whatever its name may be it does well here, and I have it in many colours : the mauve pink forms are very pretty in clumps among a bold massing of the white, and look better there than when planted among the blue form. *S. hispanica* has many good forms, too— red, blue, and white. The best of all is *maxima,* and when it has become established and likes its home, and takes a

289   T

My Garden in Spring

pride in its great spikes of cups of palest blue with deeper streaks on them, it is the noblest of all Scillas. There is a white form of *maxima* that is not so robust as the blue, but is a good thing for semi-shade. I have planted it among some good forms of British ferns in the shade of an Evergreen Oak and the effect is very good. The beds in the garden in front of the wall are edged with stone-paved walks, and I like to plant something along the edges that will grow out over the flags, so one bed has several forms of *Cheiranthus alpinus* and *Alyssum saxatile* used thus. The lemon-yellow form var. *citrinum* is very effective next to the double one of this latter plant, and contrasts well with the many shades of brown, crimson, and purple of what is often wrongly called *Cheiranthus mutabilis*, the name of a half-hardy, shrubby plant from Madeira. I know that is wrong, but am not sure it is right to call it *C. alpinus versicolor* as I do. Anyway it is a good thing, and much better than a paler form known as *C. Dillenii*. The darker and better plant has of late years hybridised spontaneously with *C. Allionii* in several gardens, and has produced some fine plants with deep orange flowers changing with age to blood red: that known as Miss King's or Newark Park Variety is the best coloured of them, but here it has a lanky habit and flowers itself to death, and we prefer one that appeared spontaneously in the rock garden and has a dwarfer habit and makes more growth. It is a fine mass of rich orange and red brown in May, and especially pleasing here on the grey stones.

Between this paved garden and the river there is a formal Rose Garden, in the centre of which stands the old

The Culmination of Spring

Enfield Market Cross dismissed from the market-place to make way for a King Edward VII Coronation Memorial. After a year or two of unhonoured repose in a builder's yard it came here for a quiet time among the roses, and makes a splendid support and background for that lovely single-flowered climber *Rosa laevigata Anemone.* The protection suits its habits and the grey of the old stones its complexion, and in the end of May and onwards it is a fine sight flinging its long growths through and over the arches of the old cross, and bearing hundreds of the glorious pink flowers as large as teacup saucers. It has now pushed its growths through to the north side, and as the last winter was so mild they bore as many and as fine blooms as those on the south side. A pergola of wooden poles and cross-pieces runs down at right angles to the wall, and divides this Rose Garden from another parallelogram of garden with stone-flagged paths, and an octagonal piece of black and white pavement round a sundial somewhere about its centre. A second and smaller pergola, devoted to Vines, divides its upper half at right angles to and leading out of the great pergola, and a flagged path leads on from the sundial across this Vine pergola up to a seat and an old stone pedestal and vase. You must come close to this, please, to admire the shower of lilac blossoms of a *Solanum crispum* that sprawls all over the Privet bushes that cut off the north wind, and hangs down over the pedestal. It is the deeper-coloured one known as the Glasnevin variety, and though it was cut to the ground here one winter has now made a trunk worthy of some tree, and I hope may never suffer so badly again, for every

My Garden in Spring

Spring since that resurrection it has been more beautiful than in the last, and it contrasts well with a neighbouring bush of golden-leaved Bramble trained over poles, which is one of the most brilliant of yellow things in its dress of young leaves. The double-flowered Apple, *Pyrus coronaria fl. pl.*, grows on the right hand of the Solanum and is now in flower. Its soft, shell-pink flowers are the largest of the Apple family, and charming next the lilac of the Tree Potato. *Arenaria montana* is climbing into *Vitis armata* on one of the pergola poles, and has got up for over a foot, and is a wonderful sight, packed so full of its large, white flowers that no leaves are visible. Various Violets and Epimediums line this shady Vine Pergola and appear in the cracks between the stones and make it look a century old instead of its actual five years. A pretty corner of the sundial opening has a carpet of the grey, finely-cut leaves of a good form of *Geranium tuberosum*, and over this a cloud of its soft, lilac-pink blossoms on tall and slender stems. Some clumps of mauve and pink Darwin Tulips are next it and among it, and behind a bush of *Ribes cruenta* is covered with its curious half-and-half dark crimson, and pure white flowers. *Euphorbia dulcis fol. var.* rises out of an edging of pink and lavender dwarf Phloxes, and is a perfect-shaped round bush of green and white leaves crowned with the mass of cream and ivory bracts of its flower-heads. A very beautiful plant, and far too seldom seen, though it needs a little looking after; the plain green shoots that appear among the variegated ones must be removed, and cuttings should be struck every two or three years for renewal, as old

The Culmination of Spring

plants are liable to be killed in severe winters more easily than youngsters.

Another unusual plant growing close by is *Bunium rotundifolium,* very much like *Thaspium aureum* but perennial instead of biennial like the latter. Both have charmingly glossy leaves of the Parsnip persuasion but not so coarse as the real members of that sect, and when old enough to flower they send up foot-high stems with brilliant yellow bracts surrounding the umbels of greenish-yellow flowers, and are wonderfully bright and suggestive of some very good Euphorbia. Both will grow happily in shady, poor ground, and furnish it in the best taste, as advertisements put it.

Parallel with the Vine Pergola and nearer the River the next paved walk has a row of Eucalypts on either side. I have tried for years to get a short avenue of them here, but some grow lanky and blow over, some are too tender for the winters, and others grow into rounded bushes, so that at present they are all heights from four to fifteen feet. *E. coccifera, E. urnigera,* and *E. obliqua* promise to make the best job of it at present. Tufted Pansies, such as Archie Grant and Maggie Mott, line the edges of this path, and the bed alongside the corresponding walk in the Rose Garden opposite is planted under the Roses with white and yellow Pansies gradually shading through pale yellow sorts edged with lilac, such as Skylark and Duchess of Fife, to the lavender Kitty Bell and then to deeper violet varieties. The white and yellow ones have a charming effect planted in blocks of varying sizes. Royal Sovereign, Maggie Clunas, Bullion, and Primrose Dame are good yellows, and

My Garden in Spring

Snowflake, White Swan, and Purity hard to beat for white. We have a good creamy white one with deep blue face-marks on it called Beauty of Hedsor, that is very useful for cutting, as like Snowflake it always has a good long stalk. I like to pick plenty of them in May, as they are so delightful in the house in their first freshness, and so doing relieves the young plants and helps them to make a better display later on. Jackanapes with red-brown upper petals and bright yellow lower ones is one of my great favourites, and we have a band of him at the back of one of the Iris beds and on the opposite side of the path to the yellow and white varieties of the Rose bed. But come back again along the Eucalyptus Avenue (how grand it sounds and how short and poor it is !). I want to show you a very beautiful Comfrey that grows at the side of the steps that form the end of this paved walk. It is the *Symphytum asperrimum*, that such great things were expected of as a perpetual forage crop many years ago, but though now turned out of the farm is worth a choice position in the garden for the sake of its exquisite turquoise blue flowers and rosy buds. It came to me from the Cambridge Botanic Gardens, where I first fell in love with it. It lasts in beauty for a very long period, and if cut down is soon up again and full of fresh flowers. The dark blue *S. causasicum* grows close behind it at this corner, and beside a large patch of the blue grass, *Elymus glaucus*, makes a very pretty picture. But then every way one looks on such a fine afternoon in May makes a picture. Even the square Georgian house as seen from a few steps further on across the pond looks comfortable and homey

The Culmination of Spring

in the golden sunlight ; the very Daisies on the lawn speak of Spring, and either blossom, or promise of it, and of fruit, is on most of the trees and shrubs ; the ground is still moist enough for planting or transplanting, weeds are young, and one feels even if left for another day or two will not do great harm, so very different from the impression one gets from the seed-laden sow-thistles and groundsels of summer days. Yes, when May is in good humour and smiling I always feel it is the moment to enjoy the garden, but once it is past and summer takes its place there is still plenty to do and more to enjoy than one has time for, and so each season brings its joys as well as its regrets, and the wise gardener will give himself over to making the most of the former and find no time for the latter. If you have enjoyed strolling round the Spring garden with me and listening to my prattle, personal and egotistical as much of it has been, and if you have any sympathy with my point of view of using the garden for the plants' welfare and not just for making the plants furnish your garden with art shades, dividing hedges, or shade to sit in, I hope later on you will accompany me on a second journey to review the summer aspect of the place and plants. For that is one of the greatest charms of a mixed collection of plants—it gives you a new garden at least once a month, and in another ten days it will be no longer " My Garden in Spring," but " My Garden in Summer."

INDEX

T 2

My Garden in Spring

Index

My Garden in Spring

Index

Index

303

Index

My Garden in Spring

Index

My Garden in Spring

Printed by BALLANTYNE, HANSON & CO.
2/14   at Paul's Work, Edinburgh   2½

NOMENCLATURAL UPDATE
by Peter Barnes

A gardening book does not have to be very old for some of its names to be considered out-of-date; indeed, nomenclature and taxonomy may both be considered rather fluid art-forms rather than precise sciences. It seems inevitable that this should be the case, since they are dealing with living organisms, by their nature also constantly varying. Consequently, the reader must not be surprised to find many name-changes from this book's original index. A few words to explain the reasons for these changes may be worthwhile.

It is a commonplace among gardeners to ask, Why must they keep changing our familiar names?, yet we must remember that names familiar to one generation may be very strange to an earlier one. All the many rules governing the naming of plants are directed towards stability of names but, inevitably, their application sometimes results in new names being required (or, more often, older names being revived) for familiar plants. There are two main justifications—taxonomy and nomenclature.

Taxonomy is the study (I hesitate to call it a science) of the relationships between different plants. It is taxonomy that encourages us to bring together, in the family Rosaceae, apparently differing genera such as *Rosa*, *Potentilla*, and *Fragaria*, not to mention *Malus*, *Prunus*, and *Spiraea*. From time to time, more detailed study, perhaps new techniques, may suggest

My Garden in Spring

that previously-held ideas can not be sustained, and a plant may then have to be given a new specific epithet, or be transferred to a different genus.

The rules ("Codes") of nomenclature determine what names may be applied to a particular plant, and especially, which name of many that may have been used for it over the years should be considered the correct one. A basic principle of nomenclature is that of priority, whereby (in general) the earliest name properly published for that plant is to be considered the correct one.

Rules notwithstanding, room often remains for argument as to the correct name for a particular plant, hence the differences between some modern publications. From time to time, proposals have been made to adopt a standard list of names, seldom with any lasting effect. Therefore, the reader must not be surprised if a name here given as "correct" is disregarded elsewhere.

The reader must bear in mind that when Bowles wrote this book the concept of the cultivar (i.e., "cultivated variety") had not been adopted. Consequently, the typography of the original index differs from what is now the norm. I have listed, in their proper style (capital initial letters and single quotation marks), those latinized epithets which are now treated as cultivar names, to distinguish them from botanical epithets belonging to subspecies, varieties, or forms. Non-latinized names, such as tulip 'Bleu Aimable', are not listed again. Bowles generally capitalised botanical epithets derived from proper nouns, a style I have not adopted. I have also corrected a few misspellings.

In general, names in this supplementary index have been brought into alignment with *The Plant Finder*, which is now

Nomenclatural Update

increasingly used as a standard nomenclator by the nursery trade, but I have reserved the right to differ in a very few instances. Furthermore, a surprisingly large proportion of the names used by Bowles represent plants not listed in that work. Some, evidently, are not currently in the nursery trade; a few others are names which, as far as I can determine, have either never been validly published or are of uncertain status. Some may be errors of the compiler of the index, of the printer, or even of the author's memory, but the text does not always help to determine their true identity. In a few instances, incorrect page references have been rectified. At the least, these supplementary notes should make it easier to track down further information about almost all of the plants that feature in this eloquent and enduringly readable trilogy.

NAME USED IN *My Garden in Spring*	PAGE	CURRENT NAME
Acer californica aurea	191, 196	*Acer negundo* 'Auratum'
Adlumia cirrhosa	158	*Adlumia fungosa*
Aegle	171, 174	*Poncirus*
Aegle hybrids	172, 173	× *Citroncirus webberi*
Aegle sepiaria	171	*Poncirus trifoliata*
Aethiopappus	194	*Centaurea pulcherrima*
Ajuga metallica crispa	189	*Ajuga pyramidalis* 'Metallica Crispa'
Allium Babingtonii	195	*Allium ampeloprasum* var. *babingtonii*
Allium Dioscoridis	261	*Nectaroscordum siculum* subsp. *bulgaricum*
Alnus incana aurea	196	*Alnus incana* 'Aurea'
Alyssum maritimum	7	*Lobularia maritima*
Alyssum saxatile	290	*Aurinia saxatilis*
Anemone alpina	219	*Pulsatilla alpina*
Anemone appenina	208	*Anemone apennina*
Anemone Blue Bonnet	214	*Anemone nemorosa* 'Blue Bonnet'

My Garden in Spring

Nomenclatural Update

My Garden in Spring

Nomenclatural Update

NAME USED IN My Garden in Spring	PAGE	CURRENT NAME
Douglasiana vitaliana	109	*Vitaliana primuliflora*
Elymus glaucus	294	*Elymus hispidus*
Epimedium macranthum	276	*Epimedium grandiflorum*
Epimedium rubrum	276	*Epimedium × rubrum*
Eranthis cilicica	116	*Eranthis hyemalis* Cilicica Group
Eranthis hiemalis	115	*Eranthis hyemalis*
Eremurus Bungei praecox	284	*Eremurus stenophyllus* 'Praecox'
Eremurus Elwesianus	43, 283	*Eremurus aitchisonii (E. elwesii)*
Eremurus Tubergenii	284	*Eremurus × tubergenii (E. himalaicus × E. stenophyllus)*
Erica hybrida	263	*Erica × darleyensis (E. carnea × E. erigena)*
Erodium lindavicum	260	*Erodium × lindavicum (E. absinthoides* var. *amanum × E. chrysanthum)*
Erodium romanum	276	*Erodium acaule*
Eryngium Lasseauxii	252, 257	*Eryngium pandanifolium* var. *lasseauxii*
Erysimum Allionii	262	*Erysimum × allionii* (complex hybrid group)
Erysimum pumilum	288	*Erysimum helveticum*
Euonymus aucubaefolius	201	*Euonymus europaeus* 'Aucubifolius'
Euphorbia melifera	270	*Euphorbia mellifera*
Euphorbia pilosa major	269	*Euphorbia polychroma* 'Major'
Euphorbia Wulfenii	269	*Euphorbia characias* subsp. *wulfenii*
Fraxinus excelsior var. *atrovirens nana*	182	*Fraxinus excelsior* 'Nana'
Fritillaria gracilis	168	*Fritillaria messanensis* subsp. *gracilis*
Fritillaria Slagswaard	167	*Fritillaria imperialis* (fasciated form)
Galanthus byzantinus	47	*Galanthus plicatus* subsp. *byzantinus*
Galanthus cilicicus	48	*Galanthus nivalis* subsp. *cilicicus*

315

My Garden in Spring

Nomenclatural Update

NAME USED IN *My Garden in Spring*	PAGE	CURRENT NAME
Iris alata	33	*Iris planifolia*
Iris Benacensis	230	*Iris aphylla*
Iris Chamaeiris	230	*Iris lutescens*
Iris florentina	223, 279	*Iris* 'Florentina'
Iris Kaempferi	7	*Iris ensata*
Iris mellita	233	*Iris suaveolens*
Iris ochroleuca	250	*Iris orientalis*
Iris orchioides	38	*Iris bucharica* (*I. orchioides* of gardens, part of the variable *I. bucharica*)
Iris persica stenophylla or *Heldreichii*	38	*Iris stenophylla*
Iris pseud-acorus	197	*Iris pseudacorus*
Iris sindjarensis	38	*Iris aucheri*
Iris Sisyrinchium	232	*Gynandriris sisyrinchium*
Juniperus sinensis	193	*Juniperus chinensis* (description suggests *J. chinensis* 'Aurea')
Lactuca (Mulgedium) alpina	269	*Cicerbita alpina*
Lathyrus magellanicus	102	*Lathyrus nervosus*
Leucoium aestivum	60	*Leucojum aestivum*
Leucoium Hernandezii or *pulchellum*	60	*Leucojum autumnale* var. *pulchellum*
Leucoium vernum Vagneri or *carpathicum*	60	*Leucojum vernum* vars. *vagneri* and *carpathicum*
Lewisia Howellii	109	*Lewisia cotyledon* var. *howellii*
Lewisia parviflora	277	Name of no botanical standing
Lilium Marhan	259	*Lilium* × *dalhansonii* 'Marhan' (*L. hansonii* × *L. martagon* var. *cattaniae*)
Linaria aequitriloba	262	*Cymbalaria aequitriloba*
Linaria Cymbalaria	262	*Cymbalaria muralis*
Linaria hepaticaefolia	262	*Cymbalaria hepaticifolia*
Lychnis dioica	201	*Silene dioica*
Magnolia conspicua	176	*Magnolia denudata*
Magnolia Lennei	176	*Magnolia* × *soulangeana* 'Lennei'

My Garden in Spring

Nomenclatural Update

NAME USED IN *My Garden in Spring*	PAGE	CURRENT NAME
Pachysandra terminalis	200	*Pachysandra terminalis* (description suggests *P. terminalis* 'Variegata')
Papaver rhoeticum	108	*Papaver rhaeticum*
Petasites japonica	159	*Petasites japonicus*
Petasites nivea	158	*Petasites paradoxus*
Petasites palmata	159	*Petasites palmatus*
Philadelphus coronaria	201	*Philadelphus coronarius*
Phlox divaricata, var. *canadensis*	258	*Phlox divaricata*
Picea pungens glauca	195	*Picea pungens* var. *glauca*
Plantago graminifolia	185	Name of no botanical standing (*Plantago graminiformis=P. maritima*)
Plantago, rose	185, 186	*Plantago major* 'Rosularis' (also an unnamed variant of *P. media)*
Polemonium coeruleum	191	*Polemonium caeruleum*
Primula acaulis	143, 144	*Primula vulgaris*
Primula Bowlesii	107, 140	*Primula × bowlesii* (*P. latifolia × P. pedemontana*)
Primula Cashmiriana	134	*Primula denticulata* var. *cachemiriana*
Primula Dumoulinii	136	*Primula × dumolinii* (hybrid of *P. minima)*
Primula Facchinii	136	*Primula × facchinii* (*P. minima × P. spectabilis*)
Primula Juribella	137	*Primula × juribella* (*P. minima × P. tyrolensis*)
Primula longiflora	136–9	*Primula halleri*
Primula megaseaefolia	134	*Primula megaseifolia*
Primula oenensis	136, 138	*Primula daonensis*
Primula officinalis	143	*Primula veris*
Primula Sibthorpei Pax	144	*Primula vulgaris* subsp. *sibthorpii* (Pax is author of name)
Primula Veitchii	145	*Primula polyneura*
Primula viscosa	107	*Primula latifolia*
Prunus Amygdalus nanus	272	*Prunus tenella* (*Amygdalus nanus*)

My Garden in Spring

Nomenclatural Update

My Garden in Spring